PLANTAGENET PRINCES

A companion volume to
Plantagenet Princesses

PLANTAGENET PRINCES

SONS OF ELEANOR OF AQUITAINE AND HENRY II

DOUGLAS BOYD

PEN & SWORD HISTORY

AN IMPRINT OF PEN & SWORD BOOKS LTD.
YORKSHIRE – PHILADELPHIA

First published in Great Britain in 2021 by
PEN AND SWORD HISTORY
An imprint of
Pen & Sword Books Ltd
Yorkshire – Philadelphia

Copyright © Douglas Boyd, 2021

ISBN 978 1 52674 306 0

The right of Douglas Boyd to be identified as Author of this work has been asserted by him in accordance with the Copyright, Designs and Patents Act 1988.

A CIP catalogue record for this book is available from the British Library.

All rights reserved. No part of this book may be reproduced or transmitted in any form or by any means, electronic or mechanical including photocopying, recording or by any information storage and retrieval system, without permission from the Publisher in writing.

Typeset in Times New Roman 11.5/14 by
SJmagic DESIGN SERVICES, India.
Printed and bound by CPI Group (UK) Ltd, Croydon CR0 4YY

Pen & Sword Books Limited incorporates the imprints of Atlas, Archaeology, Aviation, Discovery, Family History, Fiction, History, Maritime, Military, Military Classics, Politics, Select, Transport, True Crime, Air World, Frontline Publishing, Leo Cooper, Remember When, Seaforth Publishing, The Praetorian Press, Wharncliffe Local History, Wharncliffe Transport, Wharncliffe True Crime and White Owl.

For a complete list of Pen & Sword titles please contact
PEN & SWORD BOOKS LIMITED
47 Church Street, Barnsley, South Yorkshire, S70 2AS, England
E-mail: enquiries@pen-and-sword.co.uk
Website: www.pen-and-sword.co.uk

Or

PEN AND SWORD BOOKS
1950 Lawrence Rd, Havertown, PA 19083, USA
E-mail: Uspen-and-sword@casematepublishers.com
Website: www.penandswordbooks.com

Also by Douglas Boyd

Histories:
April Queen, Eleanor of Aquitaine
Voices from the Dark Years
The French Foreign Legion
The Kremlin Conspiracy: 1,000 Years of Russian Expansionism
Normandy in the time of Darkness: Life and Death in the Channel Ports 1940–45
Blood in the Snow, Blood on the Grass: Treachery and Massacre, France 1944
De Gaulle: The Man who Defied Six US Presidents
Lionheart: The True Story of England's Crusader King
The Other First World War: The Blood-soaked Russian Fronts 1914–22
Daughters of the KGB: Moscow's Cold War Spies, Sleepers and Assassins
Agente: Female Spies in World Wars, Cold Wars and Civil Wars
The Solitary Spy
Red October: The Revolution that Changed the World
Lockerbie: The Truth
Moscow Rules
Plantagenet Princesses
In preparation: Henry II – England's French King

Novels:
The Eagle and the Snake
The Honour and the Glory
The Truth and the Lies
The Virgin and the Fool
The Fiddler and the Ferret
The Spirit and the Flesh

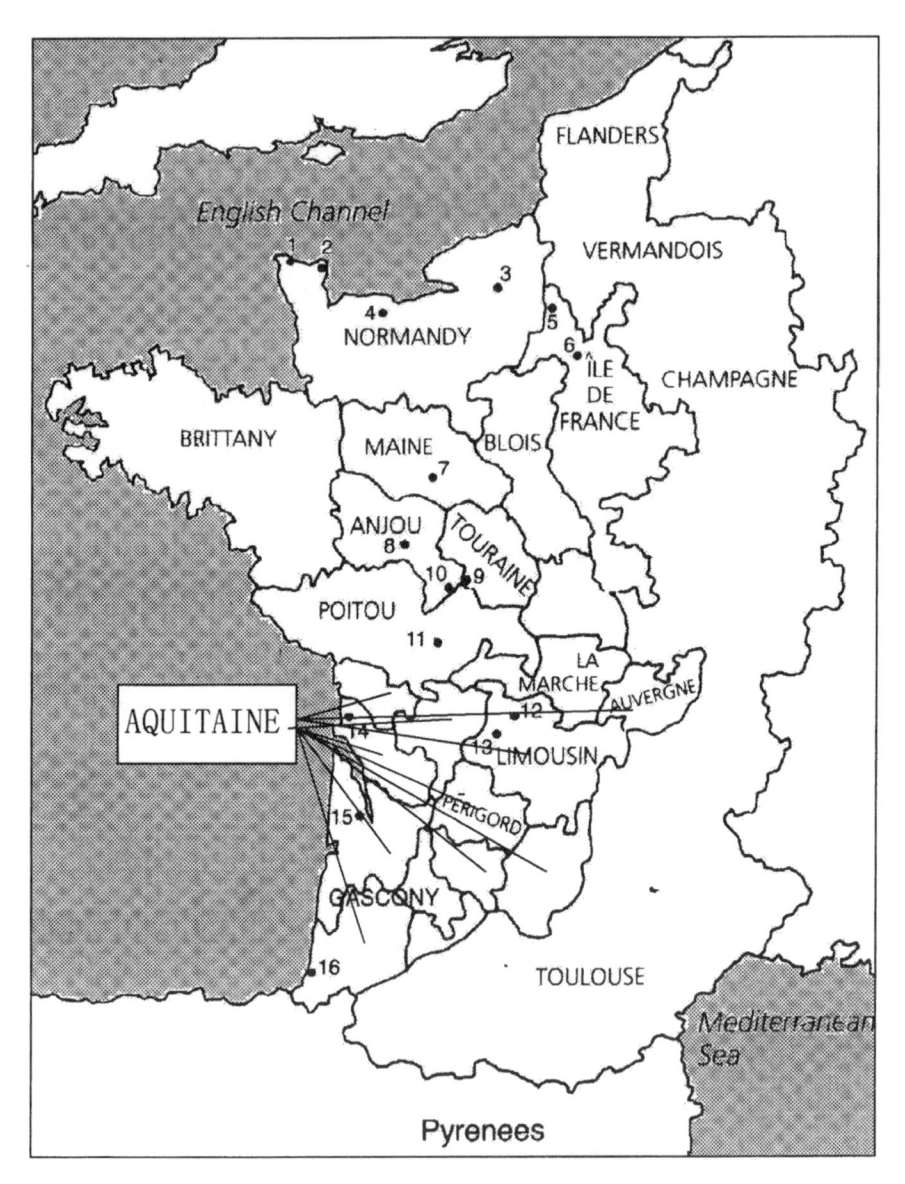

France in the twelfth century

1. Cherbourg	2. Barfleur	3. Rouen
4. Caen	5. Gisors	6. Paris
7. Le Mans	8. Angers	9. Chinon
10. Fontevraud	11. Poitiers	12. Limoges
13. Châlus	14. La Rochelle	15. Bordeaux
16. Bayonne		

Contents

Glossary ix

Chapter 1   The life of princes 1
Chapter 2   The death of kings 9
Chapter 3   The civil war 18
Chapter 4   The crusader queen 23
Chapter 5   Prince Henry 37
Chapter 6   A king with no kingdom 46
Chapter 7   Death in misery 57
Chapter 8   Prince Richard 69
Chapter 9   Richard the Lionheart 78
Chapter 10   Richard's perfect castle 88
Chapter 11   Prince Geoffrey 96
Chapter 12   Prince John 107
Chapter 13   War on all sides 117
Chapter 14   Henry III 128
Chapter 15   King v. barons, round 2 137
Chapter 16   Richard of Cornwall 146
Chapter 17   Edward I 154
Chapter 18   Edward II 164
Chapter 19   Edward III 177
Chapter 20   Edward, the Black Prince 188
Chapter 21   Richard II 199

PLANTAGENET PRINCES

Acknowledgements 203
Notes and Sources 204
Index 219

Glossary

Aketon – a protective quilted-coat worn alone or under armour

Bassinet – a simple conical helmet

Besegew – a guard for the hand on a weapon shaft

Cantle – the raised back of a medieval war saddle

Chausses – plate armour lower leg protection

Courser – a swift riding horse

Destrier – a trained warhorse

Diffidatio – the disavowal of an oath of loyalty

Excommunication – the formal pronouncement by a senior churchman that the excommunicate was no longer entitled to any benefits of the faithful

Forinsec – feudal service to an overlord

Habergeon, haubergeon, hauberk – a tunic of (chain)mail

Homage – a sworn acknowledgement of loyalty to an overlord

Interdict – the expulsion of a territory from the Christian community, with no priests allowed to say Mass or officiate in any way except the baptism of infants

Palfrey – a riding horse

Poitrail – a stout martingale that prevented a war saddle from being pushed backwards in combat

Pommel – the knob at the end of a sword hilt *or* the raised front of a medieval war saddle

Rouncy – a riding horse

Note 1: In the early Middle Ages, legitimate sons of kings were not called princes. Most were simply known as filius regis – *the king's son – or* filius henrici – *the son of Henry, for example. That said, it seems simpler for both author and reader to use the modern term.*

Note 2: So many nobles of both sexes shared a small selection of first names that people even then were sometimes confused, adding a toponym like 'Robert of Gloucester' or 'Theobald of Blois' or an epithet such as 'Geoffrey the handsome' or 'Louis the Fat'.

Chapter 1

The life of princes

The single image that epitomises the European Middle Ages is of a knight mounted on a spirited war-horse, wielding a sword. He is no gallant St George, fighting a dragon to rescue a maiden, but a trained killer. As time passed and metal-working became more skilled, his outward costume changed from padded chain mail to plate armour, although the sword in his hand seems to vary very little to the casual glance. We see the image in illuminated manuscripts, on coins and the seals of dukes and kings and their imprints on important documents. The eleventh to fifteenth centuries have been called the age of chivalry, but the knight in the image was doing what knights did best: killing people.

Male society was then divided into three estates. In Latin, they were *oratores, bellatores et laboratores*: those who prayed, those who fought and those who laboured as serfs, tied to the land, to produce the food and other necessities for the knightly classes. It has been calculated that twenty-three entire *families* of serfs were required to support one modest knight and his household, and correspondingly more for grander knights and nobles. The only profession apart from the Church for a man of noble birth was to bear arms. Knightly warriors prosecuted their bloody struggles both tactically, face-to-face with a more or less equally matched enemy, and strategically by slaughtering defenceless serfs – men, women and children of all ages – poisoning their wells with decaying carcases, laying waste their fields with fire and salt, slaughtering their animals and cutting down their orchards to bring starvation to the survivors, thus depriving a noble enemy of the support base for his unproductive way of life

In 1134 Count Philip of Flanders summed up warfare thus: 'Destroy your enemies and waste their country. Let everything be set alight by burning. Leave nothing for them … on which they could have dinner.'[1] It was, to use a modern expression, total war[2] Frequently, this was between neighbours living in the same country – not that the concept of nations and countries existed yet. Because of the enormous suffering thus inflicted on millions of innocent and uninvolved people, the Church pronounced the slaughter of farm animals and the destruction of agricultural equipment in war, preventing the serfs from setting the land in order again, to be a sin – or war crime, in our terms.

The most extravagant forms of medieval warfare were the crusades summoned by the chief priests of Christianity – the popes – ostensibly to capture the city of Jerusalem from the Muslims, but also to deflect the warlike tendencies of the knightly classes away from killing their Christian neighbours in Europe. Tens of thousands of knights and lesser fighting men enlisted for each of these costly and mostly abortive campaigns in a far-off land. If the desire to capture riches and fiefs from the infidel was a powerful motive in the First Crusade, the reason to depart on the later ones with a high risk of death from disease or in combat was a pope's assurance that all the blood the crusaders had shed in their violent past lives would be eliminated from the debit side when their souls were weighed by angels and demons after death. Killing Muslims, Orthodox and eastern Christians and Jews in the Holy Land did not count.

Most terms to do with knighthood are of Latin origin, coming into English through Norman and Angevin French after the followers of the Conqueror won the Battle of Hastings on 14 October 1066, enabling him to claim the kingdom of the last Anglo-Saxon king Harold Godwinson. The Conqueror's army had landed two weeks previously between the old Roman port of Pevensey and the town of Hastings. Then came a fortnight of foraging and laying waste the land while Harold's army fought a battle against Scandinavian invaders in Yorkshire, 300 miles to the north, after which it was force-marched south to confront another invasion. The Norman victory at Hastings was due to the undisciplined, and presumably exhausted, Anglo-Saxons abandoning their impenetrable shield wall to pursue the apparently retreating Norman cavalry and being brutally cut down when it rounded on them. In case there is any doubt how Harold's and William's men fought, the exquisite embroidery of the Bayeux tapestry shows in full detail war-horses being hoisted in slings aboard the ships of the invasion fleet for the Channel crossing, and depicts all the main participants, as well as the events that led up to 1066.[3] There were fears that the Germans would steal the tapestry

THE LIFE OF PRINCES

during the Occupation, but a team of specialists in SS uniforms contented themselves in Bayeux with making a full-size photographic reproduction to take back for the Führer, while the tapestry itself spent the war years in a bomb-proof mini-bunker – which was just as well, given all the Allied bombs that were dropped on northern France in the Second World War.[4] Who stitched the tapestry is a mystery: no one knows for certain when, or where, or by whom it was made. It was known firstly as 'King's cloth', then 'Queen Matilda's tapestry' before acquiring the name by which we know it.

The Romans and earlier peoples had fought on horseback, but Rome's word for a mounted warrior was *equitis* from *equus*, a horse. 'Chivalry', meaning knightly gallantry, comes from the French *chevalerie*, itself derived from the pejorative Latin term *caballus* – a pack-horse or nag. Yet the man riding the horse in battle and wielding the sword is not known in English by a Latin-derived word. The silent *k* and *gh* of 'knight' are relics of the Germanic *Knecht*, which had many meanings in Old German and Old Saxon, including 'boy' and 'servant', whereas the modern German for 'knight' is *Ritter*, or rider. Leaving the etymological maze, the reason why a king's seal represented the most powerful man of a nation as a knight was that all his important vassals were horse-riding warriors and he was supposedly the best of them all. In some cases like Richard the Lionheart, monarchs did have that reputation, although even Richard was bested by his eventual vassal William the Marshal outside Le Mans at the end of Lent in 1199,[73] when fighting *for* the French king Philippe Auguste *against* his father Henry II of England, whose retreat William was protecting. Recognising the unarmoured prince in the heat of battle, he chose to drive his lance into Richard's mount instead of into the rider, calling out, 'Let the devil kill you, for I shall not.' When they met later, after Richard had been crowned king of England, he accused the Marshal of trying to kill him that day. Perhaps the greatest knightly warrior of all time, William replied coolly, 'I could just as easily have spitted the rider as the horse.'

It might be supposed the control of a heavy *destrier* bearing an armoured knight in the confusion of battle with one hand and arm fully occupied by weaponry was partly a matter of luck but, as the Marshal proved that day, it was more often a question of long training and the level of strength, skill *and split-second timing* one might find in a top Olympic athlete today. Perhaps a hard-fought professional polo match comes nearest to displaying the equestrian skill of the medieval knight. To such a warrior, even in the heat of combat, every move was a precision action rendered possible by hours of tuition and practice every day of his youth to perfect the moves and the techniques of fighting with sword both on foot and when mounted on a war-horse trained to obey instantly every slightest signal by the reins held in the knight's left hand, the pressure of his legs and the spurs on his heels. Such horses being too valuable to ride to battle, or to tire by being ridden far, the knight travelled on a palfrey or courser, with his *destrier* being led by a squire mounted on a rouncey, holding its bridle in his right hand – in Latin, *dextra*. Behind them came the sumpters carrying the baggage. Comparative costs were that a destrier cost up to seven times the price of a courser.

The knight's weapons included the lance, a wooden shaft up to 12 feet long with a guard for the hand and a metal spear-head that, driven by the combined momentum of horse and rider could completely pierce an enemy's body. This weapon was too heavy to be supported just by the knight's hand and had to be 'couched' – held by the right elbow tightly into the waist, so that it projected between the rider's body and the horse's neck, pointing left; later, once plate armour came in, some of the weight was borne by a hook projecting from the right side of the breastplate. There was also the mace – a stout wooden or iron shaft ending in a solid mass of metal that could crush an enemy's helmet and skull with one blow, the penalty for failing to do that on first attempt often being death in the few seconds while the mace-wielder was off-balance after the blow. Some maces were spiked and known jocularly as 'morning stars'; others ended in a short chain or chains, at the end of which one or more iron balls, also often spiked, and known as 'holy water sprinklers', could deliver a hideous wound. The war hammer had a haft about 2 or 2 ½ feet long, with a small besagew or guard for the hand and a pommel to stop it slipping out of the warrior's gloved hand in the stress of combat. Pointed at the tip and having a clawed hammer-head 3 inches long by 2 inches square, it was balanced on the other side of the haft by a vicious curved spike that could cut straight through a coat of mail, the wielder being able to swivel it in order to present the hammer-head or the spike at will. The battle-axe was a larger weapon, requiring great strength to wield on horseback with one hand.

Of all this armoury, the weapon most familiar today is the sword, consisting of a blade usually 28-31 inches long with a cross-guard to protect the hand gripping the hilt. In cross-section, the blade could have a slender diamond shape or be flatter with a channel on each side, known as a fuller, reaching from the cross-piece to near the point. This was long thought to be for easing withdrawal from an enemy's body by allowing the blood to escape, as with a World War I bayonet, but may have been a way of lightening the blade without losing strength, since medieval swords were used more for slashing than stabbing because stabbing an enemy might make the sword difficult to remove from his body, putting the stabber at a disadvantage, whereas a slashing blow leaves the sword free immediately afterwards for another blow.

The making of a sword required the skills of several craftsmen. The pointed tang at the top of the blade fitted through a slot in the cross-piece, passed through the centre of the wooden hilt, bound with wire or cord to give a good grip, and through a hole pierced through the pommel, after which it was hammered back like a rivet on the head of the pommel making the entire weapon solid. The sword's pommel was essentially a heavy lump of iron, designed not just to prevent the sword slipping out of a knight's grip, but also to act as the essential counter-weight to balance the blade. Some sword pommels were plain, others were decorated with the owner's arms inlaid with some other metal. The whole weapon weighed about 4 ½-5 pounds. There were also swords known as 'hand-and-a-half' weapons, with longer, heavier blades and hilts about 7 inches long, enabling them to be used single-handed or with both hands, delivering enough force to amputate an entire limb or cleave an adversary from shoulder to pelvis. A swordsmith would spend several days on one blade. After forging the metal, the skill was to produce a slender blade with centre of balance close to the hand and two very sharp cutting edges without making the blade too soft or too hard and brittle, in which case it might break when colliding with another steel weapon in the clash of combat.

Set-piece battles were rare, most confrontations being more in the nature of skirmishes. Beginning the fight with his lance, the knight needed his sword ready – not usually in its scabbard, from which it would take longer to draw, but in a metal ring attached to his belt. The essence of each action in combat was speed, so prudent or pessimistic warriors also had the hilt attached by a chain or leather thong to a buckle or hinge on the breast-plate; if knocked out of their hands, it could swiftly be grabbed and put back in use. Supported on his left forearm, the mail-clad knight held a kite-shaped shield, wide at the top to protect the body, but narrowing towards the bottom to cover the left leg down to the stirrup. With the development of plate armour that covered the thigh, knee and lower leg, shields were dispensed with as an unnecessary encumbrance.

Training for mastery of this armoury began at the age of 10 or earlier, with scaled down weapons, and lasted intensively until – at about the age of 15, depending on physical development – the trainee knight was strong enough to wear armour and a helmet. Even mail armour was heavier than it looks. Once fully grown, the young warrior – who only gained the title of knight after being dubbed, with a sword belt buckled on him by a senior knight in a ceremony of initiation into the order of chivalry – had a body bulging with muscles, especially on his right side, unless he was left-handed.

That other familiar medieval weapon, the longbow looks deceptively simple, but was skilfully fashioned by craftsmen from a stave cut from the heartwood and sapwood of a yew, ash or elm tree. Drying this natural composite weapon took two years, during and after which the wood was progressively worked into a D-section profile tapering toward the ends, the whole process lasting up to four years. The heartwood belly of the stave resisted compression and was convex, the flattened outer side being the sapwood, which resisted extension. Long enough to allow the archer to draw the string to a point by the right eye, bows measured up to 6 feet long between the 'knocks' or horn tips on which the string of hemp, flax or silk was attached.[5] The force necessary to draw a medieval war-bow has been estimated at 150 pounds or even higher, well beyond the muscles of most modern archers. Made from many different woods, the arrows ranged in length from 24 inches to 33 inches, skilfully fletched with goose or other feathers to ensure straight flight and tipped with steel heads of barbed or bodkin shape. The latter had heads thin enough and sharp enough to pierce an enemy's armour. The former had long rear-facing tangs, sharpened all the way to the points, which cut their way through skin, muscle and bodily organs and were often impossible to remove, except by pushing them right through the victim's body.

Despite the accounts of King Harold's demise at Hastings, from an arrow in the eye, and of Robin Hood or William Tell, the longbow was not an accurate weapon used for single aimed shots in warfare, but was employed as artillery would later be, to make a barrage. Since archers could draw from the quiver and fire ten or twelve arrows in a minute, 200 bowmen could loose 2,000 carefully ranged arrows in a single minute in a trajectory that rose high and rained near-vertically down on advancing infantry and tightly-packed cavalry. According to the chronicler Richard of Devizes, his namesake Coeur de Lion had 1,000 bowmen at the siege of Arsuf during the Third Crusade, which gives 10,000 arrows landing on the enemy in one minute![5] Even allowing for some exaggeration, the scene is horrific, with horses struck by one or more arrows plunging and bucking desperately, breaking up the formation and unseating other riders as well as their own. Knights also learned to use longbows mounted, but this was for hunting deer and other large game, as on the day when King William Rufus was killed while hunting in the New Forest, either by a stray arrow bouncing off a tree or in a deliberate assassination. It was to counter the inaccuracy of the longbow aimed at a one-on-one target that the more accurate crossbow was invented, but not for mounted knights, as it required use of both hands to tension the weapon, load and fire it.

To handle all the other weapons on horseback, it was necessary also for future knights to spend many hours each day in the saddle – not the comfortable riding saddle on a palfrey, but the war-saddle of a lively and powerful *destrier* stallion. This was hard and had a high pommel in front and a raised cantle at the rear, between which the knight's crotch and lower abdomen were firmly gripped, so that the shock of colliding – or his firmly couched lance colliding – with an adversary would not unseat the rider and drive him backward onto the ground, where he risked being trampled to death by the horses, taken prisoner for ransom by another knight or fatally stabbed by an opportunistic man-at-arms on foot. To ease the load on the horse's spine from a fully armed and armoured knight, the saddle had lateral bars resting over the dorsal muscles,[6] which raised the knight off the horse's back, so that he was almost standing in the stirrups. To prevent the shock of collision pushing knight and saddle to the rear, there was also a stout martingale or *poitrail* attached to the saddle and passing around the destrier's chest in addition to the girth round its belly. To protect the destrier from arrows and blows from foot-soldiers, a caparison of padded material covered its chest, back and sides, later replaced by plate armour for the horse as well as the rider. Unfortunately, spending long hours on a constricting war saddle, thumping up and down at a gallop throughout adolescent and young adult years, damaged many knights' reproductive organs irrevocably.[7]

Essential in battle or a tournament was protection for the body to absorb slashing blows. This also had to be worn in training, to get the youth accustomed to its bulkiness – and the resultant heat in the summer months. The padded knee- or thigh-length gambeson or *haubergeon* arming doublet of canvas or leather, tightly stuffed with rags, tow or horsehair was, with a kettle helmet, the only protection for most foot-soldiers. Knights too wore them under their mail armour, the main part of which was the hauberk, originally thigh-length with sleeves ending at the elbows and later extending lower, the garment being slit up to the crotch, each side then being wrapped around the leg while mounted and later augmented by mail leggings or *chausses* to cover the lower leg, vulnerable to blows from enemy foot-soldiers in close-quarters combat. The sleeves becoming longer, with mail mittens attached in the twelfth century, a coif or head-piece was added. The whole outfit weighed 30-35lbs. Moving swiftly in it was tiring – hence the need for practice. Lastly the helm. In the early twelfth century this was still the conical one seen in the Bayeux tapestry, the nasal gradually being widened until it protected most of the face. Since even this left the neck unprotected, in the thirteenth century knights began adopting the great helm encasing the whole head with slits for vision and some small holes for breathing through. This was sitting on, and tightly laced to, the upper body armour, but produced a typical bull neck from supporting the weight every day.[8]

Carrying the fully armoured knight and his weapons, the destrier's need for the lateral bars of the saddle, to spread the weight on its dorsal muscles and not on the spine, becomes plain.[9]

Chapter 2

The death of kings

It is said that every child educated in England retains one date from all those history lessons. In 1066 Duke William of Normandy beat the forces of the last Anglo-Saxon king, Harold Godwinson, at Caldbec Hill, a few miles northwest of Hastings. How he did it is recorded in that exquisite masterpiece of medieval embroidery, the Bayeux tapestry – the 230 feet long and 20 inches high strip cartoon of the preparations and the battle. The result of the battle is still with us today in the bastard tongue we speak, with its vocabulary a mixture of Germanic- and French-origin words. We use Germanic ones like *cow, sheep, swine* for the living animals on our farms; when served at table, the meat is called *beef, mutton* and *pork* from French *boeuf, mouton* and *porc*. More than a thousand years after William's conquest, modern usage still reflects the society he created, with the Anglo-Saxon peasant raising, pasturing and herding the animals while French was the language spoken by those at whose tables the meat was consumed after slaughter.

Becoming King William I at his coronation, in imposing his rule on the island realm, the Conqueror went a lot further than that, with many pre-Conquest landowners being killed so that his followers could marry their widows with a semblance of continuity and obtain legal title to vast stretches of England without losing control of their possessions in Normandy. So disadvantaged was the previous native nobility that 340 shiploads of them left England under Earl Sigurd of Gloucester, sailing 3,300 nautical miles to Constantinople, where some took service in the Byzantine army and others continued a further 400 nautical miles across the Black Sea to settle on the Crimean peninsula – all this to avoid suffering under the Norman yoke.[1] It was, in its under-reported way, as significant an achievement as any of the crusades. Nor did those who stayed in England suffer quietly; the Anglo-Scandinavian region of northeast England saw widespread ethnic cleansing: killing of all inhabitants, destruction of their homes and burning down of settlements and crops, leaving a swathe of depopulated scorched earth which William carved up between his knights. Further south, he had to put down a number of rebellions and pay off a Danish invasion that arrived to win back the Danelaw with local support.

Twelfth-century England was a country where the common people continued to speak various Germanic and Celtic languages and the aristocracy spoke Norman-French. Those merchants and other natives who wanted, or were forced, to have dealings with their overlords had to learn their language. The Conqueror is best remembered today for his revision of the tax system, in which the 1086 Domesday survey assessed every corner of the realm, to ensure the maximum return for his Exchequer. It also laid bare for posterity the ownership of the entire country. The king personally possessed 18 per cent by value of the land. In four shires, he possessed over 30 per cent. In a further eight, he held 20 to 30 per cent. All over England, he owned more than 10 per cent and temporarily had the income, sometimes for years, from many other estates if an heir was under-age or an unmarried woman; also, in the case of the Church lands, if the position of bishop was vacant. [2] A quarter of England was owned by the Church and another quarter by a dozen great magnates. Title to the whole country was vested in less than 250 people, including forty prelates, who were also temporal vassals of the king.[3] Domesday Book also lists 80,000 plough teams working the land, which indicates that 14 million acres were fields producing wheat, rye, barley and oats, plus pastureland. In time of peace, England was a rich country.

The transition from the comparative chaos of Harold's rule was harsh, as were the punishments for any transgression against the new laws. Being the only important institution that survived the transition with any kind of authority, the Church played a stabilising role, so William trod softly with its bishops at first, employing the authority of obliging papal legates sent by Pope Alexander II to dismiss English prelates who refused to toe the new line. Gradually almost all the English bishops and archbishops would be replaced by Norman or other Continental appointees, some of whom, like William's half-brother Bishop Odo of Bayeux, had fought in the Norman army at Caldbec Hill. Odo it was who had commanded the tapestry to be made, telling the story of the invasion like an immense strip cartoon. Needlework historians believe that the women who stitched it were working in England, but Cambridge professor of medieval history George Garnett has counted ninety-three penises – eighty-eight on horses and five on men – in the tapestry, which inclines him to believe it must have been designed by a male person. It is perhaps significant that the largest equine penis belongs to the Conqueror's stallion and the next largest to King Harold's mount.

The Conqueror died in 1087, when his eldest surviving son Robert Courtheuse[4] inherited the duchy of Normandy. The second son, Richard, having died in a hunting accident in 1175, the succession to the English throne went to the Conqueror's third legitimate son, known to history as Willliam Rufus due to having reddish hair when young. Although he was not an incompetent king, his court was notorious for riotous behaviour and accusations of rampant homosexuality, not least because the king neither married nor sired any known bastards. His enduring memorial is Westminster Hall, the largest assembly hall in Europe when completed in 1099. One of his shrewder moves was to lend 10,000 marks to his elder brother Robert of Normandy, permitting him to answer the call for the First Crusade issued by Pope Urban II at the Council of Clermont in 1095. The loan amounted to a quarter of the annual budget of England, so its once red-haired king had to raise the money by a harsh and unpopular extra tax. The security for the loan was a mortgage on Robert's duchy, and since it was statistically likely he would not return from the Holy Land, the bargain seemed like a good way for William Rufus to acquire Normandy without having to fight his brother for it, thus reuniting the two halves of the Conqueror's land.

William Rufus' undignified lifestyle, however, made him unpopular with the nobility, and his death, while hunting in the New Forest on 2 August 1100 in a strange replay of the death there of his eldest brother Prince Richard, has been considered by many as assassination, not accident. The king and Gautier Tyrrell, an Anglo-Norman noble, were hunting together out of sight of the other huntsmen. The official record of what occurred is summarised on a memorial stone placed near the spot, which read in part:

> Here stood the oak tree, on which an arrow shot by Sir Walter Tyrrell at a stag, glanced and struck King William the Second, surnamed Rufus, on the breast, of which he instantly died, on the second day of August, anno 1100.[5]

It could have been an accident, but Tyrrell was an expert bowman, who chose to cross the Channel immediately after the event, to take refuge from English justice in his Norman estates. Even more peculiar is that the entire hunting party and the hunt servants all hurriedly rode off in the medieval equivalent of *I saw nothing!* They left their late king's body lying where it fell, later to be conveyed on a local peasant's cart to Winchester cathedral.

The immediate actions of William Rufus' thirty-something-year-old younger brother seem to indicate foreknowledge. With the only other surviving son of the Conqueror, Robert of Normandy, far away on his way back from the Holy Land, the timing of Rufus' demise was ideal for Prince Henry. He rode hard to Winchester with the intention of seizing the treasury – the first act for anyone intending to grab the throne. There, however, he had an argument with nobles loyal to Robert, to whom Henry had also performed homage. This, Henry brushed aside, claiming the right of porphyrogeniture,[6] having been born after the Conquest when his parents were king and queen of England, whereas at the time of Robert's birth they had been only duke and duchess of Normandy. Supported by a number of other barons – were they all there by chance? – his argument carried the day, permitting him to occupy Winchester castle and seize the treasury.

Archbishop Anselm of Canterbury had chosen to exile himself because he disapproved of the late king's lifestyle, so Henry and his followers rode to London, where he presented himself to the citizens as a successor to the later canonised Anglo-Saxon king Edward the Confessor and promised to correct the excesses of William Rufus, especially towards the Church. This persuaded the city's bishop Maurice of Le Mans to crown him as king of England. Returning to Normandy the following month, Robert Courtheuse was furious and planned an invasion, to claim his right to the throne of England, counting on the support of many Anglo-Norman barons who also owned lands south of the Channel and could not afford to fall out with him. Eventually landing in 1101 at Portsmouth, he wrong-footed Henry, who had guessed he would land at Pevensey, but redeemed his error by moving his forces fast to Portsmouth. There, they prevented the arrival of Robert's anticipated reinforcements from Normandy, many of whom were deterred from coming by Archbishop Anselm. Robert's partisans in England stayed away, not wanting to forfeit the privileges granted in Henry's coronation charter.

THE DEATH OF KINGS

The frustrated duke of Normandy swore an oath to renounce any claim to the throne of England and returned to Normandy, but, once there he continued to cause problems for Henry in England. Losing patience, Henry invaded the duchy in 1105, but had to return to England to sort out domestic problems with the Church. Invading Normandy anew in 1106, he defeated Robert and a number of Norman nobles loyal to him at the battle of Tinchbray on 28 September, claiming Normandy as his and thus finally reuniting his late father's empire on both sides of the Channel. As duke of Normandy, he became a vassal of the French King Philippe I, but the vassal was more powerful by far than the king to whom he owed fealty. To ensure that Robert Courtheuse could cause no more problems, Henry had him imprisoned in Devizes castle for twenty years and then taken to the more secure Cardiff castle, where he died in February 1134, aged 83, after twenty-seven years in prison. With two brothers dead and the other his prisoner for life, Henry I could afford to feel secure.

All four of the Conqueror's sons resembled each other: short by today's standards and stocky with a barrel-chest from all that weapons training when young, with darkish hair. Henry's nickname was Beauclerc because he had been raised – possibly for high office in the Church – to be literate in Latin and French. His marriage in November 1100 to the devout Scottish Princess Matilda[7] was intended to safeguard England's northern border by forming an alliance with her father King Malcolm III and to provide Henry with a legitimate heir. She bore a daughter, also called Matilda, and a son named William, possibly also a short-lived son named Richard. This was no love match: having done her wifely duty, as she saw it, Scottish Matilda left the king to 'take his pleasure elsewhere', while she occupied herself with good works like kissing lepers on the lips and distributing charity to the poor.

In 1108 Henry betrothed his 6-year-old daughter Matilda to 27-year-old German king Heinrich V. It was an important political/ military step, given the constant tensions over the duchy of Normandy between Henry and the French kings Philippe I and Louis VI, who was now faced with the prospect of war on two fronts by the new alliance. For Heinrich, Matilda's dowry of 10,000 marks or £6,666[8] was the most important element, enabling him to fund a war in Italy, adding territory south of the Alps to his possessions. Two years later Matilda, still short of her eleventh birthday, was crowned queen of Germany.

It tells much of her character that in 1111, when her husband became Emperor Heinrich V of the Holy Roman Empire – as the whole German territory was known – she awarded herself the title of empress, although not crowned as such, and kept it for life. The chroniclers taking little account of girls' births, there may have been a daughter born to Heinrich during their eleven-year marriage, but she bore him no son.

The problem for Henry I of England in having only one legitimate son was that Prince Adelin or Atheling was drowned with 140 noblemen and eighteen noblewomen in the sinking of the galley *Blanche Nef* – the White Ship – after its port side hit a submerged rock in Barfleur harbour while setting out for England on 25 November 1120.[9] The rock was a known hazard, but the fifty oarsmen and other crew-members were so drunk on wine given them by the noble passengers that no one was looking where the vessel was heading. The carousing had begun before they even boarded the fatal vessel and two monks and some other passengers prudently decided to await another ship, thereby saving their lives. After the ship capsized, only one person survived the following night in the cold seas: a butcher from Rouen clad in warm skins, who had come aboard in an attempt to dun the heedless young nobles for meat supplied, but never paid for.

King Henry I had sired at least twenty-four bastards, two named Richard and Matilda going down with the *Blanche* Nef, but since Prince William Atheling was the only legitimate son, no one dared at first to tell the king about the shipwreck. Learning eventually, the bereaved father was distraught with grief. His Scottish queen Edith-Matilda having died two years earlier, he eventually accepted his counsellors' advice to take a young bride in the hope of begetting more legitimate sons. So Henry married 18-year-old Adeliza, daughter of the count of Louvain, but he was over 50 at the time and the couple produced no children in a marriage of fourteen years. The prodigious sex drive that had produced more bastards by Henry than any other English king – at least nine sons and fifteen daughters are recorded, some of his mistresses bearing him more than one child – had either waned or a lifetime spent in the saddle had rendered him infertile, for Adeliza had no trouble bearing seven children to her second husband after the death of Henry I.

Best described as a harsh but efficient ruler, Henry had spent two whole decades closely watching his father's and William Rufus' decisions and actions. He had thus learned to keep a tight control on his barons, taxing them and his vavasours through a formal Exchequer on both sides of the Channel and raising *novi homines* – literally 'new men' with no family loyalties or feudal obligations to conflict with their duty to him – to act as itinerant justices, enforcing his laws when he was absent. However, his attempt to control the Church by appointing England's bishops – a continuing source of conflict between the Church and their temporal overlords at this time – caused him soon to fall out with Archbishop Anselm.

Bereft of an heir, and unwilling to settle on any illegitimate son as his successor, Henry was greatly relieved when Emperor Heinrich V died in 1125. Had Matilda produced a boy by the emperor, she could have ruled the Empire as regent for her son. Instead, she returned to England a year later, a forceful, experienced and intelligent stateswoman of 24 who had fully justified the considerable political power given her by her late husband. Henry swiftly decided that she was a better choice for the English throne than any of the other possible candidates. He therefore summoned his chief vassals to his Christmas court at Westminster and forced them all to swear allegiance to her as his successor, should he die without male issue, as seemed all too likely. The key word there is *forced*, for many barons resented the idea of being ruled by a woman. Grumbling but complying, they swore an oath, recognising Matilda as the lawful ruler of England and Normandy after Henry died.

The Christmas and Easter courts were important assemblies of an overlord and his chief vassals, including his bishops and maybe even an archbishop or two. The timing of these courts took advantage of the high holy days of the Christian calendar. The vassals were summoned to attend and had to show up so that Henry could personally check them out for any signs of disaffection and his regular courtiers could listen to all the gossip in the corridors. The arrangements were costly – not only to accommodate and feed the dukes and counts and their attendants, but also to feed and water their mounts, averaging three for each vassal attending.

To avoid another succession crisis when Matilda died, it was important that she should have children to inherit her lands and titles. Killing two birds with one stone, Henry married her off to Geoffrey, the handsome 15-year-old son of Count Fulk[10] of Anjou and Maine, lying to the south of Normandy. This allied the duchy with two troublesome neighbouring counties and rebuilt the relationship with Count Fulk, who had been the father-in-law of Prince Adelin. After the mariage in Le Mans cathedral on 17 June 1128, young Geoffrey seemed to his politically experienced bride like a boy and quite unworthy of the proud 24-year-old wife who called herself Empress Matilda. Whether or not she allowed him conjugal relations, is unknown. What is known – and it fits perfectly with her character – is that, shortly after the wedding, she left him and travelled back to England, against the will of both her husband and her father. A few months later, Geoffrey's widowed father Fulk, who had been a respected commander in the First Crusade, married Melisande, daughter of King Baudouin II of the Latin kingdom of Jerusalem, and succeeded Baudouin as king of the Holy City. In departing for Outremer – or *overseas* as it was termed – Fulk passed title of his lands to his son Geoffrey. In 1131 he was 18 years old and a seasoned warrior-count in his own right when Matilda returned to Anjou and either resumed, or commenced, conjugal relations, duly producing three sons: Henry early in 1133, Geoffroi the following year and William two years after that.

Unfortunately for Henry I's plans for the succession, when he died suddenly, at Lyons-la-Forêt in Normandy on 1 December 1135 – as the result of eating 'a surfeit of lampreys' against his physician's advice, if we are to believe the chronicler Henry of Huntingdon[11] – Matilda was pregnant with her last son and unwilling to risk a long winter crossing of the Channel from Barfleur to claim her right to the English throne. Instead, Henry's nephew Etienne de Blois swiftly learned of his uncle's death and immediately took ship from his port of Wissant with a small retinue of household knights for the shortest of all Channel crossings – from there to Dover – arriving in London by 8 December. Once there, he claimed the throne for himself as the dead king's favourite nephew. As to the oath that Etienne had sworn with the other Anglo-Norman vassals in his capacity as lord of Eye and Lancaster to support the succession of Empress Matilda, his brother, Bishop Henry of Winchester, obligingly said the oath was invalid because it had been sworn under duress. In corroboration, a blatantly false rumour originated with Hugh Bigod, earl of Norfolk, who swore the late king had confided in him a change of mind: that the succession should pass to his nearest *male* relative, Etienne de Blois.

Known as a valiant warrior, this nephew of Henry I also had a pleasing manner and persuasive tongue allied to an instinct for diplomacy, which won over the citizens of London, who believed they had some rights in the choice of king. At Winchester, Etienne received the approval of the Church from Bishop Roger of Salisbury, who had been Henry I's chancellor – and also grabbed the royal treasury. In return for Etienne's promise to grant more liberties to the Church, William de Corbeil, Archbishop of Canterbury, agreed to officiate at a coronation ceremony. So Etienne was crowned King Stephen on 26 December. Paraphrasing Vegetius, speed had won him the throne, allied to the dislike of many Anglo-Norman barons for the idea of being ruled by a woman.

In addition, Stephen claimed the duchy of Normandy, whose barons also viewed with disfavour the thought of becoming vassals of Matilda. In addition, many of them also held fiefs in England, and wanted the same overlord on both sides of the Channel. This incited Count Geoffrey of Anjou to initiate, in the name of his wife, an eleven-year campaign to regain the duchy of Normandy, in which he was finally successful. During this time, before heraldry in the form of coats of arms emblazoned in a knight's shield, it was impossible to recognise a knight wearing full armour in the clash of armed combat. For this reason, Geoffrey of Anjou stuck a sprig of bright yellow flowering broom in his helmet as a high-visibility rallying point for his followers in battle. It gained him another sobriquet, based on the Latin for broom – *planta genista*. The nickname was Plantagênet. And thus begins our story.

Chapter 3

The civil war

Stephen was not welcomed by all the barons of England. Although he created a power base in London and southeast England, much of the rest of the country was hostile to him. It was here that Matilda set her eye, particularly on her half-brother Count Robert of Gloucester, one of Henry I's bastards whose forces she and Geoffroi had recently been fighting in Normandy. After Robert undertook in 1139 to support her claim to the throne, she despatched an advance force that August, which landed at the town of Wareham in Dorset, lying between the river Frome and the charmingly named river Piddle, to the north. At the time Wareham was an important port on the river Frome with a Norman castle that would make an excellent base for the main invasion. When Stephen's supporters forced them to withdraw further into the southwest, in September Queen Adeliza or Adelaide, the widowed second wife of Henry I, showed what she thought of Stephen breaking his sworn oath on the succession by inviting Matilda to land in Sussex and make a base at her castle in Arundel. Matilda duly arrived with 140 knights under Robert of Gloucester – far short of an invading army. Only fifty miles from London, this was nevertheless too close for Stephen to tolerate. When Robert marched northwest, to drum up more support, Stephen struck, besieging Matilda in Adeliza's very stout castle until his brother, Bishop Henry, negotiated a truce, under which Matilda was allowed to depart with her *familia* of household knights to meet up with Robert of Gloucester. Historians differ as to why Stephen did this. Was it a tactic? Was it gallantry? We do not know.

Matilda set up court at Gloucester, with Robert basing his growing forces on Bristol. Between them, they controlled a considerable slice of west and southwest England, part of the Welsh Marches and as far east as Wallingford and Oxford. There were few real battles in this war that was fought with sieges of each side's castles and skirmishing,

THE CIVIL WAR

much of southern England being laid waste as the two sides advanced and retreated, but gradually a balance of power was established, with Stephen controlling the southeast and some eastern counties and Matilda and Robert securing the southwest and the upper Thames valley. In January 1141 a decisive battle did take place at Lincoln. The city had been occupied by Stephen's forces, while supporters of Matilda held out in the adjacent castle, hoping to be relieved, although surrounded by Stephen's army made up of vassals loyal to him and their knights, plus mercenaries from Flanders, with siege engines battering at its walls. The phrase 'vassals loyal to him' overlooks the many times a vassal changed sides. Hugh Bigod, 1st earl of Norfolk, rebelled against Stephen within a year of being granted the title, surrendered, and was pardoned. At Lincoln, he fought for Stephen, but later switched allegiance to Empress Matilda and held Ipswich against Stephen in 1153. A decade later, he had caused so many problems for Henry II, both before and after his coronation, that the king built Orford castle between 1165–1173 to remind the Bigods who was king. A year after the completion of Orford, Hugh Bigod joined the Young King's rebellion, attacking Norwich with him in June 1174.

Back in February 1141 a mixed force of Matilda's Angevins and Anglo-Norman knights under Robert of Gloucester and Ranulf de Gernon, count of Chester, plus a force of Welshmen from Glamorgan and Gwynedd, arrived to lift the siege. In the battle that followed, initial success of Stephen's supporters against the Welsh flank was followed by a cavalry charge by the Angevin knights. Stephen's cavalry being outnumbered, the Angevins carried the day and many of Stephen's nobility, deciding that discretion was the better part of valour, departed hastily to avoid being taken prisoner. According to the chronicler Roger of Hoveden, Stephen fought valiantly with battle-axe and, when the axe was broken, drew his sword and continued fighting until this was broken too – at which point he surrendered to an Anglo-Norman knight from Dorset named de Cahaignes.[1] After spending the night in the much damaged and plundered city of Lincoln, the usurper king was escorted to Gloucester for a meeting with Matilda. Forgiveness was not in her nature, nor should it have been at that moment. Taken to Bristol castle, Stephen was at first honourably treated although, when he later unwisely took to wandering outside his quarters, he was fettered to prevent him making an escape.

At this juncture, it seemed that Matilda was going to win the civil war. Certainly, she thought so, being hailed at an ill-attended council in Winchester on 7 April as *angliae normanniaeque domina* or Lady of England and Normandy – 'lady' not being a polite term, but the female equivalent of 'lord'. Arrangements having been put in hand with the blessing of Bishop Henry of Winchester for her coronation at Westminster, in June she travelled to London. Arriving in the capital on 24 June, she was met with such extreme hostility from the citizens who preferred Stephen that she swiftly back-tracked to Oxford. Bishop Henry changed sides again, prompting Matilda to set out for Winchester to force him to change his allegiance once more and crown her there.

Arriving on 12 August, she found that Bishop Henry had shut himself up in his fortified palace adjacent to the cathedral, where he managed to hold out for three weeks, his soldiers having burned down or otherwise destroyed large parts of the city that might have given cover to any attackers. Robert of Gloucester did not attack the bishop's palace, but set about taking the royal castle at the other end of the city. That done, when Matilda summoned Bishop Henry to a parley in the castle, he wisely stayed in his palace. King Stephen's wife, Matilda of Boulogne, who commanded his loyal troops during his imprisonment, arrived with a force of mercenaries from London in mid-September. With the two Matildas confronting each other, this was far from being the only time that a besieging force found itself surrounded by a relief force which, in this case roundly outnumbered Empress Matilda's and Robert's men. Seemingly, only at this point and after being rejected by the Londoners did she realise that her personal unpopularity was causing many Anglo-Normans to side with King Stephen. The country was in chaos, local nobles seizing power for themselves, building adulterine castles and issuing their own coinage. The damage to agriculture from foraging and destruction in the paths of the armies made food scarce and sickness rife in a period dubbed 'the anarchy' by Victorian medievalists.

Hearing that the London militia was also approaching Winchester, the Count of Chester deserted, as did a number of Empress Matilda's other noble supporters. On 14 December Robert of Gloucester decided to break out with him commanding the rearguard so that his half-sister could escape. Many did get away with Matilda, but Robert was taken prisoner by the count of Surrey and a cohort of Angevins from the rearguard were trapped in the abbey of Werwell after being hotly pursued

THE CIVIL WAR

for ten miles. This was not a retreat, but a rout. The worst news was for Empress Matilda to learn that Robert of Gloucester had been taken prisoner in ensuring her safety. Without her half-brother to command what forces remained, she was lost.

In November, after various attempts to negotiate a peace had failed, the two principal hostages were exchanged under conditions of truce, while Bishop Henry did a political about-turn and declared that his brother was England's legitimate monarch. In mid-1142, while Robert of Gloucester was fighting in Normandy, Matilda unwisely allowed herself to be trapped in Oxford castle. The city being occupied by Stephen's men, he settled down to a prolonged siege of the castle. Shortly before Christmas, on a night when a blizzard was blowing and the besiegers thought it too cold for a man, let alone a woman, to venture outside, Matilda and a handful of her household knights slipped out of the castle by the postern gate and descended the river bank unchallenged, the white sheets they had wrapped around themselves making them nearly invisible in the driving snow. Although they heard the alarm being sounded in the siege camp, they were not intercepted. Walking for several miles on the ice that covered the river Thames, they managed to reach Abingdon, where they acquired horses to take them the rest of the way to Wallingford castle. On the following day Oxford castle was surrendered by the Empress' garrison, its defenders being honourably treated.

A comprehensive history of the civil war would fill a thicker book than this. Essentially, for the next several years, as soon as one side gained the upper hand, defection by vassals or local truces changed the balance of power. In 1147 Stephen conferred the county of Boulogne on his son Eustace and wanted to have him crowned junior king of England too, as was the custom in Capetian France. Two successive popes refused to countenance this, as did Archbishop of Canterbury Theobald of Bec. The worst news for Empress Matilda in that year was learning of the sudden death of Robert of Gloucester in Bristol on 31 October. The one inescapable truth of the long drawn-out struggle was that she was too haughty and too arrogant to win the support of many barons – although the same behaviour in a man would have been quite acceptable. In 1148 she returned to Normandy, leaving her 14-year-old son Henry fitz Empress[2] in England, to continue the fight. A shrewd but unlovable young man, who would not be knighted until 1149 when he was 16, Henry had been taught by his mother that ruling men was like venery.

PLANTAGENET PRINCES

The trick, she said, was to show the bait to the hawk, but snatch it away before the bird could take it, thus keeping it hungry and eager to please. Applied to vassals, this policy had plainly not worked for her but her eldest son was to employ it for the rest of his life.

There was a tacit truce when vassals and other knights were summoned to court, but how did this work between men who spent most of their lives fighting? Fortunately, a poet who seems to have attended Henry's court wrote a book detailing the behaviour to be observed at court, which, by implication revealed their behaviour elsewhere. He wrote it in Latin verse 3,000 lines long. His name being *danielis becclesiensis* or Daniel of Beccles, he advised knights wishing to behave properly:

- to look up at the ceiling if they had to belch at table;
- not to attack an enemy while he was squatting to defecate;
- not to mount one's horse in the banqueting hall;
- not to urinate in hall, unless one was the host;
- if eating at a rich man's table, to say little

… and so on. The advice covered three areas of behaviour: knowing one's place in society and behaving accordingly; physical self-control; and sexual mores. A respect for women is nowhere evident. They were, he alleged, all whores, thinking of lovers when in the act with their husbands. So what should a young knight do when his lord's wife made an advance? Pretend to be ill, or diseased. If lust drove one to use a prostitute, ejaculate as quickly as possible and leave. As to choosing a wife, he recommended checking out the property she owned as the most important consideration.

Chapter 4

The crusader queen

Backtracking fifteen years, when her father died on pilgrimage to the Galician shrine of Santiago de Compostela around Easter 1137, the beautiful, educated and very forceful elder daughter of Duke William X of Aquitaine inherited the county of Poitou in her own right and thus by tradition became also duchess of Aquitaine, which covered almost a quarter of France at the time. She was 15 years old. Geoffroi de Lauroux, the shrewd archbishop of Bordeaux, hastily concluded arrangements for her marriage to 17-year-old Crown Prince Louis of the Capetian royal family, which had ruled France since 987. They were married in Bordeaux cathedral on 25 July 1137. The archbishop's messengers despatched to Paris could have done the trip in a week, with relays of horses. But Prince Louis made the journey of 400-plus miles much more slowly, having decided not to demand food and fodder from every local lord and bringing the all the necessary provisions, tents, weapons and other baggage with him transported on ox-carts. The whole cortège had to travel at the slower pace of the oxen or risk being separated in what was not always friendly territory.

When his father Louis the Fat died two weeks after the wedding, Eleanor's immature and monkish husband became Louis VII of France and she his teenage queen consort, dominating the court on the Ile de la Cité in Paris by sheer force of character. Having been raised for a career in the Church until the accidental death of his elder brother, Louis had neither the will nor the training to rule, so Eleanor, who had been raised to govern the unruly barons of Aquitaine, did her best to make him grow up and behave like a medieval monarch.

She had to drive away from court his deeply religious mother, the dowager queen Adelaide de Maurienne, and overcome the influence of the powerful northern French barons and Church leaders who had constituted the *curia* of Louis VII's father. What she could not do,

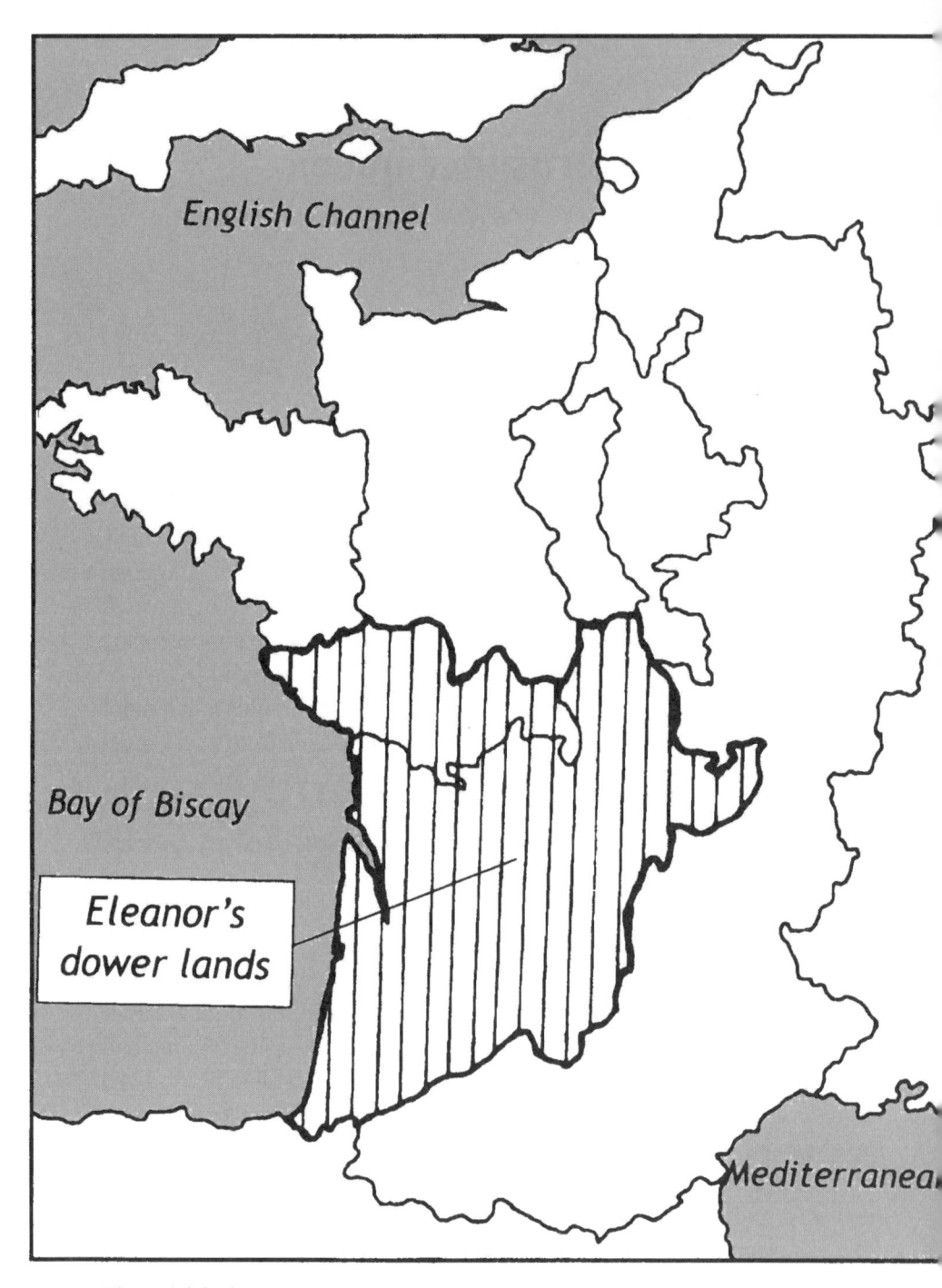

Eleanor's inheritance

was turn her husband into a powerful warrior-poet like her father and grandfather. Typical of her oft-repeated complaints were, 'I thought I had married a king, and found I had wed a monk' and 'He spent more nights on his knees at the altar than in my bed.' After one stillbirth, she did manage to produce a daughter for Louis, but the lack of any other children – especially a son – in the first decade of the marriage was regarded as her fault and increased her unpopularity in the Capetian court.

When Louis signed up for the Second Crusade in 1148, Pope Eugenius III conferred absolution on all those taking the cross. To Louis, this meant remission of the sins he had committed in warfare, egged on by Eleanor. To his horror, although Eugenius had imposed an oath of chastity on the crusaders and forbidden women to accompany them, except for 'decent washerwomen', Eleanor did not intend to miss the adventure of a lifetime. Defying both husband and pope, she assembled a court of noble ladies avid, like her, for this adventure and whose baggage train of personal effects and luxurious pavilions in which to sleep required so many ox-drawn carts that it had to set off in advance of the main body of noblemen, knights and men-at-arms, in order not to cause traffic jams on the road.[3]

Once arrived in the Holy Land, when Eleanor was prevented by Louis' chaplain and bishops from even seeing him, to prevent her influencing him in any way, she travelled north to the Latin Kingdom of Antioch. Its ruling prince was her uncle Raymond of Toulouse, with whom Louis' counsellors accused her of adultery. Although there was never any proof, they had her kidnapped in Antioch by a castrated Templar knight and forced to board a ship returning to Europe at the end of the crusade. Paying what should have been a courtesy call to Pope Eugenius, exiled from Rome and staying at his castle of Tusculum, fifteen miles southeast of the eternal city, Eleanor and Louis were greeted by the pope as returning pilgrims who had suffered much for their faith during the past two years. Louis confided to Eugenius his ambition of raising finance for another expedition to the Holy Land to carry out everything the Second Crusade had failed to achieve, but Eleanor had more personal issues on her mind. Papal secretary John of Salisbury recorded her skilful presentation in Latin of the case for an annulment of her marriage to Louis on the grounds of consanguinity, in which she cited the authority of the most famous monk in France, Bernard of Clairvaux, whom the Pope himself consulted on points of canon law.

PLANTAGENET PRINCES

Smiling but firm, Eugenius would hear none of this, ruling to the French queen's horror that her marriage was legitimate and threatening with anathema anyone rash enough to refer in the future to the matter of this consanguinity. Furious that Louis' bishops had turned Eugenius' ear against her before she had had a chance to put her case, Eleanor poured out the long list of her legitimate grievances, including her forcible abduction from Antioch and the continual constraint under which she lived as Louis' wife. Far from taking any notice of a woman desperate to escape from a hated and frustrating marriage, Eugenius ordered a double bed to be prepared for the royal couple and spread with his own bedcovers, where Louis was to perform his conjugal duty. Backed by the pope's authority, he managed to do so, with the result that, once back in the royal palace on the Ile de la Cité, Eleanor produced ... another daughter. With rumours rife about her allegedly scandalous behaviour in Antioch – and now this third failure to birth a son – she became a political problem for Louis, whose own reputation was besmirched by having wasted so much of his vassals' tax money in the failed crusade. He was under increasing pressure to divorce Eleanor and find another wife who would perform a queen's most important function: providing a son to inherit the realm.

Among many vassals who failed to pay homage to Louis after the crusade were Count Geoffrey of Anjou and his son Henry. Being a son of the late King Fulk of Jerusalem and thus well aware of the realities of the crusader states in the Holy Land, Count Geoffroi had remained aloof from the crusading fever. Recently knighted by his cousin the King of Scotland, his eldest son Henry had already proved himself in battle although only 19 years old. He was also well-educated for a layman, having been tutored in boyhood by bishops and lay scholars in both France and England. During his years in England, the famous scientist Adelard of Bath had even dedicated a book to him. After returning to Normandy with Empress Matilda in the late 1130s, he had been sent back in 1142, aged 9, to live with Robert of Gloucester. While there, Henry was schooled by the Augustinian canons in Bristol. A year later, he was back in Anjou, returning once more to England aged 14 at the head of a small invading force of mercenaries. The invasion was a failure, ending with Henry lacking the funds either to pay off his men or return to Normandy. Since neither Empress Matilda or Robert of Gloucester was prepared to bail him out, the assumption is that his futile invasion had not been approved by either of them. Desperate to escape the hole he had dug himself into, Henry turned to King Stephen, who paid off the men-at-arms and enabled his adolescent cousin to return to France. If he expected gratitude, he must have been disappointed when Henry invaded again in 1149, hoping to link up with the forces of King David I of Scotland and Count Ranulf of Chester in York – a plan that had to be abandoned when Stephen got there first, compelling Henry's return to France once more.

After Louis VII's return from crusade, Count Geoffrey needed him to invest his son Henry as Duke of Normandy, which, with Anjou, Maine and Touraine, constituted a considerable amount of territory. At the same time, he was seeking for his son a wife whose dowry would strengthen his hand against Louis on the day they came into confrontation over the heavily fortified strip of territory known as the Vexin, which divided Normandy from the royal domain north-west of Paris. Louis' Christmas court of 1151 was held at Limoges, followed by a plenary council at St Jean d'Angély, celebrating Candlemas in the first week of February. Behind the scenes the midnight candles burned as the several bishops busied themselves undoing the knots of Eugenius' validation in perpetuity of Louis' marriage to Eleanor, given at Tusculum. Her unlikely ally in this was Bernard of Clairvaux, the most famous monk in France, intelligent and learned, but so averse to women that he could not bear to look at his own sister in her nun's habit.

In Bernard's view the value of Eleanor's vast dowry, which would have to be returned to her when the marriage ended, was but dross, compared with the need to dissolve Louis' incestuous marriage to a woman in whose veins flowed the blood of the sacrilegious dukes of Aquitaine who had corrupted bishops and defied excommunication. As Christ had said in the Sermon on the Mount that an eye which sinned should be plucked out and thrown away, and that it was better to lose a hand or an eye than for the soul to be cast into eternal hellfire after death, so Eleanor must be divorced from the pious king of France …

On the Friday before Palm Sunday – 21 March 1152 – at Louis' castle of Beaugency, midway between Orleans and Blois, a council of high vassals and churchmen convened to divorce Louis from his disgraced wife. He, with a genuine nobility and charity rare among royalty of any period, still refused to accuse Eleanor of anything. It was therefore agreed for the dignity of the monarchy that the widely known consanguinity of the spouses should be the grounds for divorce. Having conveniently forgotten Eleanor's outburst in Tusculum, John of Salisbury later described this annulment as her 'repudiation'. Far from being humiliated, Eleanor was delighted. The price was that her daughters remained the property of their father, so it was extremely unlikely she would ever see them again.

The slanders that Louis had repudiated an unfaithful wife had a long life. As late as the mid-1990s the audio-commentary at the Plantagenet treasure castle above the town of Chinon still stated that *'elle trompait le roi en pleine cour'* – she had been 'unfaithful to the King in front of the whole court'. That would have taken a lot of arranging on the Ile de la Cité, where she had been spied upon since the day of her arrival by hostile courtiers, priests and servants. As to what she had done with the inevitable results of her illicit liaisons, rumours were that she had buried them in Belin churchyard, south of Bordeaux.

She rode away from Beaugency with a small escort of her own household knights, once again the confirmed and independent ruler of a quarter of France. Being no longer protected by her position as Louis' queen meant that she was, at the age of 30, fair game for kidnap and a forced marriage. On the return journey to Poitiers, two young nobles attempted to do this, and failed.

Once safe in her own territory, Eleanor welcomed to Poitiers during the second week of May the 19-year-old duke of Normandy, to sound out the possibilities. Even Alfred Richard, nineteenth-century archivist of the *département* of Vienne, stated that she was bored with effeminate Louis' platonic love and deliberately sought a brutal new lover in Henry because she was 'one of those women who like to be knocked around'.[1] This strangely misogynistic comment is baseless, like all the other slanders levelled at her, since Henry would never have married a woman he thought guilty of all the alleged misconduct.

Although generations of historians have repeated the calumnies against her, Matilda's son Henry was eager to marry Eleanor despite them. Fluent in Latin and French, he enjoyed the company of scholars, both ecclesiastical and lay, but was prone to outbursts of rage when thwarted, throwing himself on the floor among the soiled reeds and literally going berserk. This was said to be a legacy from his Viking forebears. In today's terms, he would be described as paranoid, never telling anyone his intentions until he was well embarked on their fulfilment. Becoming duke of Normandy at the age of 17, he also inherited the county of Anjou.

All Eleanor's life had been spent in the corridors of power and the agreement she made with Henry was no love match. In wedding him despite even closer consanguinity than hers with Louis, she was marrying the thirteen counties of Aquitaine to the duchy of Normandy, plus the counties of Anjou, Maine and Touraine. This master-stroke created a power bloc that stretched all the way from the snows of the Pyrenees to the waters of the English Channel and united almost half of Louis VII's kingdom, in which he personally owned very little territory. On 18 May a ceremony in due form in Poitiers cathedral made her wife to the man who not only solved her pressing need for a spouse strong enough protect her domains from present enemies, but owed her a lifelong debt of gratitude for making him the most powerful man in France. Ironically, he would become in the course of time her most implacable enemy of all.

As to Eleanor providing Henry with a son and heir, it was common knowledge how rarely Louis had slept with his wife, so the lusty young duke of Normandy had no fears that he might fail to get Eleanor pregnant again and again until she bore him a son. Should she have failed to do so by the time of her menopause, he would still be in his thirties and able to use the justification of consanguinity to discard her and take a younger second wife, hopefully keeping his hands on her dowry. Or so he thought.

Like many powerful people, Henry was a paradox. He could be generous to a captain who had lost a ship in his service or to a vassal who had lost a limb in combat or a peasant whose property had been damaged by the royal hunt, yet his forest laws were vindictively cruel. These laws had first been introduced to England by William the Conqueror and show the disdain of the conquering race for the natives, barring them from whole areas formerly exploited by local people in hunting meat for their tables, taking wood for heating and pasturing their pigs on fallen nuts. The meaning of 'forest' was not the modern one – an area of woodland – but came from the Latin *foris* meaning outside, for these areas were outside the normal jurisdiction of the realm. Many of the royal forests set aside for the king and his assigns to hunt had no trees, but were moorland. The laws governing the common people's activities there and the terrible penalties for transgression were referred to as 'laws of vert and venison', venison being the animals reserved

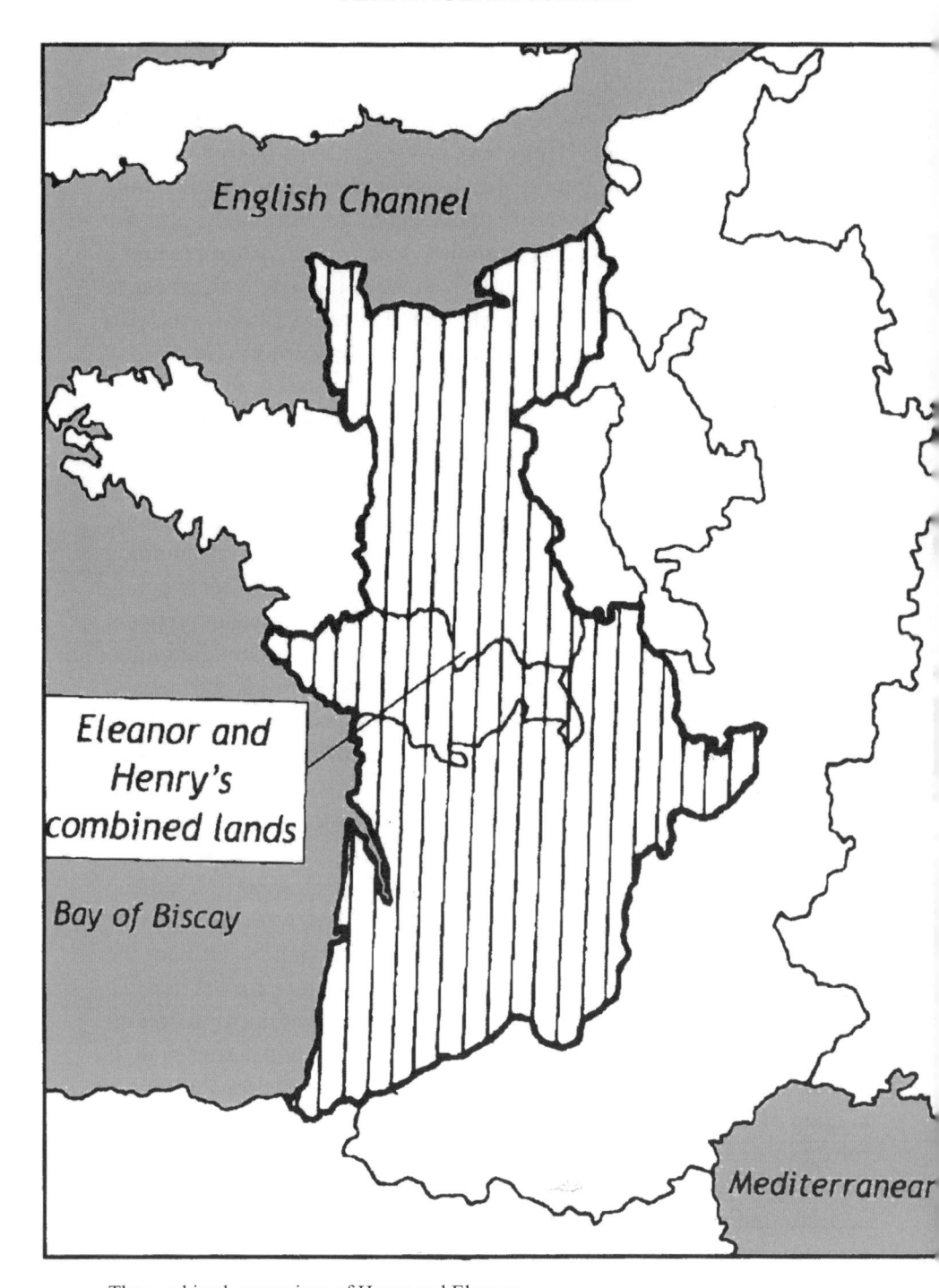

The combined possessions of Henry and Eleanor

for the king's pleasure and 'vert' being the green grazing they needed. 'Venison' from the Latin *venari* – to hunt – then covered deer but also hares, boars and wild goats taken in the chase.

Like his forebears and descendants, Henry II enjoyed hunting. Careless about his clothes, on occasion he called for needle and thread to mend a tear or replace a fastening himself. He was tolerant of Jews and heretics, but not homosexuals, once authorising torture for some Templars accused of sodomy. As to food, he contented himself when travelling with gruel or bread and expected his companions to do the same. If he thought that this lifestyle might drive Eleanor to retire from the erratic progress and wait for him in the comital palace at Poitiers, he was wrong. The woman who had ridden across Turkey on the Second Crusade was tougher than that and determined to establish her own position in the marriage from the outset, although knowing she would never have a fraction of the influence over her new husband that she had enjoyed over Louis.

After fighting off an invasion of his territory by Louis VII's brother Robert of Dreux, Henry spent the autumn of 1152 riding the length and breadth of Eleanor's Poitou and Aquitaine to impose on her vassals that he was now their duke, and so lessen the likelihood of rebellion during his future absences. His *chevauchée* as duke of Aquitane was cut short by encouraging news from England that caused him to hurry north. King Stephen's personal life was falling apart. His consort Matilda died, leaving him a 60-year-old widower, worn out by the civil war.

On 8 January 1153, Henry defied the winter storms in the Channel by setting sail from Barfleur with a flotilla of only twenty-six vessels.[2] Eleanor did not accompany him, but moved into Henry's territory by setting up in the Angevin capital at Angers the first of her own courts where comfort and pleasure meant not just good food and wine but all the other civilised pleasures of the day. In Rouen, all was sobriety and pious learning at the court of Matilda Empress. At Eleanor's court in Angers men played the gallant or were sent away until such time as they learned to. However valiant they might be in the field, Eleanor required them to speak eloquently, dress well and have their hair properly cut.

Nothing about her commended Henry's wife to his mother, who was not prepared to quietly step aside as Agnès de Maurienne had done when Eleanor arrived as Louis' bride on the Ile de la Cité. A pious autocrat, Empress Matilda accepted the political necessity for her son's marriage, but had no welcome for a daughter-in-law fresh from another man's bed and within the prohibited degrees of consanguinity. Nor was Eleanor inclined to curry favour from so hostile a mother-in-law. The two women kept their distance.

Landing in England on 9 January 1153 with an army of around 3,000 men, Henry found that being the most powerful man in France was not enough to oust King Stephen and his son, despite widespread dissatisfaction with the raping and looting of the Flemish mercenaries who kept Stephen on the throne. However, on 18 August 1153,[3] his son and heir Eustace of Blois died at Bury St Edmunds and was buried beside his mother at the royal abbey of Faversham in east Kent, an ancient Saxon 'king's town', originally founded in pre-Roman times, which was one of the Cinque Ports Stephen had wanted to make the capital of England.[4]

When Pope Anastasius IV confirmed by a papal bull the privileges of the foundation of Notre Dame de Saintes on 29 October of that same year, the list of donors included Louis VII of France, Eleanor and her sister Aelith, but of Henry there is no mention. Geoffroi de Lauroux, forever sniffing the winds of change, went on record by stating in a charter of 25 September 1153 that Aquitaine acknowledged only the authority of its duchess.[5] Never again during Henry's lifetime would Eleanor feel so secure.

Although he had another son called William, King Stephen decided it was time to accede to the pleadings of Archbishop Theobald and Bishop Henry, and make peace with Henry fitz Empress. On 6 November 1153 the treaty of Winchester was drawn up and proclaimed in Winchester cathedral. In return for Henry Curtmantle – the nickname referred to his habit of wearing short capes that gave little protection from the weather but made mounting and dismounting faster – performing homage to Stephen, the usurper king adopted him as his legal son and heir. William of Blois agreed not to dispute the succession in return for Henry's guarantee to repect his title to lands he held on both sides of the Channel. Like most of Henry's promises, the guarantee did not last, but for the moment there was no point in anyone continuing the long unrest that was ruining England in financial terms, in burned towns and in ruined agriculture as the forces of one side or the other rampaged across wide swathes of the kingdom.

On 17 August 1153 Eleanor gave birth to a son, her relief doubled by the knowledge that she had erased forever the stigma of having given Louis only daughters. She christened the boy William, after her father and grandfather and all the other Williams in her family, and honoured him with the courtesy title Duke of Aquitaine without asking Henry's opinion.[6] A few days after the birth, she learned that Eustace of Boulogne had choked to death during a meal at Bury St Edmunds. Worn out with strife, and in the hope of avoiding another civil war, his grieving father formally acknowledged Henry fitz Empress as his legal successor. At Christmas Archbishop Theobald of Canterbury enshrined the arrangement in a treaty witnessed at Westminster by fourteen bishops and eleven earls of the realm. Since Stephen of Blois was already an old man by the standards of the time, Henry was certain to be the most powerful monarch in Europe within a few years. It was a wonderful stroke of good luck for an ambitious young man of twenty-two.

Returning to France in high spirits, he summoned Eleanor and his infant son to Rouen, where they moved into the palace built by his grandfather. Henry now made peace with Louis and paid a 'fine' of a thousand silver marks for Louis to cease including 'Duke of Aquitaine' among his titles, which he had been doing on the strength of the specious argument that Eleanor had become duchess by virtue of her marriage to him. In Bordeaux, Geoffroi de Lauroux sniffed the wind again and proclaimed that the master of Aquitaine was henceforth Henry of Anjou.[7]

The city of Bordeaux, main city of Aquitaine, comes into the story many times. It had not existed before the Romans built an entrepôt port on the site near the confluence of the Garonne and Dordogne rivers. By transporting merchandise on mule-back from the Mediterranean to the watershed near Toulouse and then floating the merchandise on rafts down the Garonne, they avoided the long and perilous voyage around Spain and Portugal. Originally unwalled because the nearest enemies were hundreds of miles away on the German *limes*, it was attacked after the Roman withdrawal by Goths, Vandals and the Saracens in the eighth century, as well as several waves of Viking raiders, who penetrated inland as far as Toulouse, killing and plundering as they went. The first substantial wall enclosed little more than the Roman *castrum*. Later walls enclosed more and more space living space, dominated by the huge cathedral of St André and the ducal palace called l'Ombreyra, built adjacent to the port, which remained the city's *raison d'être*.

As duke of Normandy and Aquitaine, Henry had to lead his men into the field for Louis when called upon. After recovering from some unspecified but severe illness – perhaps malaria, which was endemic in Europe at the time – Henry rode off to help Louis pacify the ever-restless Vexin, lying between Normandy and the royal domains. It was there that messengers from Archbishop Theobald came to tell him that Stephen had died on 25 October, so the Duke and Duchess of Aquitaine and Normandy could now add 'King and Queen of England' to all their other titles.

With no intention of letting the long anarchy of Stephen's reign continue, Henry intended showing the Anglo-Norman magnates from the outset the way they were to behave with him on the throne. With a small retinue of personal servants, Eleanor travelled to meet him at the port of Barfleur on the lee of the Cotentin peninsula seven months into her second pregnancy by Henry. Surrounded by nobles and churchmen who had witnessed or heard of her humiliation on the Second Crusade, this was her moment of triumph, looking each of them in the face, and requiring the proper deference due to the mother of their overlord's son, visibly about to produce another child by him. For a whole month, Henry's court was trapped by the weather in the little Norman seaport while November gales blew in from the Atlantic day and night, making it impossible to put to sea. They were still stormbound on 7 December when, determined to celebrate Christmas wearing the crown of England, Henry ignored the lesson of the White Ship sinking in that very place and embarked himself, his pregnant wife and infant son in a virtually identical clinker-built vessel with high bow and stern, rigged with a lateen sail that enabled them to cross against the westerly swell, rolling and pitching sickeningly on a grey sea under a leaden sky.

Even with sails tightly reefed the convoy was scattered before nightfall, ships buffeted by wind and tide making landfall in harbours widely separated. Henry and Eleanor first set foot in their new kingdom somewhere in the New Forest near Lyndhurst, from where he rode hard to Winchester to secure the royal treasury, commandeering fresh horses on the way and acquiring a cortège of Anglo-Norman prelates and nobles, drawn by the news of his apparently miraculous arrival on the wings of the storm. From Winchester they progressed to London without a hand lifted or a sword drawn in protest, thanks to Archbishop Thibault of Canterbury who had assembled the bishops of the realm to acclaim their new monarch.

THE CRUSADER QUEEN

The abbey at Westminster, upriver from London and near the old crossing by a ford until the Romans built the first London bridge, was the traditional place for coronations, but had been vandalised by Stephen's mercenaries, who had also rendered the adjoining palace uninhabitable, forcing Henry to set up court south of the Thames in Bermondsey. On 15 December, the Sunday before Christmas, he and Eleanor were crowned in Westminster Abbey, walking out of it to the cheers of the Anglo-Saxon lower orders and the Norman-French and Latin acclamations of the nobility and clergy.

In his history of Britain dedicated to Eleanor, the Jersey poet Robert Wace probably based his description of the legendary King Arthur's coronation feast on hers and Henry's. While mutton was not much in favour with the Anglo-Norman nobility, beef, pork and game were consumed in large quantities. Game could be fresh all the year round, but beef and pork had to be salted for winter consumption when the animals not required for breeding were slaughtered in November. As a result, dried herbs, pepper and other imported spices were used heavily in stuffings, sauces and marinades to disguise the saltiness and cover the unpalatable taste of rotten meat.

Most bread was wheaten or rye, the latter being the cause of the disease called St Anthony's Fire when made with ergot-infected flour that caused convulsions, miscarriages, dry gangrene and death. Omelettes, stews and pies were common, and fish was consumed in quantity, with palaces and monasteries having their own fish farms to guarantee a fresh supply for Fridays, Lent and the many other meatless days decreed by the Church. To cleanse the palate there was a wide range of sweet desserts – fruits fresh, stewed and candied, jellies, tarts, waffles and wafers. While the natives preferred to drown their sorrows in ale – the fermentation process killed off many bacteria present in polluted well water – their masters preferred wine.

The waferers, whose speciality was making and serving the thin pastries eaten at the end of the meal with sweet white desert wine, were also the cabaret. There were tumblers of both sexes, storytellers, conjurers and jugglers, farters, singers and musicians playing bowed and plucked stringed instruments, harps, lyres, flutes of various kinds, shawms, bagpipes and other instruments. There were chess and backgammon boards for those who wished to gamble elegantly and fashionably, and dice for those whose taste was less refined. While many court entertainers were rewarded only with clothes and food, one who was both viol-player and *joculator* was given a life-interest in a small estate in Yorkshire. There were also some female comedians, known as *joculatrices*, who told dirty jokes. Henry's jester Herbert was given an estate of thirty acres in Suffolk and Roger the Fool doubled as keeper of Henry's otter-hounds, for which he was given a house in Aylesbury. The jesters, who owed their name to their original recounting of the great deeds of past heroes, known as *res gestae*, now amused their audience with scandalous comments on the noble guests, their irreverence being indulged so long as their wit was faster than that of their victims.

The following day, Eleanor at the age of 32 was the consort of the man who ruled from the Scottish border to the frontier of Spain. Mother of his son and heir, and conscious how great a part her wealth and possessions had played in his rise to this position of power, she had every reason to feel secure in her marriage to Henry – which was not to say she expected, or wanted, his fidelity. Queens shut their eyes to their husbands' mistresses. Indeed one of Henry's bastards by his Saxon mistress Ykenai was to be brought up with Eleanor's own children.

Chapter 5

Prince Henry

When historians wish to ascertain the character of medieval nobles and royalty, they tend to consult the writings of the chroniclers who were either contemporaneous with, or writing shortly after, their subjects. In the case of the second son of Eleanor of Aquitaine by Henry II, Gervase of Tilbury described him as tall, good humoured and of cheerful disposition – a man liked by all who knew him and the epitome of all princely virtues.[1] Yet, within a few weeks of this prince's death, Walter Map wrote of him, 'He befouled the whole world with his treasons [towards his father, and was] a limpid spring of wickedness, the attractive tinder of villainy.'[2] Ralph of Diceto, dean of St Paul's declared of him, 'sons who rise up against fathers to whom they owe everything that they are and everything by which they live ... are worthy only of being disinherited'.[3] Giraldus Cambrensis, who knew the court of Henry II, summed up Prince Henry as 'a Julius Caesar in genius, in valour a Hector, an Achilles in strength, an Augustus in conduct, a Paris in beauty'.[4] Yet, Roger of Howden's *Chronica* tells it differently: 'For this one of the king's sons was lost to all reason and feeling. He alone was to blame [for the war against Henry II], setting a whole army against his father ... for he thirsted for the blood of his father, for the death of his progenitor.'[5] With so many contradictions in the original sources, what is one to make of the prince who would have become England's Henry III, had he not died in disgrace and outlived his father instead?

When Henry II and Eleanor of Aquitaine were crowned king and consort of England on 19 December 1154, she was already largely pregnant with her second child by him. Born on 25 February 1155, Prince Henry – so named in honour of his great-grandfather Henry I – came into the world with a wondrous future ahead of him. His first state occasion came shortly after birth when he was baptised in St Paul's cathedral by Richard de Belmeis, bishop of London. As was customary with noble infants, day-to-day care of the young prince was in the hands of a wet-nurse named Philete,[6] herself supervised by a *magister* named Mainard.

To govern the Plantagenet Empire on both sides of the Channel and keep at bay the Scots and Welsh was already proving difficult for Prince Henry's hyperactive father. So, as the second son, it seemed likely that his older brother Prince William would one day inherit the throne of England with expectations of ruling also Wales and Ireland, if they could be subdued by force of arms. Since that would be more than enough for one king, it therefore seemed logical for the second son, if he survived childhood, to inherit the Continental possessions also ruled by Henry II, which together comprised more than half of France.

But the young prince's elder brother William was a sickly child, so when Henry II ordered the barons of the realm to swear allegiance to him for the kingdom of England on 3 April 1155 at Wallingford castle, he prudently obliged them also to recognise the infant Prince Henry as crown prince in the event of William dying. Just over a year later, in the spring or early summer of 1156, Prince William did die at Wallingford of some childhood ailment and was buried before the high altar of Reading Abbey beside the grave of his illustrious great-grandfather Henry I, who had founded the abbey.[7] It then seemed that Prince Henry might even eventually inherit all his father's lands. From early in his life Prince Henry accompanied his parents in visits to Normandy, travelling in the royal galley, known as *esnecca* – the snake ship. Although this was a relatively rapid way to cross the Channel, it was still not without risks. In 1170 a vessel travelling in the royal convoy was sunk in a gale with the loss of 400 passengers. Seven years later, Young Henry's chancellor was among those lost during a Channel crossing, with some 300 others, in another sudden storm that blew in from the Atlantic. However, between February 1157 and late 1158, although Henry II was busy putting down resistance to his rule on both sides of the Channel and fighting a minor war in Wales, Prince Henry stayed in England, his mother giving birth on 11 September 1157 in Oxford to another boy, christened Richard, who was to be her favourite son. On Easter Sunday 1158, Henry and Eleanor were re-crowned at Worcester following the French custom of confirmatory coronations.[8]

PRINCE HENRY

In August 1158 Henry II charged his chancellor Thomas Becket with an important mission. In Paris, Louis VII's second wife Constance of Castile had given birth to a daughter named Marguerite – and this after his two daughters by Eleanor of Aquitaine during his first marriage. When his fourth daughter was born a couple of years later, the devout king of France took to pacing the corridors of his palace on the Ile de la Cité muttering about *le nombre effrayant de princesses* – the frightening number of princesses – with which God had blessed him.[9] The infant Marguerite seemed to Henry II indeed a gift from God that might enable him to kill two birds with one stone, if she could be betrothed to Prince Henry. The problem was that Louis' *curia* would hardly approve any link with Queen Eleanor, the woman they still called 'the whore of Aquitaine'. But Becket had worked wonders during Henry II's reign already, so maybe …

Becket accordingly rode in great pomp from Rouen, the capital of Normandy, to Paris in early summer 1158 with a baggage train that included ten wagons loaded with his personal effects, including his travelling chapel and several pack horses laden with precious plate, to grace his table, and his personal library of books and scrolls. To avoid the temptation of theft or pilfering, armed guards ran alongside each wagon when entering Paris and grooms led finely bred hounds on the leash with falconers bearing their birds on gauntletted wrists. Knights of Becket's household in full armour and grandly attired bishops were followed by squires bearing their shields. Groups of singers in the costumes of every region governed by Henry II danced and sang as they progressed through the streets. Lastly came Henry II's chancellor, so magnificently robed – in contrast with his king, who took little interest in fine clothes – that the crowds in the streets marvelled, 'If this be only the chancellor of England, how much more splendid his master must be!'[10] So many people were in his train that Becket had to be accommodated in the Templars' halls outside the city, since there was no sufficiently large accomodation within the walls. Becket loved luxury and played his part well, distributing lavish gifts on all and sundry as well as charity to the poor and to monks and priests at the shrines he visited. To the English students of the schools, of whom he had been one in his youth, went purses of coin to fill their bellies with food and pay their rent. Subtly, as was his wont, Becket implanted the notion in the minds of the *curia* that the daughter of Louis' Spanish queen might be the instrument to bring about a *rapprochement* between the royal houses of France and England. Chancellor Becket fulfilled his mission impeccably.

In the summer of 1160 Archbishop Theobald of Bec in Canterbury urged Henry II to return and resume his duties in England, but Henry was too busy playing his Continental game, which involved an invasion of the county of Toulouse, once part of Aquitaine. In the autumn, Henry II ordered Queen Eleanor to bring Prince Henry and Princess Matilda to Normandy, not that their mother was to be present when Prince Henry performed an act of homage to Louis VII, for that would have been too embarrassing for the French king. With Constance of Castile shortly to give birth again, Henry II planned to betroth his daughter Matilda to her new child, if male. After Constance died giving birth to yet another daughter for Louis VII, on 2 November 1160 Prince Henry was betrothed to Princess Marguerite, the first daughter of Queen Constance and Louis VII.

Henry II's motive in tricking her father into this arrangement was to get his hands on Marguerite's dowry: the three castles at Gisors, Neaufles and Châteauneuf-sur-Epte in the Vexin, that disputed territory between Plantagenet Normandy and Louis' royal domains. Since Louis did not want a child of his second marriage to be brought up by the first wife who had dishonoured and divorced him, he made it clearly understood that his daughter was not to be brought up by Queen Eleanor, but be placed *ad custodiendum et nutriendum* in the household of Roger of Neubourg, the justiciar of Normandy. Henry installed supposedly neutral Templar castellans to hold all three fortresses in the Vexin, then completed the ensnarement of Louis by inviting him to visit Neubourg,[11] where Marguerite was supposed to live.

The highlight of Louis' visit to Normandy was a trip to the shrine of Mont St Michel, lying just off the western coast of the Cotentin peninsula. Welcomed there by the chronicler Robert de Torigni,[12] sixteenth abbot of the monastery, after being cut off by the high tide the two kings ate with him in the community refectory, sharing the monks' simple fare as the devout king of France loved to do – and Henry never cared what he ate as long as his belly was filled.[13] Crossing back to the mainland at low tide, in Bec that night Henry gave up his bed to Louis, causing that innocent man, who was Henry II's suzerain for the duchy of Normandy, to declare that he loved the king of England more than any other man, and looked forward to enjoying long fraternal relations with him. What the wily abbot of Mont St Michel made of this apparent rapprochement is unknown, but he was well rewarded by Henry's gift of several rich properties to the monastery, perhaps for his silence. He at least cannot have been surprised when Henry II ignored the marriage contract, assembled his family at Neubourg and took advantage of two papal legates soliciting his support for the new pope Alexander III against the antipope Viktor. The two cardinals – Henry of Pisa and William of Pavia – obligingly ignored the need for a papal dispensation for child marriages and were present when Archbishop Hugues of Rouen married 5-year-old Prince Henry to 3-year-old Princess Marguerite. They also kindly overlooked the consanguinity of the two children. Louis VII had been given to understand that the marriage would take place several years later when his daughter reached puberty, but since they were now technically married, Henry II demanded to take possession there and then of her dowry, the three Vexin castles, which the Templars obediently vacated.[14]

Furious at the deceit to which he had fallen victim, Louis banished the three Templars from his kingdom and assembled a force of knights and soldiery from Champagne and Blois – neither county having any love for the house of Anjou – to punish Henry II. Suspecting that he would invade Normandy in an attempt to recover Princess Marguerite, Henry had her moved further away from the border with Louis' territory and placed with Queen Eleanor in direct defiance of the betrothal contract. In an oblique revenge, Louis VII and Theobald of Blois fortified the castle of Chaumont on the river Loire, just twenty-five leagues or two days' easy ride from Chinon. With the speed that would become legendary, Henry captured Chaumont castle before Advent ended campaigning until the end of Lent. Understandably, he was cock-a-hoop at the Christmas court of 1160, held in Le Mans. After the 1161 Easter court in Falaise, he ordered Chancellor Becket to take Prince Henry and the infant Marguerite back to Britain and bring them up in his household there so that Louis had even less chance of ever recovering his daughter. At Whitsun in Winchester, Becket obediently convened the barons and bishops of the island realm to do homage to 7-year-old Prince Henry.

One year later the bishops of England were enraged by Henry II overruling the wishes of the community of Canterbury by appointing Becket, who had only taken minor orders as a deacon in 1154, to the see of Canterbury, vacant since the death of Theobald of Bec in April 1161.

Since it was impossible for him to jump from that rank to archbishop, Henry II had him ordained a priest one day before his installation on 3 June 1162. That winter, the king had intended holding his Christmas court in England, to impress on the Anglo-Norman barons that he was back and personally in charge again, but the elements were against him. It was not until 25 January 1163 that he and Eleanor crossed the still troubled seas of the Channel. Archbishop and Chancellor, Becket was waiting to greet them on the quayside with Prince Henry shielded from the weather under his cloak. At first, all seemed in order, but it was not long before Becket quoted to Henry II the phrase from the Gospel of Matthew 6:24 to the effect that a man cannot serve two masters. In the choice between God and his monarch, he chose to resign the chancellorship. The king was furious, for Becket had been not just his chancellor, but also the man closest to a friend in the whole Plantagenet Empire, so that his renunciation of secular office felt like a betrayal. There is also another possible reason to explain Henry II's violent reaction. He and/or Eleanor had a grand design, using the betrothals of their sons and daughters to weave a network of alliances with powerful dynasties across Europe, in which Becket may have been their intended candidate to become pope.[15]

Far-fetched as this sounds today, at the time the papacy was not a monopoly of Italian cardinals and the Anglo-Saxon Nicolas Breakspear had recently served as Pope Adrian IV 1154–59. If he could climb that high despite being illiterate in Latin, the educated Anglo-Norman Becket could certainly do it. Being schooled by the Augustinians at Merton, he was an accomplished Latinist, spoke French and English, was highly intelligent and had a quick lawyer's brain. So, whether for some or all of these reasons, his frustration of Henry II's plans triggered the king's *iram et malevolentiam* or kingly anger and ill-will as no other vassal or churchman ever did. Prince Henry and Marguerite were summarily removed from Becket's household and Henry deprived the intransigeant archbishop of all the sources of his considerable worldly wealth, accumulated during his term as chancellor.

In keeping with the medieval custom of compelling the presence of his growing sons in council, as an important part of their education, in January 1164 Henry II jointly presided with Young Henry at the palace of Clarendon where the Constitutions of Clarendon were drawn up, radically limiting the powers and customs of the Church in England despite Becket's protests. A complication in the rift between Becket and the king was that Young Henry and the justiciar had released Becket of all secular obligations at the time of his consecration, but Henry II's fury was such that he proclaimed their action to have been *ultra vires* and therefore void. He insisted that Becket repay enormous sums which, he said, were owing to the Exchequer. Young Henry, having been the most privileged member of Becket's household, was understandably disturbed by the rampant hatred of his father for his former guardian, never more than when he travelled in February 1162 with the royal household to Canterbury to celebrate Palm Sunday on 17 March in Becket's cathedral.

This was shortly after his eighth birthday. It was said at the time that a boy who could not ride at the age of 7 would never make a knight, so Mainard other royal administrators had purchased ponies for Prince Henry to learn on and also miniature suits of armour and scaled-down weapons, of which he could be taught the use. In addition to this training for knighthood, he already enjoyed the noble sports of hawking and hunting, taking his falcons and goshawks with him when crossing the Channel with his father. Since two of Henry II's greatest pleasures were venery and the chase, he must have approved Young Henry's keenness for these sports.

In early January 1168 at Montmirail in the Champagne region Henry II met his suzerain Louis VII to obtain Louis' consent to passing title for Anjou and Maine to Young Henry – who had already done homage for Normandy – as well as Aquitaine to Richard and Brittany to Prince Geoffrey, to whom Louis gave permission to marry the Breton Countess Constance. Each prince performed homage to him on the second day of the meeting. Curiously to modern minds, Young Henry also performed homage for Brittany, which Geoffrey was to hold as his vassal.

As far back as 1162 Henry II had expressed the intention of crowning Prince Henry as associative king, emulating the Capetian custom of crowning the eldest son of the reigning king as 'the young king'. The advantage of this was that, in the event of the father dying, the succession passed automatically to the already crowned son, avoiding any dispute by other possible contenders. With Becket in his chosen exile and coronations traditionally conducted by the archbishop of Canterbury, what was Henry to do? A solution came from Pope Alexander III: Henry must restore Becket to his see and Becket must crown Young Henry, who could then give the archbishop the symbolic kiss of peace that his father refused to do. To back up the proposal, Alexander III wrote to all the bishops of England forbidding them to crown Young Henry unless he first swore to rescind the Constitutions of Clarendon and restore Becket to the primacy of Canterbury.[16] However, as so often, Henry held a trump since 1161, when the see of Canterbury was vacant before Becket's appointment, in the shape of permission from the pope for Archbishop Roger of York, a long-standing rival of Becket, to crown Young Henry.

After a meeting in Bayeux with papal legates who urged him to try and end the feud with Becket, at a meeting with the renegade archbishop in November 1169 at St-Germain-en-Laye near Paris, Henry II restored all Becket's confiscated property in England and asked him to officiate at a coronation service for Young Henry – which was not strictly necessary. Becket, however, did not grasp this olive branch that could have ended the dispute on the spot. His body was by then covered in sores from wearing punishing horsehair shirts day and night and undergoing daily flagellation, ostensibly for having impure thoughts. He also had an agonising osteomyelitis of the jaw after being locked into the sewers of the monastery at Pontigny with a dental abscess. During an operation by a monk to remove two bone fragments from the jaw, he refused any pain relief. So far did his self-ordained penances exceed the norm that people were beginning to say he was mad.

So furious at the rejection of his offer was Henry II that, after the Christmas court in Nantes, a site chosen to impress on the Bretons that Geoffrey and Constance were indeed their count and countess, he crossed the Channel in the teeth of a storm that sank the largest vessel in the royal convoy, drowning 400 passengers and crew. After four years spent restoring order in the Continental possessions, he held his Easter court of 1170 at Windsor, summoning all the barons and bishops including Archbishop Roger of York to attend a grand council to discuss *inter alia* the coronation of Young Henry. It was known that Becket was bombarding Anglo-Norman vassals with so many contrary missives that the southern English ports had been made subject to strict censorship to prevent any letters from the exiled archbishop in France entering the country. Henry II also forced all the senior vassals and churchmen of the realm to refuse to accept any communication from Becket, should it by-pass the censorship. In addition, any person likely to carry a papal inhibition against the coronation on his person was refused permission to cross the Channel by Queen Eleanor in Normandy. Conversely, Young Henry was escorted from Normandy to England by two compliant Norman bishops, although Marguerite was not allowed to accompany him, which was taken as an insult by Louis VII. Another person refused permission by Henry II to cross and attend Young Henry's great day in Westminster Abbey was his mother, left in Normandy to punish her for investing Prince Richard as duke of Aquitaine – which was, after all, in her gift.[17]

On 14 June 1170 the great and good gathered at Westminster to attend the coronation. The first ceremony, on the previous day, was the dubbing of Young Henry with the arms of knighthood. At the time, the 15-year-old prince was said to be tall but well-proportioned, broad-shouldered with a long neck, his skin pale and freckled, his eyes bright blue and his hair reddish-gold. This was according to a eulogistic poem which was hardly going to say he was ugly and lazy. After a night-long vigil, Young Henry was washed and dressed in a linen undershirt and costly robe, his legs clothed in silk stockings, gold-embroidered slippers on his feet. In the cathedral before the altar, the sword belt was buckled on him by his sponsor and golden spurs buckled on his feet. Surprisingly, we do not know for certain who performed the ceremony. Most probably, it was his father.[18]

On coronation day, the youthful knight walked between Archbishop of York Roger de Pont-Levé and Hugh de Puiset, bishop of Durham, on a woollen carpet spread from the palace to the adjacent cathedral, flanked and followed by richly attired senior clergy with their cross-bearers and torch-bearers and attendants swinging incense censers, while choirs chanted the anthem *Firmetur manus tua* – a prayer that his right hand should be strong in proclaiming the law. Present in the cathedral were Henry II's other three surviving sons: Richard, Geoffrey and John. Also present were the reigning kings William the Lion of Scotland[19] and Godred, king of Man and the Isles, whose presence expressed ambiguously a relationship with the Angevins akin to, but not exactly, vassalage. As Young Henry swore the traditional oath, a bishop asked the asembled barons whether they accepted the new king and would obey him, to which they replied, *'Volumus et concedimus'* – we wish it and submit. Next, after the removal of his outer garments, came the annointing on head, breast and arms with holy oil and the clothing in richer raiment, then the heavy gold crown, its weight partly borne by a noble standing on either side, and the placing of the orb and sceptre into his hands.[20]

Chapter 6

A king with no kingdom

At this point Young Henry must have believed that he was a king equal to his father, who had allowed him little personal freedom hitherto. In corroboration of that, Matthew Paris tells of his arrogance at the coronation feast, when Henry II symbolically insisted on serving his son at table and presumably expected some sign of gratitude. When none came, Archbishop Roger of York, sitting beside Young Henry, observed what a privilege that was, to which Young Henry insolently remarked that there was nothing strange about the son of a duke waiting on the son of a king.[1]

Hostile reaction to the coronation by Roger of York came from many sides – Becket's supporters of course and especially strongly from Louis VII in Paris. He was deeply insulted that his daughter Marguerite had not been crowned at the same time as her husband and mounted an invasion of Normandy to make his point. This forced Henry II to cross the Channel, leaving the Young King as regent in England, under the control of several *tutores* appointed by his father including the archdeacons of Canterbury and Poitiers. A series of routine charters were sealed in his name and witnessed by the *tutores*, but the regent himself was more prone to go hunting or hawking with his friends than sit in council as his court travelled from palace to palace.

Across the Channel in Normandy, Henry succumbed to illness in repelling Louis' force. Two months after the coronation, he collapsed near Domfront and lay in sickbed, shaking with ague, probably from malaria. Rumours ran throughout Europe that 'the old king' was dying, or already dead. Feeling near death himself, he confirmed the division of his possessions similarly to the arrangement he had made at Montmirail and disposed of his mortal remains to the abbey of Grandmont in the Limousin. Had he died then, the world would have marvelled at his prescience in arranging the succession with such impeccable timing.

Back in England, Young Henry's feelings are not hard to discern: if his father died, he would be truly king of England, duke of Normandy and count of Anjou and Maine; Richard would be count of Poitou and duke of Aquitaine; Geoffrey would be count of Brittany. The youngest son, Prince John, known as John Lackland, was only 3 years old and had no inheritance, but was be put in Young Henry's care and tutelage until adult.

The Young King's dreams faded as news came that Henry II was recovering and indeed travelling all the way to the shrine of St Adour at Rocamadour in the Quercy region with an entourage as large as an army for the good reason that he was, while there, very near enemy territory. It was also a sign to the restive lords of Aquitaine to behave because he was both alive and fighting fit again. Another meeting with Becket at Amboise was followed by the archbishop's long delayed return to England, marred by his continual stream of letters written in his capacity as papal legate, excommunicating more bishops, few of whom supported him by then. Trying to re-establish his former closeness with Young Henry, Becket made several attempts to see him face to face, but all were blocked by the Young King's *tutores*. On Christmas Day Becket excommunicated all the bishops associated with the coronation on the grounds that only he had the right to place the crown on an English king's head. News of this being relayed to Henry II's Christmas court in Normandy by Gilbert Foliot and two other excommunicated prelates reignited the smouldering stand-off between monarch and archbishop, leading to Becket's murder on 29 December.[2]

Although Henry II had never expressly ordered the killing of Becket, Pope Alexander III appointed a papal commission to examine the extent of his responsibility. To place himself beyond the reach of the Church, Henry II decided to implement a long held plan to invade Ireland and make Prince John its overlord. He summoned the Young King to Normandy at the end of July 1171 to act as his regent in the Continental possessions during his time in Ireland, especially because the pope's displeasure might well encourage Louis VII to invade. As the campaign in Ireland progressed from victory to victory, the Young King seemingly took his responsibilities more seriously, criss-crossing the Channel several times. In Ireland, Henry II reformed the Irish Church and informed Alexander III, hoping the gesture would go some way to cancel the opprobrium for Becket's murder. Then the start of winter gales in the Irish sea virtually ended communications and certainly made it impossible to bring the king and his army back to England.

When in England, Young Henry was accompanied by his wife, still uncrowned, but spent Christmas at Bur-le-Roi, holding his own Christmas court with due ceremony and extravagant gifts to important guests. A legendary event during the festivities was the feast of the Williams, when all the men whose names were not William were turned away by the palace staff and 110 knights with the right name sat down to eat with the Young King. If that sounds fun for a pleasure-loving young man, the chroniclers Ralph of Diceto and Geraldus Cambrensis reported that Young Henry's Christmas court was also where the seeds of the 1173 rebellion against the Old King were sown by Queen Eleanor taking advantage of her husband's absence.[3] Before those seeds could germinate, Henry II crossed the Irish sea in February 1172, having learned that two papal legates were on their way to examine him. Almost certainly – for keeping secrets in a medieval court was near to impossible – he had heard at first or second hand some rumours of unrest among his barons and his sons. The legates had to be dealt with first. After losing his temper with them, Henry II eventually consented in the cathedral of Avranches, across the bay from Mont St Michel, to swear at the altar that he had neither wished for, nor ordered, Becket's murder. At the same time, he accepted that his evident anger at the intransigeant primate's defiance might have been what motivated the four household knights to travel to Canterbury with the initial intention of arresting Becket, which turned to violence only when he resisted.

His penance imposed by the legates was fourfold: to pay for 200 knights to go on crusade and serve for a year in the Holy Land; at the pope's discretion, himself to join the *reconquista* driving back the Moors in Spain; to restore the much despoiled lands of Canterbury cathedral to their former condition; and to compensate all who had suffered as Becket's supporters. Doubtless, fasting and other obligations were also imposed, but privately.[4] The old king was also required to abrogate the Constitutions of Clarendon. Promises came easily to him, so he promised to do this. Young Henry was present in Avranches when his father was led out of the cathedral to the place where penitents were whipped. The sources are obscure, as to whether he underwent this public humiliation. As associative king of the English realm, Young Henry swore before the legates to implement the various undertakings of his father.

A KING WITH NO KINGDOM

To remove one king from the now long list of his enemies, at the same time lessening any hopes of his Continental vassals for support from Louis VII, Henry II agreed that Young Henry should be re-crowned with Marguerite beside him, making her the junior queen consort of England. Together, they crossed the Channel on 24 August, landing in Southampton. Three days later Archbishop Rotrou of Rouen crowned the Young King again and anointed and crowned Marguerite in the presence of Queen Eleanor, Henry II having stayed in Normandy. The Young King resuming his duties as regent, his court then rode to Canterbury for the election of Becket's successor. While charming with smooth talk and his easy-going manner the community – which regarded the choice of new archbishop as its prerogative – Young Henry prevaricated and continued to do so at a further council at Windsor in October, instead commanding the monks to send representatives to Henry II's court in Normandy for a council on 30 November, where the matter could be settled.

Commanded by his father to attend this court, Young Henry could not have guessed that the days of his regency were at an end. He travelled with Queen Marguerite to Paris, where Louis VII advised that the time had come for the Young King to demand from Henry II untramelled rule over either Normandy or England, since otherwise his regal title was a mockery. In the event this was refused, Louis said, the young couple were more than welcome to return to French territory. Henry II was not so easily outwitted, however, and the only difference after returning to Normandy was that the Young King was allowed to hold his own 1172 Christmas court at William the Conqueror's castle in Bonneville-sur-Touques while his parents held a frigid one of their own with Richard and Geoffrey in the castle at Chinon, dominating the valley of the river Vienne. The mood grew worse after news came from Rome that Becket was to be canonised on 21 February 1173.

His festivities over, Young Henry was summoned to travel with his father for an important meeting with Count Humbert of Maurienne at Montferrand[5] in the centre of modern France – the twin city of Clermont, where Pope Urban II had proclaimed the First Crusade. Humbert's possessions straddled the Alps and controlled several important passes. The intent was to betroth 6-year-old John Lackland to Humbert's 4-year-old daughter Alix, her dowry giving him some wealth of his own when they were married. The last straw for the Young King was to hear

Henry II's quid pro quo: the three Angevin castles at Chinon, Loudun and Mirebeau were to be the bride's dower lands. She would have no rights over them during the husband's lifetime, but could expect to take possession of them in the event of his death, to provide for her own upkeep. Not only had Young Henry no clear domains of his own, but his father was giving away three castles he regarded as his because they lay in the county of Anjou. This was far from being his only ground for complaint. In an additional humiliation, Henry II had also sent away some of Young Henry's household knights and imposed his own men as spies in the Young King's household. With no territory to tax, the only way the Young King could get money to pay his household, was by asking his father for allowances. The list of his complaints was long.[6] Among other voices encouraging the Young King to stand up for his entitlement was that of Queen Eleanor, increasingly sidelined by Henry II as her menopause made her incapable of providing any more sons for her husband to pit against each other.

It was Count Raymond of Toulouse who told Henry II outright that there was a coalition plotting against him. Leaving Limoges with Raymond on the pretext of a day's hunting, Henry made a tour of his castles in the Limousin, ordering all the castellans to put them on a war footing. Returning to Limoges, whence Young Henry's partisans had departed to summon their vassals for war, he dismissed the Young King's remaining household knights.[7] Forced to ride with his father to the fortress at Chinon, and sleep in the same bedchamber, Young Henry was under no illusion of the fate that awaited him. Accounts of what happened there vary. The simplest one is that he stole quietly out of bed before dawn on 6 March, joined some supporters waiting with horses on the river bank below the castle walls and rode his mounts into the ground, changing them frequently. Their way led to Le Mans and Argentan. Furious when he awoke to find the small party gone, Henry II thundered north in pursuit, also riding mounts into the ground.[8]

Hearing that Louis VII was in the county of Le Perche, Young Henry changed course, arriving at Louis' court on 8 March and placing before his suzerain, the king of France, his dispute as duke of Normandy with Henry II as count of Anjou. Heading back to Paris, to put a decent distance between father and son, he was at Louis' court there when Henry II's emissaries arrived, saying that they came from the king of England. Louis affected surprise, replying that the crowned king of England was both his son-in-law and his guest, the old king having resigned. Young Henry having left his great seal behind in Chinon at the time of the hasty departure, Louis ordered that a new one be made for him, so that he could seal charters rewarding with grants of land the supporters who came flocking in, in anticipation of loot and reward. Given the Young King's lack of political sense, it was probably Louis VII or his *curiales* on the Ile de la Cité who suggested he involve the pope. In a letter to Alexander III justifying the dispute with his father, Young Henry wrote that although he had been crowned at his father's wish, he had never been given the power that went with the title of king, enabling him to fulfil his coronation oath to protect the oppressed and exercise justice.[9] Alexander III refused to be drawn into the dispute. Advised that his position would be all the stronger if he recruited also the princes Richard and Geoffrey, both of whom hated him thanks to their father's manipulations, Young Henry rode to Poitou, meeting Queen Eleanor. She decided that the more support he had, the better, and took it upon herself to reconcile her three adult sons.

At 15, Richard was already called Ricart Oc-e-No in Occitan, or Richard Aye-and-Nay, for his habit of changing his mind frequently and Geoffrey, one year younger, was reputed to be as slippery as an eel. Somehow, after Young Henry had listed all the nobles he said were supporting him, Queen Eleanor persuaded them both that this was the ideal chance to take their revenge on their father, and opened her treasury, to provide the necessary funds. All three brothers rode to Paris, attended by the young knights of Eleanor's court, to ask Louis' support against their father. Eleanor did not accompany them. Did she believe that she was quite safe in Poitou because her three hot-blooded sons could outwit and out-fight their father? Or was she simply too proud to beg the protection of the first husband she had not seen for twenty years, despite being entitled to do so as duchess of Aquitaine, and as such a vassal of Louis VII? Whatever her reasoning, she was to pay dearly for not going with to Paris with them.[10]

Henry II having commanded all his Continental cities and fortresses to be provisioned and garrisoned, the uprising began on the Sunday after Easter, 15 April 1173, when all the Plantagenet possessions south and west of Normandy declared against him, with the exception of a few cities like La Rochelle, where the shrewd governing burgesses sat out the conflict in the expectation that Henry II would win the confrontation with his sons. He, meanwhile, recruited 20,000 mercenaries from Brabant, whose neighbour Count Philip of Flanders took the field with Young Henry, attacking Normandy from the east and taking Gournay and Aumale while Geoffrey brought Breton troops into the conflict in the west and Richard led his Poitevin supporters, driving into Henry II's lands from the south. In each case, the technique was similar, with skirmishes and the burning of crops and destruction of everything of value to the enemy in addition to a few grander sieges of castles and cities. Young Henry's campaign ground to a halt after Count Philip's brother was killed and the count had to arrange for his other brother, the bishop elect of Cambrai, to change career and take up arms in the field. At a loss what to do next, Young Henry rode south and west through French territory for some 125 miles to join Louis' siege of Verneuil on the southern fringe of Normandy.

Although there were certainly sufficient forces on the princes' side, there was no overall command, and therefore no strategy. Also, Young Henry, Richard and Geoffrey lacked military experience, Louis was no general and Henry II had the geographical advantage, able to move himself and his forces quickly from one front to another. The war was also being prosecuted in England, where the city and castle of Leicester and associated strongpoints in the fief of the Young King's supporter Earl Robert of Leicester, were under siege. The earl himself having fled to France, the defence was conducted by his constable, Leicester being Henry II's first objective among the several Midland and northern castles and cities rebelling against his rule. After a fire within the city forced the burgesses to seek a truce, they were fined and expelled, to seek asylum in other towns and cities loyal to Henry II. With the town gates and walls partly destroyed, the lesson to other rebellious cities was plain. Further damage was delayed by a truce to last until Michaelmas after news was received on 28 July of the Scottish invasion of Northumberland and the siege of Carlisle.

South of the Channel, the siege by Louis VII and Young Henry of the well-defended castle and several walled boroughs of Verneuil was not going well. The usual tactic of filling in moats to make a level surface across which huge siege towers could be wheeled up to the walls not having succeeded, the besiegers turned instead to one of the walled boroughs, in which the inhabitants were starving. As was customary, Louis and Young Henry took hostages and granted a truce of three days:

if aid had not come by the end of that time, the borough would yield. Given the shortness of the truce, the besiegers did not expect any aid to come, but Henry II force-marched a considerable force of knights and mercenaries to take up position just seven miles away within the three days. To make a point, it was on land in a fief of Robert of Leicester. From there, he sent Louis an ultimatum: to meet him in battle or withdraw from Norman soil. Louis was no last-ditch fighter and Young Henry faced a dilemma spelled out by historian Matthew Strickland. At the siege of Gerberoi in 1079 Robert Courtheuse[11] had unknowingly unhorsed his father William the Conqueror, wearing full armour. Recognising his father's voice coming from the man on the ground, he dismounted and gave him his own horse, permitting William to escape further harm. The possibility of Henry II being killed in a battle by men under Young Henry's command was remote, but if it happened, it would make the Young King an object of universal opprobrium by pope and monarchs throughout Europe.[12]

In the event, after agreeing with Louis' emissaries a truce of one day, Henry II awaited Louis' negotiators on 9 August. Nobody came. Instead a cloud of smoke rose from the besieged borough as Louis' men broke in, robbing indiscriminately and carrying off their loot into French territory before retreating precipitately, to save their skins. The rearguard was taken prisoner by Henry II and the French camp sacked by his forces, but he decided not to pursue Louis and his own rebellious son. As to who persuaded Louis to break his word at Verneuil, we do not know, but it was a flagrant offence against one of the canons of medieval warfare.

Gradually throughout the summer, Henry II's generalship and decisiveness repeatedly carried the day, until a peace conference was arranged for 24 August in the traditional spot beneath an ancient elm tree outside Gisors castle. He opened with generous settlements – or, rather, the promise of such. From experience, Louis VII warned the princes not to trust their father's promises, but take them as proof that the titles he had previously given them were worthless. After the conference broke up in disarray, Henry II swiftly returned to the attack, leaving much of western France a scorched and shattered wilderness, its surviving inhabitants starving. Queen Eleanor being one prize that eluded him, he ordered Archbishop Rotrou of Rouen to write a letter commanding her, like a willful adolescent, to return to the husband who had insulted and rejected her. She refused, and fled, too late, towards Paris. Riding astride with a small escort, dressed as a man, she might have made it to asylum on Capetian territory, had she not been betrayed within a few leagues of safety by four of her most trusted courtiers, and taken prisoner to face her husband's fury.

The war ground on, large tracts of Brittany being laid waste by Henry II's Brabanters while Young Henry's supporters on the western and southern fronts were whittled away. The new peace conference that began on 25 September at Gisors was initiated by Pope Alexander III because he wanted the belligerents to stop killing each other and go east to kill Muslims in the Holy Land. On the second day, despite the presence of the papal legates, the conference broke up in exchanges of insults between Henry II and Robert of Leicester. Abandoning his possessions in Normandy, he rode hard to Wissant in the county of Boulogne and joined a force of mercenaries, mounted and on foot, already assembled there by Count Philip. Embarked in a waiting flotilla, they landed on the estuary of the river Orwell in east Anglia, joining forces with the elderly Earl Hugh Bigod of Norfolk and marching to relieve Leicester. Ambushed on 29 September by a posse of knights loyal to Henry II near Bury St Edmunds, they suffered much slaughter with Earl Robert and other important prisoners afterwards transported to Henry II's prison castle at Falaise in Normandy.

One by one the insurgent fortresses fell to his forces until Advent in December ended campaigning for the year. After a truce was concluded between Louis VII and Henry, the Young King defied the Church's ban on campaigning during Lent by declaring that he was not bound by Louis' truce and led a force of some 500 knights to besiege the city of Sées. It was an ill-conceived initiative that failed.

During the truce, wiser heads in Paris advised the Young King to assemble a great host to be led by him in an invasion of England simultaneously with another invasion of Normandy by Louis. Across the frozen battle lines, Henry II used the time well in preparations and, when hostilities recommenced, he took Le Mans, Angers and Poitiers in rapid succession. Richard, as titular count of Poitou, fled south to Saintes, thinking himself safe there. His father's habitual speed of attack caught him unprepared. Having broken into the walled city and invested the cathedral that was serving as Richard's arsenal and treasury, Henry II captured sixty ransomable knights and 400 sergeants-at-arms, together with all his son's treasury. Richard had abandoned his troops and taken refuge in the redoutable castle of Taillebourg. Never one to waste energy or resources, Henry left him there and dragged his captives back north – with good reason. A coalition of French and Flemish nobles had judged him too busy in Aquitaine to stop them and chose Young Henry as their figurehead for an invasion of England supported by King William of Scotland. On 8 July they were still awaiting favourable winds at the Flemish port of Gravelines, near Dunkirk, when Henry II not only reached the Channel coast at Barfleur but, leaving his Norman vassals to take care of Louis' invasion, embarked several thousand of his Flemish mercenaries on ships at Ouistreham and landed them in England. It was an expensive gamble: the cost of keeping so many mercenaries so long in his service had emptied his treasury to the extent that he was reported to have mortgaged even his bejewelled coronation sword.[13]

While Henry II sought to placate the Church by making an ostentatious penance for Becket's death in Canterbury cathedral, the Young King was landing with an advance guard of his troops in East Anglia. With Earl Hugh Bigod having declared for him and the Scottish King William the Lion heading south in Yorkshire, victory seemed feasible until King William was captured by Henry II's men at Richmond, which both he and much of the population took as a sign from God that his penance had been accepted on high. After this, Young Henry's invasion fell apart with Count Philip and the main body of his troops never setting foot in England. After Hugh Bigod surrendered and swore fealty anew to Henry II, he pleaded for a safe conduct for the Flemish mercenaries with him, who were allowed to return to Flanders.

Next, Young Henry headed for Rouen, under siege by Louis in the expectation that the Norman capital would shortly fall. It did not. On 8 August Henry II was back in Normandy, landing at Barfleur with the ranks of his Brabanters strengthened by another 1,000 mercenaries from Wales. Three days later, they raised the siege, Louis and Young Henry fleeing back to Paris, where the ageing French king, born in 1120, announced that he could no longer finance the rebellion of the English princes, and advised them to make the best deal possible with their father. Henry II agreed to a meeting on 29 September at Montlouis, shrewdly reasoning that, if he brought the Young King to heel, his other sons would follow. And so it was, both Richard in Poitou and

Geoffrey in Brittany abandoning most of their followers and heading to Montlouis. There, they humbled themselves before their father, Richard weeping copiously as was his wont on these occasions, before swearing fealty to him. Both were pardoned, as was Young Henry, who was excused performing homage because his title was equal to that of his father. At Louis' insistence, a treaty was drawn up, giving Young Henry a stipend of 15,000 pounds Angevin per annum and two castles in Normandy; Richard was accorded half the revenues of Poitou and two castles; and Geoffrey received half the revenues of Brittany and a promise of the other half later. Of all the princes, 7-year-old John came off best. Not having been involved in the rebellion, he kept title to the three disputed castles of Chinon, Loudun and Mirebeau and was granted other lands on both sides of the Channel. As part of the settlement, Henry released 1,000 of his ransomable captives. Among the major figures of the rebellion who stayed in prison was Queen Eleanor. None of her sons asked any awkward questions as to her whereabouts, locked away in Old Sarum castle near Winchester.[14]

Chapter 7

Death in misery

In the way of things in that period, the end of open hostilities between Henry II and his sons and their supporters saw knights and nobles who had lately been facing each other in lethal combat now at least pretending to be civilised. Paranoia being such a central part of Henry II's make-up, this did not lessen his suspicion of the legitimate sons, as a result of which their illegitimate half-brother Geoffrey the Bastard, who had remained loyal, was appointed bishop-elect of Lincoln despite not having reached the minimum age of 30 and being, of course, illegitimate – two details which the pope pardoned in this case. Keeping the Young King close to him, Henry II despatched the new bishop to France.

What Young Henry made of his father's undertaking to go on crusade as part of his penance for Becket's death, we do not know, but by now no one expected the old king to fulfil his promises. In any case, departing for months or even years abroad would have been to invite a renewal of the intra-dynastic contest. Partly caused by the destruction of crops by the royal and rebel soldiery in the north and east of England, a famine occurred there and plague broke out. Translated into cash, this meant reduced income for the Exchequer at a time when damage to besieged cities and castles needed repair. Little goodwill accrued to Henry II for attempting to make good some of the shortfall by sending his justice officers far and wide to impose fines for actions taken during the civil war and afterwards. Young Henry's name was equally blamed, for the wording of the writs clearly associated him with the authority for this measure.

Perhaps the cruellest retribution was inflicted on 1 August 1175, when Young Henry and his father were in York for the abasement of the Young King's erstwhile ally William the Lion. The Scottish king, his brother and chief vassals swore fealty to Henry II and the Young King and undertook to observe the provisions of the December 1174 Treaty of Falaise, to which William had agreed in order to get out of prison there. Under this, five strategically important castles in southern Scotland were handed over to Henry II, with William having to tax his people to pay the costs of their English garrisons. The Scottish king had not invaded during the rebellion for love of the Young King, but to recover his father's earldom of Northumberland. Yet, it must have felt odd for him to see Young Henry standing beside his father at this moment of ignominy – which was to last for fifteen years until Richard the Lionheart released William from these obligations in payment for a substantial contribution to the costs of the abortive Third Crusade.

By Easter of 1176 Young Henry had had enough of being tied to his father's coat-tails – apart from the humiliation, he had always been bored by the business of state – and came up with a request to leave England on a pilgrimage to Santiago de Compostella. The old king rightly suspected this was an excuse for regaining his freedom of action, thought up by some of his son's *familiares*. He refused permission, but, with his twentieth birthday approaching, Young Henry persisted. After Henry II's Easter court at Winchester, at which Richard and Geoffrey were also in attendance, Young Henry eventually won permission to cross the Channel with Marguerite and his household knights. It has to be recognised that this was not so much Henry II giving in, but rather so that Young Henry could join Richard in putting down the increasing unrest in Aquitaine. However, once landed at Barfleur, the Young King and Marguerite went first to Louis VII's court in Paris and then to Count Philip of Flanders, who provided horses, arms and other equipment for Young Henry to lead his knights in a major tournament. Tournaments being illegal in Henry II's England, this was the life for his bored son and heir!

While Prince Richard was campaigning successfully against dissident vassals with an army of mercenaries in the Limousin, Young Henry was jealous of his brother's comparative freedom of action. Until then, his charters had been witnessed by *tutores* appointed by Henry II. Starting in 1175, his charters bore the seals of members of his own court. After a shared siege of Châteauneuf, the two princes separated at Poitiers and went their separate ways. Among the spies Henry II had implanted in the Young King's household as his vice-chancellor was a cleric named Adam of Churchdown. Some of his letters reporting on

DEATH IN MISERY

Young Henry's association with nobles hostile to the old king were intercepted and read by Young Henry, who decided to make an example of the unfortunate vice-chancellor. The choice lay between hanging him for treason or flaying him alive until the bishop of Poitiers saved his life by pointing out that Adam was exempt as a deacon of York cathedral from judgement in a civil court. Instead, Young Henry ordered that he be taken to prison in Argentan and whipped naked through the streets of every town along the way – which could have had the same result.[1]

Furious that 'his man' should be treated in this way, Henry II sent four household knights to France to secure Adam's release and bring him back to England. Learning there more about the substance of the incriminating letters, the old king decided that Young Henry was attempting to re-kindle a rebellion. After the feast of Michaelmas at the end of September, he placed garrisons loyal to him in all the important castles of England and Normandy. Such was the atmosphere of suspicion in England that many nobles who had rebelled in 1173–74 chose the excuse of going on crusade to avoid the wrath of the king after being dispossessed. Others of the princes' former allies also went east, but Young Henry's impulse for that great adventure was dampened by his wife's first pregnancy. Further to spite him, Henry II compelled the wealthy Earl William of Gloucester, son of his uncle Robert of Gloucester, to betroth his 3-year-old daughter Isabel to 10-year-old Prince John and make the prince his heir, no longer to be known as Lackland. The prince was also in line to become the king of Ireland, with which in mind, Henry II despatched a force thought powerful enough to subdue the Anglo-Norman nobility ruling the occupied east of the country.

Another girl child was to bring about a sort of reunion between the two Henrys. Early in 1177, Young Henry was commanded to proceed with sufficient force into the county of Berry, where Count Ralph de Déols had died, leaving his 3-year-old daughter Denise as heiress to the castle of Châteauroux in the centre of modern France. Certain of the late count's relatives had in effect kidnapped the infant heiress, whom Henry II declared his ward, to dispose of to whom he pleased. This was not just a local dispute, but was also a way of demonstrating to Louis VII that, although Marguerite had returned to the Ile de la Cité to give birth, her husband the Young King was the obedient son of his father. Henry II's emissaries demanded that Louis return Marguerite to

PLANTAGENET PRINCES

Plantagenet territory for the birth, but her child – a son named William – lived just three days. Deaths of infants and stillbirths were so common that Young Henry's reaction is not noted anywhere. The death of the child meant that Henry did not have any specific *casus belli* against Louis and halted his moves in that direction, despite having transported a considerable army to Normandy. Instead, he met with him and Young Henry on 11 September to sort out the continual squabbling over Louis' daughters, of whom Princess Alais had been in Plantagenet custody for years, betrothed to Richard, who had no intention of marrying her or anyone else. To strengthen his case, Louis VII invoked the powers of papal legate Cardinal Peter, who threatened to place all Henry II's lands on both sides of the Channel under interdict. Henry stalemated this by an appeal to that long-lived Pope Alexander III and a three-way conference near Nonancourt concluded a peace with Louis, officially ending the hostilities between the French and English crowns of 1173–74. To impress Cardinal Peter, both kings took an oath to go on crusade, which neither of them had any intention of doing.

Henry II split his army to give a reasonable force with which Young Henry marched into the Berry, always eager for 'enterprise of martial kind' in any cause. Richard was also given men to suppress rebellion in Poitou and Geoffrey similarly reinforced to put the Bretons in their place. Young Henry having failed to capture Denise de Déols, his father moved fast, captured Châteauroux and La Châtre, where the girl was being brought up and sent her off to Chinon. At the end of the year 1177 Henry II could feel pleased with himself and held an expensive Christmas court in Angers, which was graced by all three of his adult sons. Peace seemed likely for a time, Young Henry's thirst for combat was for the moment satisfied by participation in tournaments, said to have been invented by an Angevin knight named Geoffroi de Preuilly[2] as a test of all the martial skills a knight should possess. Although Henry II forbade tournaments in England, fearing the potential for rebellion in a gathering of several thousand knights and nobles, there were at this time regular tournaments in northeast France, where Young Henry's personal involvement and his generosity to his household knights who fought alongside him made him a popular figure. Everyone who was anyone in the world of chivalry was to be seen at these meets, William the Lion of Scotland and some of his nobles once travelling all the way to France to take part in them.[3]

DEATH IN MISERY

The troubadour lord of Autafort castle in Aquitaine Bertran de Born described them thus:

> *Bela m'es pressa be blezos*
> *coberts de teintz vermelhs e blaus*
> *d'entresens e de gonfanos*
> *de diversas colors tretaus*
> *tendas e traps e rics pavilhos tendre*
> *lanzas frassar, escutz trancar e fendre*
> *elmes brunitz, e colps donar e prendre ...*

> The *mêlée*, with its thousand charms:
> shields vermillion and azure
> standards, banners, coats of arms
> painted in every bright colour,
> the pavilions, the stands, the tents,
> shattered lances, shields split and bent,
> blows given, taken, helmets dented ...

In modern terms, the spectacle was a cross between a rock concert and a sports meeting, with all the side shows that would appeal to men of war, especially gambling and the buying and selling of trained warhorses and arms and armour. The tournament itself was not the Hollywood set piece of two armoured knights thundering towards each other on their destriers, separated by a stout barrier so that the only contact was by the lances they wielded. It took the form of the *mêlée*, in which two teams of combatants charged at each other with lances, the fray spreading out for miles after breaking up into small groups seeking a ransomable opponent to bring down, take him prisoner and gain the price of his liberation, or at least acquire his horse and trappings as winner's booty. To enhance the performance of Young Henry's team, Henry II had appointed the prominent knight William the Marshal – who had taken 103 knights prisoner in one tournament year – to combine the duties of instructor, master-at-arms and bodyguard on the team that often numbered 100 or more combatants. In a tournament at Lagny to celebrate the coronation of Louis VII's son Prince Philippe, Young Henry fielded twice that many in an attempt to win by sheer weight of numbers.

PLANTAGENET PRINCES

Since all the personal weapons of war were being used after lances shattered in the first shock – with splinters of oak frequently penetrating the eye slits of the helms and blinding the combatants – the many fatalities were regarded as honourable deaths. Men were also unhorsed and trampled to death. Although deliberately setting out to kill a man was forbidden, there were many cases of deaths where it was unclear what had been the winner's true intent. Henry II's prudence in assigning William the Marshal to the Young King was manifest after Young Henry's brother Geoffrey died two days after being unhorsed and trampled by the horses in a tournament at Paris, arranged for his entertainment in 1186.

Taking part in this expensive sport cost money for entrance fees, the necessary equipment and subsistence for one's team, payable from the moment they set out for the venue. In the Young King's case, his budget came from his father's allowance, sufficiently generous to attract knights and nobles who had fought on both sides in the war of 1173–74 as well as French, Flemish and other *bacheliers* wanting the prestige of being seen in such noble company with him. His taste for the grand life frequently outstripping his income, he was reduced to borrowing large sums of money and buying equipment and paying for lodgings and food on credit.

Because of the confusion after combat had been joined by several hundred men, it seems to have been in these lethal mock battles that the nobility took to flaunting easily recognisable emblems on shields and banners, so that their followers could support them – and rescue them, if need be, as the Marshal did more than once for Young Henry, whose emblem was probably a single golden lion rampant on a red field – in the archaic language of heraldry, *gules, a lion rampant or*. Ever eager to outdo his elder brother, Richard made his arms three golden lions – *gules, three lions passant guardant or*. They are still there on the royal standard today.

After three years south of the Channel, frequently indulging in tournaments, Young Henry returned to England in February 1179, when Henry II showed his pride in his son's tourneying reputation by restoring all the grants of land and castles previously given and taken away. In return, Young Henry at the age of 25 at last participated in the administration for a couple of months before returning to France at the end of April. He missed what must have been a great surprise to all the nobility of England: an unplanned visit of Louis VII. This was due to his son Philippe, shortly to be crowned as the Capetian young king, falling ill after spending all night lost in a forest – whether from exposure or the shock of being entirely alone for the first time in his life. His father, already ill, came to pray for a miracle at the tomb of Becket in Canterbury, and Henry II rode through the night to greet Louis affectionately after his landing at Dover on 22 September, riding with him and Count Philip of Flanders to the cathedral, where Louis VII made rich offerings to the community. Afterwards, Louis VII was accompanied with equal pomp back to his ship at Dover on 26 September. Although Prince Philippe recovered, Louis could not attend the coronation on 1 November 1179, having finally suffered a stroke that paralysed his right side.

Young Henry was not only present at Rheims, but played a significant part in the ceremony, carrying the crown from the palace to the cathedral and supporting it when placed on the 14-year-old's head. Both Geoffrey and Richard were also there in their capacities as vassals of the French king. At the following coronation feast, Young Henry made a point of serving his Capetian counterpart and cutting up his food. Lest anyone take this as indicating subservience, he also fielded a team of 200 knights, including nineteen counts, in the following tournament, to show the world Plantagenet superiority. Also fielding an impressive team was Count Philip of Flanders, whose increasing influence in France after Louis VII's stroke was worrying Henry II. Summoning Young Henry back to England, he ordered him to join a new expedition in France, in which he was to obey all his father's commands. Father and son sailed from Portsmouth and Dover respectively before Easter. Raising an army to back up his diplomacy, Henry met the young French king at Gisors and persuaded him to restore his kinsmen and kinswomen who had been disadvantaged by Count Philip, whose wounded pride was healed by Henry II accepting his homage and pledging 500 knights, if called, in return for a generous annual subsidy of £1,000.[4] Seemingly a master-stroke, it failed to achieve its aim.

After Henry II's return to England, Young Henry had full powers as duke of Normandy. As in every other royal or ducal court, jealousy was rife – in this case targeting William the Marshal, whose prowess was legendary and who had accumulated considerable wealth from ransoms of knights and nobles he had bested on the tournament circuit. It was alleged that he even paid a herald to announce his participation beforehand. Jealousy too arose from William's closeness with Young Henry and the respect shown to him by his master. After a great tournament at Lagny in 1179 five members of the Young King's *familia* conspired to bring him down. They put their heads together and thought up a plot based on the Arthurian legends so popular in knightly circles, particularly the story of King Arthur being cuckolded by his best knight, Sir Lancelot. Since neither Marguerite – cast as Guinevere – nor the Marshal had a reputation for amorous dalliances to give credibility to the accusation, they decided to spread the rumour that William had become Queen Marguerite's lover, so that it might become general gossip.

When this reached Young Henry's ears the conspirators expected an outburst. But this was not a re-run of the punishment of Adam of Churchdown six years earlier. Whereas the vice-chancellor had been a mere functionary, the Marshal was almost a father-figure to the Young King, who had taught the younger man everything he knew about knightly combat over the thirteen years of their association and saved both his pride and his life on several occasions. Instead, Young Henry began distancing himself from the Marshal with a cold hostility. Whatever his initial feelings, he had grown up in the ambiance of his father's perpetual paranoia, which may have rubbed off on him. Whether or not William knew the reason for this, it is hard to tell, but his instinctive reaction was to keep away and avoid rubbing salt in Young Henry's imagined wound.

In late autumn of 1182 Young Henry and the Marshal fought their last tournament together north of Paris, others in the team noticing the awkwardness between them. As the Marshal prepared to take his leave afterwards, Count Philip of Flanders took the Young King aside and advised him not to lose the Marshal's loyal services over a piece of unsubstantiated gossip. However Young Henry could not bring himself to restrain the Marshal from leaving his court, a fact evidenced by his charters no longer bearing the seal of William as most important witness, replaced by those of the conspirators.

At Henry II's Christmas court in Caen, with all three princes present, the Marshal caused a stir by appearing – and being welcomed by many of the nobles present. He had come to plead with Young Henry for a chance to clear his name by the old, and deadly, ritual of trial by combat. His offer was to take on in sequence three champions proposed by his old pupil; if defeated, he was prepared to acknowledge guilt and end on a gallows. The Young King refused, which left the Marshal no option but to go into exile. He must have had reasons to suspect an attack on the way, for he asked for safe conducts to the limits of Plantagenet territory, which were given by Henry II. Among the offers from noble tourneyers prepared to employ him, he chose an offer from Count Philip of Flanders.

In Caen, after his departure, the mutual hatred of Henry II's sons erupted. Lacking William's moderating counsel, the Young King admitted publicly that he had sworn to support by force of arms the barons of Aquitaine against Richard, their unpopular overlord. Incandescent with rage, Richard dared him to do his worst. Geoffrey, as always slipped between the two traps awaiting him. At a further meeting in Angers, Henry II tried to smooth things out, to no avail. By the end of February, the Young Queen had been despatched to her half-brother's court in Paris, Young Henry was in Limoges and Geoffrey had allied himself with Count Aimery of Limoges. Richard was in Poitiers prepared for a full-scale war against his brothers, crushing Geoffrey's Breton mercenaries and executing all prisoners before doing the same in the Limousin with Young Henry's Gascon mercenaries.

The citadel of Limoges still holding out in early May, Henry II ended the siege as increasing local support for Young Henry – or rather against Richard – made it prudent for him to leave Aquitaine. Somehow, in all the chaos of warfare, a knightly messenger named fitzGodfrey did find the Marshal, who agreed to return to the Young King's service. Henry II did not interfere, presumably hoping that his eldest son might see reason at last with the Marshal to counsel him.

Summoned to Henry II's Christmas court of 1182 in Caen, Young Henry received the homage of his brother Geoffrey, but Richard argued that they were both issue of the same conjugal bed and therefore equal. Insulted by this, Young Henry allowed himself to be incited by the lies of the trouble-making troubadour Bertran de Born to tell his father that the most important vassals of Poitou and Aquitaine had asked him to depose Richard, whose depredations were greatly damaging their territories. They wanted, he said, that he should replace Richard as duke of Aquitaine. To unravel this, Henry II sent Geoffrey into the duchy, summoning the chief vassals to his court at Mirebeau. Once there, Geoffrey obeyed not him but Young

Henry, who had ordered him to raise the duchy against Richard. Where this might have led, we cannot know, but, playing the game both ways, Bertran de Born composed a *siventès* or satirical verse naming all the chief conspirators. When this reached Henry II, he correctly deciphered its references to reveal the other princes' plot to assassinate Richard.

To short-circuit this challenge to his own authority, the old king rode to Limoges, where his small escort was attacked. Before this was stopped by an Anglo-Norman, who had recognised his standard, he suffered a sword-cut to his outer garments, although fortunately no actual wound. Young Henry appeared that evening to say that the attack was a case of mistaken identity. Refusing to listen, Henry II retired to the castle of Aixe-sur-Vienne and Young Henry retreated behind the walls of Limoges. In the absence of siege engines, torrential rain preventing their movement over the sodden ground, it was a stand-off until King Philippe sent a troop of mercenaries to intervene at the request of Marguerite. In the usual way, they so plundered the countryside for miles around that Henry II was forced to withdraw, seeking forage for his horses. Young Henry took this as his cue to exact revenge on the townsfolk of Limoges after begging them for loans to pay his mercenaries in place of his allowance, which Henry II refused any longer to pay.

When this source of finance also was exhausted, he turned to looting churches and monasteries of their treasury – and even shrines, including the most famous one in France at Rocamadour. Falling ill shortly afterwards, he finally collapsed with dysentery in the town of Martel. Tracked there by the bishop of Cahors and other clerics, he was on the point of death, declaring himself ready to make his confession and receive absolution. Learning of this, Henry II wanted to travel to Martel, but was dissuaded by his councillors from going in person, and despatched instead Bishop Bertrand of Agen and Count Rotrou of Le Perche, giving them a ring that the Young King would recognise as being his father's. Near death, Young Henry kissed it and dictated to the clerics present a plea that his father might pardon him and his supporters in the recent revolt. Doubting that Henry II would indeed forgive them, they prudently fled. Having failed to go on crusade despite the oath he had sworn, the dying Young King begged William the Marshal to go in his stead, which the Marshal swore to do – an oath he kept for the good of the Young King's soul. That done, after confessing his sins and receiving the viaticum, Young Henry died at four o'clock on 11 June at the age of 27.

The few household knights remaining loyal to him escorted the bier with the body in a sealed lead coffin, stopping first at the abbey of Grandmont. The entrails had been removed to delay putrefaction, but at the abbey the bishop of Limoges – who knew exactly what the Young King had been doing prior to death – refused to allow any part of the excommunicated prince to be buried in hallowed ground. The decision was reversed after the prior of the monastery swore that Henry II would make good all his late son's plundering, and the eviscerated corpse was packed with salt and spices in the hope that this would enable it to withstand the midsummer heat until it could be delivered to Rouen cathedral in accordance with the Young King's dying wish.

Instead, at Le Mans the bishop took possession of the coffin and had it interred within his cathedral, where Young Henry's paternal grandfather Geoffrey of Anjou already lay. Henry II was enraged, giving the dean of Rouen a warrant for the remains to be disinterred and brought to the Norman capital for a second burial on the north side of the high altar in the cathedral.

Prince Richard, acting as duke of Aquitaine, arrived with Alfonso of Aragon and several siege engines at Bertran de Born's castle of Autafòrt, to punish him for betraying the princes' conspiracy to Henry II. Bertran managed to hold out for a week before capitulating, when Richard awarded the damaged castle to Bertran's brother, whom he had swindled out of his half-share. Taken under guard to Henry II to be punished for his part in the revolt, the troubadour/warrior touched the heart of the old king with two *plans* or eulogies he had composed during the siege, including

> *Si tuit li dolh e'lh plor e'l marrimen*
> *e las dolors e'lh danh e'lh chaitivier*
> *qu'òm anc auzis en est segle dolen*
> *fossen emsems, semblaran tuit leugier*
> *contra la mòrt del jove rei engles ...*

> If the sadness of all the grief and tears,
> the pain, the suffering, the misery

> that afflict a man in a hundred years
> were added up, they would weigh
> less than the death of the young English king ...

So affected was the grieving king by these laments that he reversed Richard's verdict and restored Autafòrt to both brothers, to share equally – a formula that was never going to work, given their mutual hatred. Satisfied that the recent round of hostilities was over, he rode north to Normandy, leaving behind the devastated city and county of the Limousin, its people starving.

Chapter 8

Prince Richard

Even today, with all the science we have at our disposal, millions of people still believe that the positions of the constellations, as seen from our planet at the moment of their birth, influence their character and affect the whole course of their lives. On the night of 8 September 1157 Queen Eleanor, consort of Henry II, countess of Poitou and duchess of Aquitaine in her own right, gave birth to her third son by King Henry II in the King's Houses, later Beaumont Palace, outside the gates of Oxford city. A woman known only by the fashionable Norman French name of Hodierna also gave birth to a son on that night. The son of Queen Eleanor grew up to be King Richard of England; the boy born in St Albans on the same night became one of the foremost philosopher-scientists and theologians of the time, Alexander Neckam.[1] So perhaps there is something in astrology.

In those times noble mothers did not breast-feed their babies, who were put out to wet-nurses, with the birth-mothers' breasts tightly bound to keep them small and high. The mother of a boy born on the same night as Prince Richard seemed eminently qualified by astrology for the post of *nutrix* to the new-born prince, so Hodierna was chosen for that honour. Queen Eleanor enjoying an itinerant lifestyle, usually in the company of the king, Hodierna was installed in the King's Houses, bringing her own son with her. Her plentiful supply of milk sufficing for both infants, Prince Richard was accorded the right breast, thought to make richer milk. Hodierna's position in the royal household was an important one, but the honour of her selection was double-edged: should the prince die from an accident or a childhood disease, she would be held accountable. It was customary for infants to be breast-fed until the age of 2 or older, after which she would be expected to chew all his solid food before placing it in his mouth until his own teeth were adequate. She washed him and dressed him and, if he fell or had a pain, she would comfort him. She was, in short, the source of all the affectionate attention today labelled 'maternal'. In return, she became the woman for whom he felt the most affection. Thirty-three years after her arrival in the King's Houses, he remembered her with the gift to *Hodierna nutrix* of the benefit of a house between Chippenham and Bath, worth an annual rent of £7 10s.

With child betrothals being the fashion at the time, Richard was betrothed at the age of seventeen months to 9-year-old Berengaria, daughter of the count of Barcelona – not to be confused with Berengaria of Navarre, to whom he was later married. In January 1169, when he was 11, another betrothal to a French princess, whom Henry II had tricked the French King Louis VII to hand over, saw him meet face-to-face the teenage Alais Capet, whom also he did not marry, but who became one of his father's mistresses. The royal family in which he grew up was frequently changing, with some children being sent away – like his brother Henry, sent to live in Chancellor Becket's household – and others arriving as strangers. His father's court led a peripatetic existence but, when summoned to a Christmas or Easter court, the children too young or ill to ride a horse were packed into barrel-roofed carts with leather curtains to keep out the weather, together with their minders, wrapped in furs. Night after night, they slept in different places, none of which was 'home'. It is not surprising that growing up in a constantly changing environment like this made them suspicious and unable to trust anyone in later life. At the Christmas court of 1164, held in Marlbrough, Richard was 6 years old when his father learned that Thomas Becket, whom he had made archbishop of Canterbury, was in Rome to enlist Pope Alexander III in his dispute with Henry II. The fury of King Henry at this news was such that he fell on the soiled rushes covering the flagstone floor, foaming at the mouth, in one of his many fits of berserker rage. It must have been a terrifying sight for his young son.

Peter of Blois, who served as Queen Eleanor's secretary for a while, described life in the court as resembling that of the *milites herlewini* – soldiers of the mythical English king Herla, always on the move. If any man fell out of the ranks exhausted, he was turned to dust, according to the legend.[2] A similar pressure in Henry II's court saw that restless monarch dismiss any courtier who failed to come running when called at any time of the day or night – a rejection that was the social equivalent of being turned to dust. Another courtier, the chronicler Walter Map, described how the king would frequently announce an early start the following morning and then stay in bed till noon, leaving 100 men and women, or more, dozing beside their harnessed mounts or draught animals since before dawn. Alternatively, the king might proclaim a day of rest for everyone, then rise before daylight and depart with an escort of household knights in a cloud of dust, leaving the court and hangers-on to make a hurried toilet and hasten after them as best they could. To know what was in the king's mind, Peter of Blois said, meant 'running to the court whores, for this breed of courtier often knows the palace secrets'.[3] Even when staying several days in the same castle or palace, life was hectic with 200 people or more coming and going, plus the noise of farriers, armourers and wheelwrights hammering, horses neighing, hunting dogs barking, shod hooves and iron-bound wheels on the courtyard cobbles. And the stench of so many people and animals in close proximity – there were never adequate washing facilities – was added to the stink of night soil being carried out in earthware pots and wooden tubs and animal dung being removed each day. It was enough to make one yearn for the fresh air on the road.

It could be that Richard found the chaos and confusion of the court difficult. Maybe that was why his mother – hardly a maternal figure – kept him close to her as much as possible. She seems to have decided early in his life that he was the son destined to become a warrior-poet like her grandfather Duke William IX of Aquitaine, known as William the Troubadour. The word did not mean an itinerant musician travelling from castle to castle with a lute slung over his shoulder; that was a *jonglar*. The troubadours who composed poetry and songs were mostly of noble descent. So Queen Eleanor insisted that, in addition to his training for knighthood, her favourite son be taught to read and write in Latin, the northern Frankish tongue and Occitan, the language of southern France, more akin to Spanish than the *langue d'oïl* spoken in Paris. If writing poetry sounds effeminate, Prince Richard also heard court jesters declaiming the tales of martial prowess, as when Godefroi de Bouillon leaped from a siege tower onto the walls of Jerusalem during the First Crusade and hacked his way through living flesh and blood with a handful of knights to reach the gates of the city and open them for the mass of Christian fighters to pour inside and murder every Muslim, Jew and eastern Christian living there. The lesson that the young prince was absorbing was that no less would be expected of him, when grown up. It was a lesson that would cost thousands of lives.

Probably the first time he actually went to war was after the meeting with Louis VII at Montmirail on 6 January 1169. After having his sons swear fealty to Louis for the lands their father had given them – and which he would take away when it suited him – Henry rode south, taking 11-year-old Richard, now nominal duke of Aquitaine, with him to have a taste of the bloody reality of war in punishing with fire and sword the perpetually squabbling vassals in Poitou and Aquitaine. In August, as his twelfth birthday approached, the prince accompanied his father to acquire a taste for another blood sport: hunting in a forest near Angers. Leaving Eleanor, who knew well the province she had inherited at 15, to guide the young duke's footsteps, Henry headed north for an infuriating meeting with Becket at St-Germain-en-Laye, outside Paris.

If Henry had 'blooded' Richard in the field, his mother introduced him to the elegant southern way of life at her court in Poitiers, where she behaved as a queen in her own right, not just a consort. There were up to sixty eligible heiresses at the court at any one time and she exercised her right to arrange their marriages to the young knights who came there, hoping to catch her eye. To do that, they had to be as one flesh with their mounts when in the saddle, acquit themselves well in combat and know how to set a falcon on its prey. If, in addition, they could turn out a poem or make music on lute or flute, they stood a chance of pleasing their demanding duchess and marrying a rich heiress. A contemporary song, still sung today, catches the mood:

> *A l'entrada del tens clar, per jòia recomençar*
> *e per gelos irritar, vol la reina mostrar*
> *qu'el es si amorosa. El'a fait pertot mandar*
> *non sia jusqu'a la mar pucela ni bachelar*
> *que tuit no vengan dançar en la dança joiosa.*

> In Spring, the queen worries her husband
> by showing him she still knows what love is.
> She summons to her from far and wide
> every unwed knight and maid
> to join her in the joyous dance.

PRINCE RICHARD

The ambiance of the Poitiers court was the epitome of *gay saber*. France's most influential monk, abbot Bernard of Clairvaux disapproved of its luxury, the ladies wearing floor-length dresses with sleeves so long they had to be knotted up out of the way even for dancing, to avoid tripping over them. Unlike his father, who dressed carelessly, Richard adored dressing up and, on occasion, penned a polite verse or two for some young girl. The knock-on effect of all this sartorial fashion was that even bishops in the southwest required their outer sleeves to be slashed, revealing the costly cloth beneath. Abbot Bernard deplored also in women 'the beauty that is put on in the morning and taken off at night'.

Eleanor, no longer deferring to Henry II, summoned all her vassals to Richard's Easter court of 1170, where the 12-year-old duke accepted their homage, for what it was worth. Afterwards, Eleanor rode with him to Poitiers, where the counts of Poitou were ceremonially proclaimed *ex ufficio* abbots of St Hilaire. Archbishop Bertrand of Bordeaux and the bishop of Poitiers presented the young prince with the traditional lance and standard of a count of Poitou in the cathedral, after which the choir sang and hailed him as *princeps egregie!* Their titular abbot of St Hilaire would indeed turn out to be an egregious prince.

Mother and son continued their grand progress to the twin towns of Limoges, where Geoffroy du Vigeois, a monk in the abbey, described how his bishop placed on Richard's finger a ring, making him the symbolic husband of the city's patron saint, the Roman martyr Valeria, killed there because she refused to renounce Christianity. There was more to all this than simply conforming with tradition. Eleanor was going through all the formalities so that Richard could swear fealty directly to Louis VII, making it difficult for Henry II to cancel Richard's title to the duchy, as he was prone to do with his sons. To spite her for this, when she travelled north to accompany Prince Henry to England for his coronation as Young King, Henry II did not invite her to come, ordering her instead to prevent any emissary from Becket crossing the Channel and disturbing the ceremony.

What Richard was doing meanwhile is a mystery. Historians trying to discover where a prince was on a certain date consult the charters sealed in his name around that time. Despite his new status, Richard seems to have refrained from sealing charters for a while, leaving that boring business to Queen Eleanor. In fact, prudent benficiaries of charters accorded by Ricart Oc-e-No – his nickname from Bertran de Born – always had them confirmed by Eleanor, to ensure they were valid.[4] We know Richard was always bored with the minutiae of office. So, was he hunting? Was he fighting? Either is equally possible, and the truth obscured behind the great drama of Becket's murder on 29 December 1170 by four of Henry II's household knights in Canterbury a few days after they had attended the king's Christmas court at Bures in Normandy. We know the young duke of Aquitaine was at Argentan in Normandy in the first week of January 1171, witnessing Henry II's display of contrition, protesting to Alexander III that he had done everything to prevent the murder. Shortly afterwards, he and Eleanor rode back to Poitiers, where Eleanor sealed charters in her own name, with Richard's appearing secondarily.

At the end of the year, with Henry II staying on the far side of the Irish Sea, to avoid papal legates harassing him about Becket, Richard held his own 1171 Christmas court in Bayonne. The honour for the citizens was tempered by his imposition of taxes on the fisherman working the Bay of Biscay, and for taking whales, abundant there until hunted to extinction in the nineteenth century.[5] Eleanor having fallen ill on the way, her 13-year-old son was in his element, with no one to curb him, albeit frustrated that the peacekeeping army stationed in Aquitaine to keep the barons under some semblance of discipline was controlled by the seneschal appointed by his distant father. Henry II returned to southwest France for a meeting with Count Raymond of Toulouse, who confessed that he held the county as the vassal of Henry II, Henry the Young King – and Richard as duke of Aquitaine. When summoned in time of war, Raymond had to attend his overlords with 100 knights for forty days and pay an annual tribute of 100 silver marks, which could be replaced by ten trained warhorses valued at ten marks each.

Richard was not present, being in Paris with Louis VII to be knighted by his suzerain, but obeying the summons to attend Henry II's Christmas court in Chinon castle. The atmosphere in the exposed and draughty castle on the cliff overlooking the river Vienne was made even more frigid for Queen Eleanor, Geoffrey and Richard by the king's fury that Young Henry refused to attend. The news from Rome that Becket was to be canonised on 21 February 1173 added to the chill. On that day all three princes were in Limoges as Henry II welcomed King Alfonso II of Aragon and King Sancho VI of Navarre arriving on pilgrimage to the tomb of St Martial.[6] Killing time together, the three princes found that their mutual jealousy was outweighed by a seething resentment at the way their father had controlled and manipulated them all their lives. Young Henry was 18, Richard 15 and Geoffrey 14. In that time of brief life expectancy, the two elder brothers were considered men and Geoffrey nearly so. He was also more intelligent than his elders and took some persuading to join them in a conspiracy to raise the Limousin against Henry II in a rebellion that was also high treason.

Normally, Henry II's paranoia would have alerted him to the conspiracy between his sons, but he was too busy pulling the wool over Count Humbert's eyes and sending the count's young daughter to be brought up in Eleanor's household as an important element in his plan to gain access to the disputed territory of northern Italy. As we have already learned, after learning of the conspiracy, he immediately ordered the castellans of his nearby castles to ready them for sieges before returning to dismiss Young Henry's household knights and bring the prince to heel. After the uprising began on 15 April 1173, Henry II assembled an army of 20,000 mercenaries from Brabant and outmanoeuvred the forces against him, each castle taken providing the money to pay the Brabanters for the next stage.

After the capture of Eleanor, he pursued Richard south into Aquitaine and brought him to bay at Saintes, the western terminal of the great Roman highway across the middle of France. Abandoning sixty ransomable knights and 400 men-at-arms, Richard slipped away, leaving his treasury to swell his father's coffers. After performing an impressive penance for Becket's death, Henry II concentrated on subverting the Young King, knowing that the other princes would give up, if he did. He was right. Richard left his loyal supporters in Poitou and arrived at Montlouis near Tours on 29 September to throw himself at his father's feet, weeping. Lifting him up and giving him the kiss of peace, Henry led him like a captive to a peace conference with Louis VII where Geoffrey and Young Henry also humbled themselves before their father and their suzerain.[7]

Twelve months later, Eleanor was still incomunicada, locked up in Old Sarum with a single maidservant for company and showing no signs of giving in to Henry II. His Christmas court of 1174 was held in Argentan, with all three sons obliged to attend in a show of loyalty that continued afterwards with them compelled to accompany him in a tour of Poitou and Aquitaine, during which castles that had been held for him were improved in any way necessary and manned by garrisons sufficient to put down any further trouble. But castles strengthened by vassals and vavasours who had declared for the princes were reduced to their *ante bellum* status. According to Alfred Richard, nineteenth-century archivist of the Vienne *département*, Henry II regarded Richard as having, true to his nickname, changed his coat to his father's colours. He was therefore equipped with a small army of knights and men-at-arms to conduct a punitive *chevauchée* throughout the southwest, attacking his supporters from the war against Henry II as viciously as he had treated barons loyal to the king during the war, tearing down their castles and laying waste their lands. As always, the serfs suffered worst, being deprived of their sustenance for the following winter.

One of his allies who suffered particularly was Geoffroy de Rancon, who had given him asylum after Henry II chased him out of Saintes. Alfred Richard recorded events thus:

> As soon as he was on the lands of the lord of Taillebourg, he tore up the vines, burned down isolated houses and laid waste whole villages, reducing the population to poverty and leaving the men no alternative but to join one of the bands of *routiers*. Knowing the weaknesses of the castle from the time he had spent there, he installed his siege engines on the most vulnerable side. Geoffroy made a sortie to destroy them, but was beaten back by Richard's troops and a horde of attackers managed to pour through the gate before it could be closed, forcing de Rancon to retreat to the donjon. A long defence was out of the question, so de Rancon surrendered and, to avoid being taken prisoner, yielded all his castles, every one of which was razed to the ground.[8]

The ultimate irony of a long siege was illustrated at Arnaud de Bouville's castle of St-Puy,[9] which held out for two months resisting all attacks and a battery of siege engines. Richard took prisoner thirty knights and many sergeants-at-arms, whose ransoms repaid his costs in the siege. In addition, the castle was razed to the ground and de

PRINCE RICHARD

Bouville's land spread with salt to make it infertile for years to come. Bertran de Born summed up the pleasure of this kind of campaign. In a poem that could have been written by Richard, he wrote:

> *E platz mi quan li corredor fan las gens e l'aver fugir.*
> *E platz mi quan vei après lor gran re d'armatz ensems venir.*
> *E platz mi em mon coratge quan vei fortz chastels assetjatz*
> *e los barris rotz et esfondratz ....*
> I love to see the skirmishers putting the common folk to flight.
> A host of armed men riding them down is a grand sight.
> It warms my heart to see great castles under siege
> and ramparts gaping at the breach ...

After Richard failed to pay off his Basque and Navarrese mercenaries, they started southward but stopped at Bordeaux. They could not attack the walled city, but vented their spite by looting the dwellings and commerces outside the walls before setting fire to them.[10] Richard was in jocular mood at some time in this punitive expedition. The cook was an important member of a noble's household because his mistakes could kill his master. Particularly pleased with his cook after one meal, Richard summoned him and made him kneel, to be dubbed a knight and 'lord of the fief of the kitchen of the counts of Poitou'. His spell of fun and games in all-male company was threatened when a papal legate arrived in Rouen to inform Henry II that Pope Alexander III had taken up Louis VII's cause in the matter of Princess Alais' still uncelebrated wedding to Richard. In the case of any further delay, the girl and her dowry must be returned to her father. The current complication was that she was Henry II's mistress. As usual, he spun out negotiations and totally confused the legate by swearing an oath to go on crusade, adding that Richard and the unfortunate princess would be married immediately after his return.

Chapter 9

Richard the Lionheart

The only king with a statue[1] in the Palace of Westminster or British Parliament is the most popular of all English monarchs: Richard the Lionheart. Seated on a warhorse with sword held aloft, the statue in Old Palace Yard is the perfect image of a Christian king, whose greatest fame came from departing on the Third Crusade to recapture Jerusalem from the Muslims under Salah ed-Din, known as Saladdin in the West. Yet, after arriving in the Holy Land with a huge fleet, a large army and considerable materiel, and an allied army under French King Philippe Auguste – and causing thousands of deaths both military and civilian – he failed to achieve any change in the political/military situation there and had to borrow a single ship from the Templars to start the lonely journey homeward.

The respected historian of the crusades, Steven Runciman,[2] writing in the 1950s, summed up the life of King Richard succinctly thus:

> He was a bad son, a bad husband and a bad king, but a gallant and splendid soldier.[3]

Ideas about 'splendid soldiery' have changed in seven decades, but one might think that the very influential Victorian divine Bishop William Stubbs, who did so much for medieval scholarship in his long career, would see King Richard as a great Christian hero. Yet his verdict, written in a far more religious time nearly a century earlier reads:

> [Richard was] a bad ruler, his energy, or rather his restlessness, his love of war and his genius for it, effectively disqualified him from being a peaceful one; his want of political common sense from being a prudent one. [He was] a man of blood, whose crimes were those of one who long use of warfare had made too familiar with slaughter ... and a vicious man.[4]

RICHARD THE LIONHEART

It is ironic that Richard, the renowned warrior and champion of Christendom owes his fame to a battle at which he was not present. On 4 July 1187, Saladin as commanding general of a coalition of emirs trapped the army of Guy de Lusignan, king of the Latin Kingdom of Jerusalem, between two hills called the Horns of Hattin, which lay east of the re-fortified Greek city of Sepphoris, then known as Saffuriya, and Tiberias on the western shore of Lake Galilee.[5] Saladin's generalship was exemplary and that of King Guy, under the influence of his bellicose vassal Prince Arnaud de Châtillon, a catalogue of all the faults a commander can commit. The result was near annihilation of the crusader host – some 1,200 knights from Jerusalem and Tripoli and a handful from Antioch. News of the consequent fall of Jerusalem brought to Europe by Archbishop Joscius of Tyre caused Pope Gregory VIII to issue a bull entitled *audita tremendi* on 29 October 1187.[6] The bull called for a new tax known as the Saladin tithe – the payment of 10 per cent of all income and moveable property with the exception of a knight's weapons, armour and horses, the clergy's vestments and Church treasures. The aim was to finance a third crusade to re-take Jerusalem from the Muslims. Like most additional taxes, it was widely resented, so an exemption was made for all men who swore to join the new crusade.

Crusading fever erupting like the plague, Richard would have joined in this great adventure in any event. At the time, he was conducting a minor war of his own in the county of Toulouse and, with his customary brutality, killing any unransomable captives, until his chaplain Milo persuaded him to let them live on condition they swore to accompany him on his 'pilgrimage to Jerusalem'. On 22 January1188, while Henry II was negotiating a truce at Gisors with the new French king Philippe Auguste, Archbishop Joscius killed three birds with one stone, pinning red crosses to the cloaks of Philippe's retinue, with white ones for Henry's men and green ones for the followers of Count Philip of Flanders. The count had already been to the Holy Land and returned totally disillusioned, calling the rulers of the crusader states *poulains* or foals forever looking to their mares – the European countries of their origins – for help and finance, instead of fighting their own battles.

Henry II had no intention of actually going on crusade and could always find a compliant churchman to free him from his oath. Philippe delayed any action in the logical belief that leaving his realm for two years would see it attacked by Henry despite the pope's protection.

PLANTAGENET PRINCES

The first European ruler to actually depart was the Holy Roman Emperor Friedrich Barbarossa, who drowned in a Turkish river and never reached the Holy Land. Two-thirds of his army returned home, leaving a rump force of 5,000 men to continue under his son Duke Friedrich VI of Swabia. When he in turn died at the siege of Acre early in 1191 command of the German-speaking troops was assumed by Duke Leopold V of Austria – of whom more later. As for the kings of England and France, that troublesome troubadour Bertran de Born accused them of forgetting the 'journey they had sworn to make' – *el pasatge qu'an si mes en obli.*

A reluctance to leave their lands for the crusade was the only thing the two kings had in common. Henry was now 55 years old and increasingly enfeebled with a damaged leg, spinal problems and haemorrhoids that made it painful to sit on the unyielding saddle of a *destrier*. Philippe Auguste pressed home the advantage this gave him. The end of Lent in 1189 saw hostilities break out again after a truce, but with many of Henry II's vassals, including Prince Richard, fighting against him. On 3 July the fortress-city of Tours fell to them. Richard, suspecting his father of some trick, was surprised to see a frail old man, who had to be supported on his horse, at the truce meeting on the following day. Henry was dying. No longer with the strength to argue, he agreed to pay the costs of the war and pardon all who had fought against him – with one exception. Miming the kiss of peace for Richard, he hissed into his ear, 'May God let me live to avenge myself on you.' The prayer went unheard. Carried back to Chinon castle on a litter, on 6 July 1189 he died, making Richard king of the dual realm.

Travelling south to Fontevraud abbey, not to pay his respects but to ensure Henry was really dead, Richard returned to Chinon to grab the treasury, but found it empty – every *denier* spent in the recent war. Respecting William the Marshal for his loyalty to Young Henry and Henry II, he betrothed him to Countess Isabel of Striguil, one of England's richest heiresses, who had been kept a ward of the Crown in the Tower of London for thirteen years, and ordered the Marshal to head north and release Queen Eleanor from house arrest. That amazing woman aged 67, Henry's prisoner for a quarter of her long life, did not wait for the Marshal's arrival, but declared herself the crowned queen of England – which she was – and took the reins of government into her hands, requiring that every free man in the whole realm swear that he would bear fealty to the Lord Richard, lord of England, son of the lord Henry and the lady Eleanor, in life and limb and earthly honour, as his liege lord against all men and women who might live and die, and that they would be answerable to him and help him keep the peace and justice in all things.

With her habitual prudence and statecraft, she required the Archbishop of Canterbury to witness the barons' oaths of loyalty. To bring the general population on-side, she announced an amnesty releasing thousands of men languishing in jail under the cruel forest laws although never tried and sentenced. Richard did not hurry to England for his coronation. It was a country in which he had no interest, and which he had visited only twice in his adult years, at Easter 1176 and Christmas 1184. First, he had himself absolved by the archbishops of Sées and Canterbury from the sin of bearing arms against his father when both had taken crusaders' vows, and was also invested as plenary duke of Normandy in Rouen. To ensure that his illegitimate half-brother Geoffrey the Bastard could not claim any right to the throne, in an echo of Becket's death he despatched a posse of his household knights to Geoffrey's manor in Southwell to 'persuade' him to accept consecration as archbishop of York, debarring him from secular office.

After spending two months putting his Continental affairs in order, he stepped ashore in Portsmouth and hastened to Winchester to supervise the weighing of the treasury, estimated at £90,000.[7] From this, a little less than £14,000 was set aside to defray Philippe Auguste's costs in the recent war in fulfilment of Henry II's promise at Chinon and another 4,000 marks added to be quit of any claim from Philippe.[8] Probably under Eleanor's guidance, with the intention of mollifying his only surviving brother on 29 August he had Prince John married to the rich heiress Isabel of Gloucester in defiance of the Church's ruling on their consanguinity. When the southern Welsh under Rhys ap Gryffydd took advantage of the change of king in London to burst into the Marches, it was Eleanor who curbed Richard's immediate reaction, to ride off and put down their uprising. Instead, she accompanied him to Westminster for his coronation on 3 September. With poor Alais discarded in Winchester, never to wear the promised crown, it was Eleanor who played the part of queen in the abbey, surrounded by her court of ladies. Repairing to Westminster Hall for the coronation feast, where women and Jews were not welcome, Richard may not have noticed that members of the latter community bearing presents were turned away from the hall peremptorilly. This led to a pogrom, in which men, women and children were murdered and the only perpetrators punished were two Londoners who had accidentally burned down a Christian house when setting fire to a neighbouring Jewish property.

Was it Eleanor's influence or his own impatience to let nothing delay his departure on crusade that caused the new king to send 13-year-old John off with an army to sort out the Welsh? In the following month, it was again John who gave Rhys a safe-conduct to attend a truce conference at Oxford.[9] If Eleanor had thought that kingship would in any way change her favourite son, she soon learned that his interest in the island realm was purely financial, as an asset to be plundered to finance his dream of waging a war of violence and savagery unfettered by any other sovereign and even the pope. Indeed Pope Clement III accorded absolution of all past sins to men departing on the Third Crusade and none of their murderous violence on the crusade mattered, because it was intended to kill non-Christians. The result was the sale of the century: heiresses who were wards of court, offices high and low. He reputedly said, 'I would sell London, if I could find a buyer.'[10] In case that sounds like exaggeration, the towns of Berwick and Roxburgh were sold back to William of Scotland for £10,000, which included his release from vassalage to the English Crown. Years of Henry II's prudent governance were undone by the sale of permission to build castles for any baron who could pay. Henry II's 77-year-old justiciar Ranulf de Glanville was thrown into jail to squeeze out of him a fine of £15,000 of silver, and saved from execution by Eleanor, whose jailer he had been, pointing out he was corrupt but astute. Glanville was replaced by Bishop Hugh of Durham for northern England after purchasing the earldom of Northumberland and his enemy William de Mandeville, earl of Essex for southern England. Richard's unpleasant chancellor of Aquitaine joined in the feeding frenzy, buying the chancellorship of England and the bishopric of Ely for £3,000.

Thoughtlessly, Richard ordered Prince John to join his crusade – a move that Eleanor crushed. She had no liking for John, but foresaw the possibility that both her sons could die in combat or disease, leaving the Angevin Empire up for grabs. Instead, Richard tried bribery, giving John a chain of castles, the town of Nottingham and the whole of Derbyshire, Devon, Cornwall, Somerset and Dorset.[11]

He would have done better to lock up in jail his treacherous younger brother.

Already in the Holy Land were numerous English barons and knights, Sicilians, Germans and Austrians, Danes, Frisians, French, Flemish, Sicilians and knights from a dozen other lands without any overall command and many openly refusing to obey the ousted King Guy of Jerusalem at the siege of Acre. When a sortie from the city by 5,000 Muslims took in the rear the crusader force already fighting Saladin's encirclement of their disease-ridden camp, more than 4,000 crusaders died.[12] In the intervals between major battles, men covered in boils and with teeth falling out of bleeding gums died from sand-tick fever, from dysentery, from plague. Knights slaughtered their own horses for meat and the common soldiery was reduced to eating grass and weeds. The bishop of Salisbury had men flogged for resorting to cannibalism, cutting up their dead comrades' corpses. What fresh food remained was subject to terrible inflation. A handful of peas cost a silver penny; a small sack of corn went for 200 gold *bezants* instead of the normal price of six.[13] The men suffering and dying under Acre's walls had come seeking the kingdom of Heaven on earth and found themselves in hell.

As to how they got there, maritime historian John Pryor observed that accounts of medieval campaigns assume

> they took place in a geographic, meteorological and oceanographic vacuum. Military forces move from one place to another without the slightest difficulty. Naval forces ... leave the West and arrive in the Holy Land as though their commanders had merely engaged the engines on their cruise ships and set course by the shortest route. For the First Crusade, the only fleet to attempt to make the passage to the East was a Genoese flotilla of twelve galleys and a transport ship. It took four months to make the voyage.[14]

To avoid paying the exorbitant rates demanded by the ship owners of Pisa and Genoa, Richard scoured the English ports from Hull to Portsmouth and assembled in Dartmouth a motley collection of merchant shipping of the type called 'cogs', to which were added fore- and after-castles for maritime conflict en route. They cost between £50 and £66 each, paid two-thirds in cash and the balance by remission of taxes to their owners, and had to be bought outright because none would ever return to England or Normandy, but were to be scrapped in the Mediterranean. Food for the crews and passengers included live animals and fowls for slaughter on the voyage.[15] It was necessary to put into land several times for fresh water for men and horses, the supply on board swiftly becoming stagnant and undrinkable. Scurvy, of course, was an ever-present threat.[16]

On 11 January 1190 Richard and Philippe Auguste swore to depart on the crusade together, since neither trusted the other. Queen Eleanor caught up with her headstrong son shortly afterwards, bringing across the Channel Prince John, Geoffrey the Bastard, Richard's chancellor William Longchamp and a pride of prelates as well as Princess Alais, who had been Henry II's prisoner for twenty-one of her thirty years. Eleanor wanted Richard to marry her and beget an heir in case he died on this insane expedition. Alais was known to be fertile, having born at least one child to Henry II, and the marriage would have formed an alliance between the houses of Capet and Plantagenet – surely a good thing between brother crusaders – but Richard argued that it was against nature to marry his late father's former mistress. In the generalised crusading fever, England's Jews were targeted as unbelievers. One of the worst pogroms, at York on 16 March 1190 – the feast of *shabbat ha-gadol* at the end of Pesach – the survivors of previous violence killed their wives to avoid them being raped by the mob outside Clifford's Tower, where they had taken refuge, and a rabbi also killed sixty of the men. The remainder were beaten to death by the mob after emerging from the tower with safe conducts, having volunteered to convert to Christianity as a last resort. Similar massacres occurred in King's Lynn, Stamford, Colchester, Bury St Edmunds, Thetford and elsewhere.

Richard had no illusions about the conduct of his army during the long voyage. At Chinon in June he proclaimed rules of conduct and penalties for misdemeanours: for murder at sea, the murderer was to be bound to the corpse and thrown overboard with it; for murder on land, the murderer was to be buried alive with the victim; for an attack without bloodshed, the aggressor was to be keel-hauled three times, and so on. On 1 July 1190 the French and Plantagenet armies rendezvoused at Vézelay in Burgundy: thousands of barons and knights, each with four horses – his destrier, a palfrey for him and one for the squire and a sumpter horse for carrying his arms and armour. There was also a long wagon train pulled by oxen to transport tents, food, and dismantled siege engines. With no sanitation, the enormous mass left a wide trail of human and animal excrement behind it on the 200-mile journey from Vézelay to Lyons and the countryside was plundered for miles around.

Richard's army embarked at Marseilles, Philippe Auguste's smaller force taking ship at Nice on galleys, cargo vessels and specially constructed *chalendres* – galleys carrying forty horses each, with a long ramp at the stern that was let down for embarcation and disembarcation. In theory, this would have enabled them to be ridden ashore, straight into battle – a medieval amphibious attack. In fact, fed on dry grain while on board and suffering from sea-sickness – horses cannot vomit – and with only stale water to drink, all the horses required a long rest at the end of the voyage. Over-wintering on Sicily, to avoid the Mediterranean's winter gales and also to repair ships damaged by the teredo wood-boring mollusc and which needed timbers replaced,[17] conflicts broke out between members of the two armies, echoing exchanges of insults between the two kings. Bearing in mind the likelihood that he might die on the crusade, Richard drew up a will and named his brother Geoffrey's son, Arthur of Brittany, as his heir. That would have been as good as handing the Plantagenet Empire to Philippe Auguste, who was Arthur's suzerain. To undo this gross lack of statecraft, 76-year-old Queen Eleanor rode south to Navarre and then back to France and down the length of Italy bringing a bride for Richard. With impeccable timing, on the day after the departure of the French fleet, Eleanor crossed from the mainland to Messina, bringing with her a bride with whom Richard *might* just father a child because 25-year-old Princess Berengaria of Navarre was reputed to be submissive, prudent, gentle and docile. Suspecting Richard would wriggle out of the marriage contract if given the chance, Eleanor brought her in person to her future husband. His first excuse was that weddings could not be celebrated during Lent; the second was that women were barred by the pope from travelling with crusaders. Taking all this in her stride, Eleanor arranged with the bishops of his party that the couple would be united after Lent during the scheduled stopover at Cyprus. She then hastened back to England, where Prince John was subverting many barons who expected Richard to die in the Holy Land. On Sunday 12 May Richard was married to Berengaria in Limassol after doing penance for sodomy and receiving absolution. Whether the marriage was ever consummated is not known; to Queen Eleanor's frustration, there was no issue and some historians believe that Berengaria was England's first Virgin Queen.

The mass of the English fleet arrived at Acre on 8 June 1191, Richard immediately throwing himself into the siege of the Muslim fortress. Apart from the heat of midsummer, the lack of hygeine and bad food, there was an epidemic of *arnaldia* – which, in the case of Philippe Auguste, caused sweating with loss of his teeth and nails and whole strips of his skin rotting away. Conflict was intermittent and morale was low. During a truce, Richard sent a Moorish prisoner under a flag of truce to request a meeting with Saladin. Instead, Saladin sent his brother Al-Adil to the meeting with the message: 'Kings meet only after an accord, for it is unthinkable for them to wage war once they have broken bread together.'[18]

Richard's siege engines were erected to bombard the city walls. Sappers also dug tunnels under them, so that fierce fires of fatty pig carcasses could be lit there, burning through the props and causing breaches when the walls above fell in. At times, Saracen counter-mines broke through into the tunnels. About to kill the 'enemy' digging them, the crusader sappers were startled to hear them talking *lingua franca*, and found they were Christian prisoners, forced to dig in shackles. After one successful mine damaged the wall near the Accursed Tower, from where prisoners were thrown to their deaths, Philippe Auguste's marshal Albéric Clément cried, *'Aut hodie moriar, aut in Achon, deo volente ingrediar!'* This day I shall die or, God willing, enter Acre. Seemingly, God was not willing for, after he clambered onto the walls, the scaling ladder broke under the weight of the following knights and he was hacked to death all alone.[19]

An account of the siege of Acre could fill a book,[20] but two events stand out. When the city was finally taken, Richard was enraged that Duke Leopold of Austria, leader of the German-speaking contingent, managed to find quarters as good as his own, and some English knights threw Leopold's standard into the sewage-filled moat. Profoundly insulted, most of Leopold's force abandoned the crusade and rode north on the long journey home. Secondly, after the surrender of the city, Saladin agreed to ransom all the inhabitants. Impatient with the time it took to assemble the ransom, Richard ordered 2,700 of his captives to be executed, sparing only 300 individually ransomable individuals. The French also killed all the soldiers of the garrison and 300 of their wives and children. Distraught parents were forced to watch children and friends killed with sword and lance, clubs and stones before being dragged to their own death in full view of the Saracen camp, which triggered an impromptu attack to stop the carnage. This was beaten off, and the killing went on.

Chapter 10

Richard's perfect castle

On 22 August, when thousands of corpses were still being cut open before being burned in case they had swallowed any jewels, Richard departed with an army of 20,000 men for the strategic port of Jaffa. They rode and marched in a long column, keeping close to the coast and paced by a flotilla sailing close inshore bearing supplies and taking off the wounded. The column could only be attacked from the left, or inland, side by Saracens commanded by al-Adil, who rode in armed with short recurved bows and galloped away after loosing their arrows, inviting pursuit that would turn to ambush. This was Richard's finest hour. The Norman chronicler and poet Ambroise, who was present, was the first admirer to use the epithet 'Lionheart'. Riding in the middle of the column that moved only between dawn and noon to avoid the afternoon sun, he forbade any knight to leave the column after being attacked in this way. This was went against the grain for warriors who prided themselves of never suffering a blow without immediately returning the violence. Despite thickly padded covers, many horses were killed by arrows. According to Saladin's historian Baha al-Din, some crusaders had up to seven arrows sticking in their padded protective clothing.[1] Nineteen days after leaving Acre, and after a full-scale battle at Arsuf on 8 September, the army reached Jaffa, to find it a ruin, destroyed when Saladin's garrison had withdrawn. To re-build the fortress-cities, Richard recruited 20,000 native mercenaries called Turcopoles and set them to work.

Saladin withdrew inland to Jerusalem, which had suffered much damage during the siege of 1187. This was the moment when Richard could have attacked the Holy City before the walls were repaired but, in a major strategic error, he lingered at Jaffa, intent on making it a secure rear base with its own port. Among visiting Saracens whom he welcomed in a spirit of gallantry that was widely disapproved, was al-Adil, whom he called 'my brother'. On 8 December the army moved to Latrun at the foot of the Judean mountains, about twenty miles from the Holy City. Winter in the mountains is cruelly cold, even for Europeans, and Saladin's army had left it a scorched wilderness devoid of food for horse or man. Torrential winter rains made foodstocks rotten and turned the ground into a sea of mud, churned up by thousands of hooves, through which dismounted knights had to drag their horses when combating skirmishes.

Moving to Beit Nuba, a couple of miles nearer Jerusalem, negotiations with al-Adil through the Arabic-speaking crusader noble named Humphrey of Toron led nowhere. In ultimate desperation, Richard offered al-Adil the hand of his sister Joanna, the former queen of Sicily who was in Acre with Constance of Brittany. The idea was to make them king and queen of a Christian Jerusalem. Joanna, in an outburst of fury rare in a medieval woman, refused the idea of marrying a Muslim. So Richard offered to his 'brother' as bride his niece Constance of Brittany. As his chattel, she was his to dispose of as he wished. However, al-Adil refused to convert to Christianity, so that led nowhere.

On 13 January, riven by in-fighting between the various political and national factions, the crusader army turned tail and headed back to the milder weather on the coast at the ruined fortress of Ashkelon, where the squabbling continued. News from England of Prince John inciting rebellion and from France of encroachments by Philippe Auguste into Plantagenet territory might have inclined Richard to return and 'put his own house in order'. But he could not resist pressure from the nobility of the Latin Kingdom to make one last attempt on Jerusalem, which was bound to be futile because there was no way of re-constructing the arc of fortresses required as outworks. On 7 June the army nevertheless abandoned Ashkelon and marched into the mountains, setting up camp at Qalandiya, from where there was a clear view of the Holy City, ten miles distant. Here, dissension between the contingent commanders prevented an attack until on 31 July news reached them that Saladin had outflanked them and broken into Jaffa. Grabbing at straws, Richard decided on a seaborne counter-attack, which, with his customary courage, he led in person. On 5 August Saladin led an attack, reputedly by 7,000 men, but then desisted and returned to Jerusalem, leaving some of the coastal cities in crusader hands.[2]

PLANTAGENET PRINCES

A treaty was drawn up, ending the crusade, and leaving Richard's prestige at an all-time low and the army's morale non-existent. An invitation for him to visit Jerusalem as Saladin's guest was rejected and Richard, having alienated all the other national contingents, left the Holy Land in a single galley borrowed from the Templars, who furnished him with a small bodyguard. It was a humiliating departure for the king who had arrived with a fleet and an army. Putting into an Italian port after deciding not to travel on land because that entailed crossing many miles of German territory ruled by Duke Leopold's suzerain, he learned that Count Raymond of Toulouse and Philippe Auguste had set ambushes for him all along the French Mediterranean littoral. He back-tracked, hiring two Romanian pirate galleys to escort him northwards up the Adriatic.[3] Disaster struck when the vessels were stranded in a storm on the coast of Istria.

This was Leopold's territory, so Richard disguised himself as a merchant but was duly recognised and the journey became a hell-for-leather ride, in which fourteen of the Templars were sacrificed as rearguards. Suddenly coming down with malaria, he was betrayed on 21 December, when disguised as a scullion, turning the spit on which a brace of spatchcocks was roasting. Declaring his true identity, he refused to surrender until Duke Leopold left his Christmas court in Vienna and came to take his sword in person and order the sick monarch to be nursed back to health, well-guarded in the castle of Dürnstein. After the German emperor Heinrich VI Hohenstaufen ruled it improper for Leopold to hold a king prisoner, Richard was transferred into imperial custody. At the emperor's Easter court he was tracked down by Queen Eleanor's emissaries, who found him in good spirits, popular with his guards and treating imprisonment as no worse than being held for ransom like a knight taken in a *mêlée*. In front of the whole court, he pleaded his case in elegant Latin, kneeling in submission before Heinrich and bursting into tears, as he often did at such moments.

Noblesse oblige! Heinrich lifted him to his feet and led him to share the dais. There remained the awkward question of the ransom for his release, set at 100,000 marks, plus ships, weapons, the release of Richard's prisoners and the offer of his niece Eleanor of Brittany as a bride for Heinrich VI's son. With Prince John and Philippe Auguste conspiring to beat that offer in return for Richard being locked up in Germany for life, and England in upheaval due to Richard's

RICHARD'S PERFECT CASTLE

long absence, Queen Eleanor was desperate to secure his release and set to personally to amass the considerable sums raised from a reluctant population. Coinage and bullion raised from the population already impoverished by Richard's crusade tax were stored in sealed bags in a cellar of St Paul's Cathedral. When the first levy proved insufficient, she ordered a second, and a third, to squeeze every last penny out of his vassals, vavasours and common people, who were well aware that their monarch's problems were all of his own making. It was she at this time who created the myth of the great Christian hero that has endured until today.

The shortfall in cash and bullion had to be made up by 200 noble hostages, to be held in Germany until the ransom was all paid, plus a supplementary 50,000 marks. Richard's conditions of confinement at Worms on the Rhine were luxurious, but he had little patience for his English subjects delaying payment and complained in a *sirventès* addressed to his half-sister Marie de Champagne:

> *Ja nuls hom pres non dira sa razon*
> *adrechament, si com hom dolens non*
> *mas per confort deu hom faire canson.*
> *Pro n'ay d'amis, mas paure son li don.*
> *Ancta lur es, si per ma resenzon*
> *soi sai dos yvers pres.*

> No prisoner can put his case for long
> without self-pity making it sound wrong,
> but still for comfort he can pen a song.
> My many friends offer little, I hear.
> Shame on them all if they leave me here
> unransomed for a second long year.

On 6 January 1194 considerable numbers of Richard's religious and lay English vassals arrived in Cologne, some of them designated as hostages until the ransom was all paid. Meeting her son at Mainz on 2 February, Queen Eleanor learned that Philippe Auguste and Prince John were offering £1,000 per month for Richard to be held in captivity. German Emperor Heinrich VI was tempted until Richard's unpopular chancellor William Longchamp shrewdly pointed out to the German court that Philippe and John had no way of raising these sums. A compromise was for Richard to pay homage to the German emperor, declaring himself a vassal of Heinrich VI *and* promising to pay an annual tribute of £5,000. Promises cost nothing, so the deed was done and England's crusader king released on 4 February, by when John, deprived of all his English possessions by the Great Council, had fled to Paris.

Back in London, Richard stayed only a few hours before setting off to punish all those who had declared for John. Fearing that his arrogance which had caused all the problems in the Holy Land and on the return journey would exacerbate the political tensions in the island realm, Eleanor accompanied him. On Wednesday 30 March in the great hall of Nottingham castle she was proven right. Far from taking his duties as king seriously, he regarded the Anglo-Norman vassals as a source of finance that would enable him immediately to cross the Channel and wage a new war in the Continental possessions. Everyone who had purchased an office or privilege five years earlier had to re-purchase in cash or in kind, or lose it. The final debate of the council in Nottingham was of the disgrace of Richard's oath of fealty to Heinrich VI, ending with the decision that he should be re-crowned king at Winchester to restore the dignity of the Crown. Although Richard adored dressing up and ceremonial, the political reasoning behind this was probably his mother's. On 17 April, seated on a dais in Winchester cathedral surrounded by a court of eligible heiresses, she played the part of queen – Berengaria being relegated to her convent near Le Mans – as he was re-crowned. Queen Eleanor had done all she could for him.

Some historians have commented on the wealth of good laws passed during Richard's reign, but most of these became law during his absences, like the *avoirdupois* unified system of weights and measures[4] that served Britain well for 800 years until the country went metric halfway through the twentieth century. His impatience to get back to France and in combat was such that he seized as much as possible of the money collected to complete the ransom and liberate the hostages in Germany. One week later he was in Portsmouth, planning a fleet of galleys to blockade the French ports, and set sail on 2 May with 100 ships transporting his army of levied Anglo-Norman knights supported by Flemish and Welsh mercenaries – into the teeth of a storm that drove them all back into English ports. Ten days later, he finally arrived at Barfleur, where Eleanor's return was regarded almost as a reincarnation on account of her great age as she rode with her son through Normandy. Richard, too, had long been thought dead by vassals who transferred their loyalty to John and Philippe Auguste. For the next three months, those who delayed reaffirming their allegiance to the royal duke of Normandy suffered by fire and sword.

One who did not was 26-year-old Prince John, who came to beg forgiveness after being dumped by Philippe Auguste and abandoned by everyone else. Although often employing floods of crocodile tears himself, Richard was moved by John's penitential weeping and forgave his 'little brother', blaming instead the councillors who had led him astray. Ahead lay months of total war across Normandy and south into Anjou, Poitou and Aquitaine,[5] Richard's army being composed largely of Flemish mercenaries, paid by the loot, and a contingent of Navarrese knights led by Prince Sancho, brother of Berengaria. At Vendôme, Philippe Auguste fled so closely pusued that he had to abandon all his siege engines, personal chapel and his secret list of Richard's vassals who had changed sides during his long absence.[6] With tax after tax being levied both in England and south of the Channel to finance Richard's wars against Philippe Auguste and his own vassals, civil unrest grew. Paying no heed, Richard initiated construction of the most costly castle ever built on a limestone spur overlooking the Seine one third of the way from Rouen to Paris at Les Andelys. Determined that it would be impregnable, he incorporated every device known in Europe and the East, including a walled town at the base of the cliff. He drove his work force hard to finish construction within two years at the cost of £12,000 – figuratively speaking, another 'king's ransom' – and twice the amount spent on all the castles in England during Richard's reign.

That the land on which it was built was not his to occupy, but belonged to the Archbishop of Rouen, worried him not at all. Nor did the fact that, under the Treaty of Louviers, he and Philippe had sworn that neither would fortify the site, since a castle there would be a provocation to the other. The Pipe Rolls[7] list huge sums disbursed to miners, quarrymen, stone cutters, carpenters, masons, water-carriers, lime-workers, smiths, hod men, diggers who hacked out the dry moats by hand through the solid rock and carters who transported the building stone from quarries and all supplies that had to be brought up to the site. Soldiers are mentioned too, but it is unclear whether they were employed to protect the workers or ensure they did not abscond under the draconian regime necessary to complete the castle and new town on so difficult a site in so short a time. The Rolls make no mention of a master mason or architect, so it is possible that Richard himself supervised the work on what he dubbed 'Château Gaillard'. The adjective is hard to translate, having many meanings. Certainly, it means 'strong' but verging on 'insolent', since it was intended as a threat to Philippe Auguste after both kings had agreed not to fortify this site. Richard called it in Latin his *bellum castrum de rupe* – the fine castle on the rock. The description serves well: a castle perched on a bare limestone outcrop 300 feet above the river Seine. With its own walled town down at water level, it certainly incorporated all the refinements he had seen in other castles, in England, France, the Holy Land and those in which he had been confined in Germany and Austria. Its cost was staggering. Never one to cut his coat according to his cloth, Richard borrowed – among others from Geoffrey of Val Richer, the moneylender of Rouen who had played an important part in the transfer of money for his ransom.[8]

Yet, perpetually broke and improvident, Richard complained in a *sirventès* addressed to the count of Auvergne, who was currying favour with Philippe Auguste:

> *Vos me laïstes aidier per treive de guierdon.*
> *e car saviès qu'a Chinon non a argent ni denier.*
>
> You no longer support me since my pay ceased to flow.
> My treasury's empty, as you very well know.

Shortly before Easter 1199, he learned that a hoard of Roman gold had been unearthed on the land of Viscount Aymar of Limoges and taken for safekeeping to the castle of Châlus. After Richard's demand that the gold be handed over to him was refused, he was incensed that a mere viscount dared defy him and set 100 mercenaries to work, besieging the castle. Inside it were two low-born sergeants-at-arms and a total of thirty-eight men, women and children, it being Lent, during which the Church banned warfare.

After inspecting the progress of sappers undermining the curtain wall, he withdrew, wearing a helmet but no body armour and having a small buckler, with which to fend off stray missiles fired from the arrow slits high up in the keep. Relaxing his guard, being out of bowshot, he was hit in the junction of the neck and left shoulder by a quarrel from a crossbow fired from the keep.[9] Being more accurate and powerful than longbows, crossbows had been banned by the Lateran Council of 1139 as unchivalrous because they allowed a peasant deliberately to kill a king. Richard was among those monarchs who had defied the ban, and now paid the price. Concealing the fact that he had been wounded, he rode back to the house that had been commandeered for him, where the mercenaries' medic attempted to remove the quarrel. The wooden shaft broke off, as it was designed to do, revealing the mark of Richard's armoury at Chinon, but the pointed metal head was still deeply embedded. Fortified with alcohol, the only analgesic available, the royal patient, who had put on weight, had to suffer the medic cutting deeper and deeper through fat and muscle until he could pull the quarrel out.

With a poultice held over the wound by bandages, Richard continued supervising the siege but, by the morning of 28 March the stench of gangrene and increasing pain foretold an agonising death. Having seen thousands of men, women and children dying at his command or in his cause, he despatched a sealed letter written by his chaplain Milo, summoning Queen Eleanor from the abbey of Fontevraud. Setting out with the abbot of Turpenay and a small escort, by travelling night and day she covered the 100 miles to Châlus. On arrival, the stink of bacteria in the wound and discoloration of the necrotised tissue made clear that Richard had little time to live. The dying king had not confessed and received absolution since before his second coronation in 1194 since he could not claim to have given up his forbidden practices. Now, he could finally make an act of contrition, swearing never to sin again. After receiving absolution and communion from chaplain Milo, he died in a peasant's hovel on 6 April, nine days after being wounded.

Chapter 11

Prince Geoffrey

In 1148, on the death of Duke Conan III of Brittany, known as Fat Conan, a civil war broke out between the unruly lords of the duchy, which, although geographically and politically a part of France, had retained its Celtic identity, language and traditions. The teenage successor Duke Conan IV, grandson of Conan III, found his inherited vassals as unruly as the barons of Aquitaine, and fled to England, where he had inherited also the honour of Richmond in Yorkshire through his wife Margaret of Huntingdon. Once there, he begged military aid from Henry II to gain a semblance of control over Brittany and force out his regent Eudon II de Porhoët. This was done by Henry II in 1156, but there was a heavy price to pay. Although proclaimed duke in that year, young Conan IV could not control the English king's incursions with a mixed army of Normans and mercenaries, which penetrated far into Brittany. Henry II dealt with the dissident Breton lords with his habitual harshness, and claimed overlordship of the duchy on the grounds that his grandfather Henry I had been its suzerain.

One reason for doing this was because the sparsely populated duchy might just rise up and threaten the western flank of Normandy in concert with an attack by Louis VII on the south and east of the duchy. In that case, Henry would find himself waging a war on two fronts, something he wished to prevent, but that was very unlikely because, like the Welsh, the Breton nobility was too involved in internecine struggles to form an effective alliance. Henry II also saw Brittany as presenting new territory for him to rule through a marriage alliance. After the death of Conan IV's uncle Count Hoël III, who governed the county of Nantes on the marches of Brittany and Normandy, Conan wanted to add the county to Brittany, but Henry II moved faster and annexed Nantes into Normandy, forcing Conan to abdicate in 1166 in favour of his only daughter, Constance de Ponthièvre. It seems that she may have had a brother, who would have inherited the duchy, taking precedence over Constance, and that Henry II's forced abdication naming Constance as successor was a way of circumventing that possibility on the death of Conan IV.[1] It also had the advantage that Conan IV's daughter could then be betrothed to Prince Geoffrey, named for his grandfather Count Geoffrey of Anjou. The young prince was 7 years old at the time and the nominal duchess of Brittany and countess of Richmond was just 4 years old on 31 July 1166, when she was handed over to the Plantagenets to await her marriage. When the long stand-off between Henry II and Louis VII erupted into open warfare in 1167, Louis invaded Normandy in an uneven alliance with Welsh, Scots and Breton forces. As usual, Henry II refused the obvious counter-move and attacked instead Louis' principal arsenal at Chaumont-sur-Epte in the Vexin, burning the adjacent town to the ground, after which the French king abandoned his allies and made a private truce, following which Henry rampaged through Brittany, to punish the Bretons who had been fighting for Louis.

At Montmirail early in 1169 Louis VII accepted the hegemony of Henry II over Brittany. Because Henry II refused to kneel in homage before Louis for Normandy, Maine, Anjou and Brittany, Young Henry did it for him. This made his younger brother Geoffrey a vassal of the Young King. That Christmas in Nantes, Geoffrey accepted the homage of the Breton nobility, but little power accompanied his title, Henry II having appointed his own proxies to govern Brittany. For the following twelve years he effectively ruled the duchy, leaving Prince Geoffrey as discontented as the Young King, with whom he joined in the rebellion of the princes in 1173, all being pardoned by their father in 1174 at Gisors. Either then or in the next year, Henry II sought Geoffrey's loyalty by promising him half the revenues of Brittany. Given Henry II's record of broken promises, whether Geoffrey ever received some or all of this money, is unknown. He was at the time not quite 16 years old. In 1177 and 1179 uprisings of various Breton barons were put down by Geoffrey and his seneschal Raoul II de Fougères, an old enemy of his father, as bloodily and violently as Henry II would have done. Two of Raoul's sons were held hostage for his good behaviour.

In July 1181, aged 22, Geoffrey was at last invested with the duchy, being known as Duke Geoffrey II. His marriage to Duchess Constance was duly celebrated, also in July. It produced three children, the first and the third being cursed with the unhappiest lives imaginable. Eleanor, known as the Fair Maid of Brittany or the Pearl of Brittany, was born in 1184. In 1185 a sister was born for her and named Mathilde or Maud. She died aged 4.[2] In 1186 Geoffrey did come into possession of Nantes, but it did him little good as he died in the following year. After Geoffrey's death, Eleanor's ill-fated brother Arthur was born and named for the mythic King Arthur of Breton legend. There may have been another son of the marriage, a charter of Constance's mother mentioning someone called William, described as *clericus*.[3] In 1183 Geoffrey reconciled with his father and joined Henry the Young King in a war against their brother Richard, then the unpopular duke of Aquitaine.

Following Young Henry's death at Martel, Henry II decided to re-apportion the Plantagenet Empire, giving Richard Anjou, Maine and Normandy and naming Prince John duke of Aquitaine. When Richard refused to play this game, Henry II sent Geoffrey and John into Aquitaine to persuade him, by force of arms if necessary. They failed. In 1185 Geoffrey gained the loyalty of many of his Breton vassals by drawing up what seems to have been the first legislation covering the whole duchy. The main effect of the *Assise au Comte Geoffroy* was to put an end to the wholesale erosion of the great estates by plural inheritance.

Geoffrey had been cultivating for years the friendship of Louis VII's son and heir Philippe Auguste, who was seven years his junior, frequently visiting him at the court in Paris, where he was received with great honour. After Louis VII's death, Philippe was crowned king on 1 September 1179, aged just 14. Where this friendship might have led the Plantagenet presence in France, is hard to say because Geoffrey died in Paris five years later. The version of his death reported by the Anglo-Norman chroniclers is that he was unhorsed while taking part in a *mêlée* on 19 August 1186 and trampled so severely by the mounts of the other knights that he died two days later. During the burial service in Notre Dame cathedral, King Philippe was said to have have been so grieved at the loss of his friend that he tried to jump into the grave with the coffin. The cause of death was disputed by French cleric Rigord, who seemed to believe that Geoffrey died of a seizure after boasting that he would lay waste to Normandy – stricken by God, so to speak, for the sin of betraying his father.

PRINCE GEOFFREY

Two of Geoffrey's half-sisters by Eleanor of Aquitaine's first marriage to Louis VII were Alix de Blois and Marie de Champagne, the latter paying for masses to be said for Geoffrey's immortal soul. As to his mortal remains, his tombstone was destroyed in 1699 or 1797, when the skeleton was measured at 5ft 6in – a good height for the time. Despite the Ancient Greek aphorism, best known in its Latin form as *de mortuis nil nisi bonum*[4] – of the dead, say only good things – neither in France nor England could any chronicler find anything nice to write about Henry II's fourth son, but portrayed him as oily, deceitful and disloyal. In part, this may have been their way, being clerics, of damning his memory in posthumous punishment for him having repeatedly plundered churches and monasteries to finance his various military enterprises, the tax base of Brittany being inadequate.

In any event, Geoffrey's death left Duchess Constance a potentially eligible widow – potential because she was pregnant with Geoffrey's son at the time of his death. Waiting until 1188 Henry II married Constance, who was then 27 or 28 years old, to England's second-greatest landowner Ranulf de Blondeville, earl of Chester, who became duke of Brittany *iure uxoris*. The marriage was not fated to last, and there were no children. After succeeding his father, the Lionheart continued Henry II's aggressive policies in Brittany, ordering de Blondeville to arrest Duchess Constance in 1196 so that she could not seek asylum in Paris after Arthur was spirited away to Philippe Auguste's court there. Released in 1199, Constance had her marriage to Earl Ranulf dissolved, and swiftly took another powerful husband, Guy de Thouars, marrying him in September or October of 1199. To him, she bore two more daughters named Alix and Katherine and possibly one other daughter.

A great future was already prophesied for Arthur when, overwintering at Messina on Sicily 1190–91 while on his way to the Holy Land on the Third Crusade, King Richard named his 3-year-old nephew as his heir, to inherit England and the Continental possessions in the event of his death.[5] When the news reached her, this appalled Queen Eleanor. The only reason for Prince John to behave during Richard's long absence on crusade and afterwards a prisoner in Austria and Germany was his expectation of inheriting the dual realm if his brother died on crusade. Now, he had nothing to lose and everything to gain in seducing by bribery and promises as many as possible of the stay-at-home Anglo-Norman barons from their loyalty to the absent king.

It was true that the property of a crusader was under the protection of the Church, but John was an atheist and, as his subsequent behaviour bore out, cared not a jot about that. When the news from Messina reached Brittany, the most important Breton barons swore fealty to him at St Malo de Beignon in the manor house that was the summer residence of the bishop of St Malo.

In 1196 on Richard's orders Ranulf de Blondeville captured Constance, to whom he had been married for seven or eight years. Richard invaded the duchy, but Arthur was not present, having travelled to Paris, preferring his late father's friend Philippe Auguste to his unpredictable uncle. It was a strange tangle. Aged 10, Arthur returned to Brittany, where his mother involved him in the government of the duchy. Where this extraordinary childhood might have led, remains a mystery because of his premature death. Whether Richard, when dying at Châlus, changed his will made on Sicily, which appointed Arthur as his heir, nobody knows. Present at the death of her favourite son with only his chaplain and the abbot of Turpenay as witnesses, Queen Eleanor refused for several days to say what had been in his deathbed testament: a confirmation of Arthur as heir or, by a change of mind, the appointment of Prince John, the only one surviving of the five princes born to Henry II and Eleanor.

Apart from the chaplain and the abbot, only she *knew* what Richard decided while dying at Châlus. It was an evil choice. Nobody thought that John would make a good king and there was no indication in his life so far that he was capable of ruling the dual realm. As events were to prove, he could not. But giving all that power to Geoffrey's adolescent son must have seemed like handing the whole Plantagenet Empire to Philippe Auguste. Otto of Brunswick, son of Richard's sister Matilda, was another favoured nephew of Richard. He had held Aquitaine for some years, during which time he had made many enemies, and seemed devoid of statecraft. That ruled him out, despite Matilda coming in person to Fontevraud to plead his cause. Her failure to gain him the English crown was of little moment, since he had been elected German king in 1198 and became German Emperor Otto IV in 1209.

After mulling it over until she could no longer put off the decision, Eleanor made what she considered the best of a poor choice by herself naming John Lackland king of England. Richard's chaplain, who had written down the dying monarch's last words regarding the succession, was richly rewarded for his silence when Eleanor eventually announced that Richard had changed his will before dying and that his brother John was to inherit the Crown of England and all the Continental possessions. The barons of England – among whom John did have some support – and of Normandy, Poitou and Aquitaine accepted the succession, but the nobility of Anjou, Maine, Touraine and Brittany invoked the right of primogeniture to refuse John as their new overlord. In May, just a few weeks after Richard's death, Arthur swore allegiance as duke of Brittany to Philippe Auguste, with the support of his mother and the principal bishops and lay vassals of Brittany. As his seneschal, he named an old enemy of Richard, Guillaume des Roches, who attempted to negotiate some sort of agreement between John and Arthur. This failed. In September Arthur fled to Paris, Philippe Auguste proclaiming as his suzerain that the son of Henry II's fourth son took precedence over the fifth son.

In May of 1200 Arthur's only protector was obliged to recognise John as ruler of the whole Plantagenet Empire by the Treaty of le Goulet, signed on 18 May 1200 on the neutral island of Gueuleton in mid-Seine near Vernon – incidentally severing the *îles normandes* from the duchy of Normandy to become the English Channel Islands. The treaty required John to pay 20,000 pounds or marks[6] for the right to become overlord of Brittany and a vassal of Philippe Auguste.

This must have come as a great shock to Arthur, forced with his mother to do homage to his uncle John for Brittany. Whether he already realised that Richard had been a relatively benevolent tyrant and John was very different, we cannot tell. When Constance died in September 1201 at Nantes, Arthur did not inherit his mother's claim to the county of Richmond, which went to his half-sister Alix de Thouars. There is some mystery about Constance's death. Rumour held that she had leprosy, which might have killed her slowly but, since she had recently given birth to her twins by Guy de Thouars it is more likely that she died from the complications of a difficult birth, death in childbed or *post partum* being common at the time, especially for a woman aged 40 like her.

Philippe's mistress Agnès de Méranie having also died in childbirth, he was no longer living in sin, so from Rome Pope Innocent III revoked the excommunication of the French king and legitimised his bastards. The revocation of the interdict seemed like good fortune for Arthur of Brittany, who was betrothed to Princess Marie, but it seems that his new expectations rather turned the head of her betrothed, who lacked the shrewd brain of his father Geoffrey Plantagenet. Rashly invading Normandy at the head of only 200 knights and some foot-soldiers, he was chased off and retreated into Touraine, where he was informed by the disaffected Lusignan family that Eleanor had left Fontevraud, where she was protected by the Peace of God, and was heading for the temporal safety of her palace inside the walls of Poitiers.

Currently in the border town of Mirebeau, she was under the personal protection of King John, but Arthur ignored saner counsel and allowed the Lusignans to persuade him that together, they could capture Eleanor and force her to confer the county of Poitou and the duchy of Aquitaine on him, after which he could hand her over to the Lusignans as a very valuable hostage. When Arthur's small coalition broke into Mirebeau, Eleanor retreated to the citadel with a small number of loyal knights and men-at-arms after despatching messengers to find John, who was known to be near Le Mans, eighty miles to the north. Coming to the gate of the citadel to speak with her, Arthur seemed to find nothing wrong with besieging his own grandmother, who did not lose her head, but dragged out the negotiations. King John, for once, did not hesitate, but rode day and night with a band of knights and mercenaries under Guillaume des Roches, arriving at Mirebeau before dawn on 1 August.

Arthur's men had forced the citizens to wall up all the town gates except one, through which supplies and reinforcements could be brought in. Thinking himself far from any enemy, Arthur had left that gate open and unguarded, allowing his uncle's men to steal quietly into the town. Half-asleep, Arthur's Breton and Norman knights and men-at-arms were cut down in the streets. Reacting fast, Guy de Lusignan, who had been eating breakfast with Arthur, managed to mount his warhorse and head for the gate. The horse was killed under him by Guillaume de Braose,[7] who took him prisoner and went on to capture Arthur too.[8] De Braose may have thought that taking so valuable a prisoner was the next step in his rise to fame and fortune. It was instead the first step on his path to disgrace, dispossession, bereavement and the grave.

Defying feudal custom that ransomable hostages were the property of the knights who had captured them, John demanded that all the male captives taken at Mirebeau – including many who were related to knights who had helped him take the town – be handed over to him. To overcome the reluctance of the captors, he gave promises that the prisoners would be well treated by him and that he would share out the ransom money, when received. Instead, driven in chains to various of his castles in Normandy, many suffering castration and/or blinding, Arthur's knights were shuttled backwards and forwards to confuse any possible rescue attempt.[8] With John's vindictiveness finally alienating all those who had fought with him at Mirebeau, Eleanor must have despaired anew at the inappropriate behaviour of her sole surviving son. John had, after all, even been pardoned by King Richard for conspiring with Philippe Auguste to keep Richard a prisoner in Germany. She left Mirebeau and returned to Fontevraud, where she took the veil and put the Peace of God between her and 'the evil that men do'.

In England the barons who resented being taxed for John's putative invasion to recapture Normandy from Philippe Auguste gathered 2,000 of their knights and men-at-arms on 13 April 1215 at Stamford, led by two of the nobles on whose wives John had forced himself in their absence, Robert Fitzwalter and Eustace de Vescy. Their king delayed attending, cancelling several rendezvous and attempting to weaken the opposition by subverting or bribing individuals in clandestine one-to-one meetings. On 5 May the barons' patience was exhausted and they formally declared *diffidatio*, revoking their oaths of loyalty to the king. On 15 June a temporary truce permitting the meeting at Runnymede saw the dissident barons force John to agree the terms of the original Magna Carta, the great charter that created a council of twenty-five nobles who assumed many functions of the monarch. On 24 August John's technical overlord Pope Innocent III declared it invalid and excommunicated thirty of the principal barons responsible.[10]

Henry II had legitimised the Angevin concept of *ira et malevolentia*, or ruler's right to indulge his anger and ill will against a subject of whatever rank. This accorded perfectly with John's personality. He was an embittered, deceitful and jealous man, to whom Arthur was a threat: having been named successor to Richard in the treaty of Messina, his children would have a prior right to the Crown over John's offspring. Confining Arthur in the castle at Falaise in Normandy,[11] which still glowers down at the town below, must have caused John's prisoner to fear the worst; there was no chance of rescue and his uncle's recent defiance of custom in grabbing all the ransomable captives at Mirebeau hinted that worse was to come. It did.

To remove the risk of his 15-year-old nephew ever having children with a claim on the throne, John ordered him to be castrated and blinded. Three men-at-arms were ordered to inflict the grim punishment. Two of them refused to carry it out after recognising the victim. The third man botched his first cuts – perhaps because Arthur was not held down with enough force by the others – before stopping his grisly work on the order of Hubert de Burgh, castellan of Falaise. Partly mutilated, Arthur was again shackled hand and foot and fed starvation rations of bread and water. Reports of his resulting emaciation caused Guillaume de Braose to resign from John's service after swearing in front of three witnesses that Arthur had been in good health when he handed him over to the king.[12]

Ownership of knights taken in battle could be complicated. Although often ransomed and released by their captors, it was also customary for the king to claim them on condition of sharing the ransom with the original captor.[13] In February 1203 John wrote to Hubert de Burgh regarding a prisoner exchange of one Peter for John's engineer named Ferrand: 'If Ferrand be whole, let Peter be delivered whole also; but if Ferrand be lacking in any limb, Peter must first be deprived of the same limb (*eodem modo demembratus*) and then delivered in exchange.'[14] This was an instance of the application of *lex talionis* – the medieval law of revenge – which is still an important element in Sharia law.

The poet William the Breton, in his ode *Philippide* in praise of Philippe Auguste, related that King Richard was so angered by news that a body of his Welsh mercenaries had been murdered by the French that he threw three prisoners from the rock of Les Andelys and had fifteen others blinded before sending them back to Philippe, guided by a sixteenth prisoner who had been blinded in one eye. In retaliation, Philippe blinded fifteen of his prisoners and sent them back to Richard, guided by the wife of one victim.[15]

In the case of Arthur, John had his nephew secretly transferred in shackles to Rouen castle, whose castellan was one Robert de Vieux Pont, known in England as Vipont, who was to be richly rewarded by John for his collaboration. On a Thursday in April 1203 the enfeebled count of Brittany, whose sixteenth birthday was less than a week past, was taken out of his cell through the postern gate at dead of night and forced into a small boat with just his uncle and the castellan, for John could not afford to have witnesses who might talk. There was some doubt as to which of his captors stabbed him twice. Shackled and enfeebled, the youth could hardly resist. The annals of Margam abbey, founded by Robert of Gloucester, are quite definite that John *propria manu intefecit* – killed him with his own hand. A large stone was tied to his nephew's neck and the corpse tipped overboard into the Seine, where Arthur's emaciated body sank out of sight.[16] The act may have been performed for John by his close associate Peter de Maulay,[17] but at John's command and probably in his presence, to make sure there was no sleight of hand at the last moment. A few days after the death of Arthur, Queen Eleanor received a confidential letter from Guillaume de Braose telling her that a monk named Brother Jean de Valerant was bringing from Rouen an oral message for her, which was far too dangerous to put in writing.[18]

For the part he had played in the carefully orchestrated murder, Robert de Vieux Pont was rewarded with the castles of Appleby and Brough in Westmorland, plus many other honours and renumerative offices. After Guillaume de Braose's wife inadvertently admitted her knowledge of John's responsibility for Arthur's murder,[19] her husband was fined the colossal sum of 40,000 marks or more than 25,000 pounds, which he had no way of paying. De Braose fled with his family to his estates in Ireland,[20] where John had his wife and 40-year-old son hunted down, brought back to England and starved to death in a dungeon below Windsor castle.[21] For once John prepared an elaborate 'alternative truth' in the royal records, alleging that de Braose owed the Crown 5,000 marks for the lordship of Munster and city of Limerick, which he refused to pay, defying repeated deadlines over five years. 'With great regret', the king summoned an armed force to pursue de Braose to Ireland. Just before crossing the Irish sea, de Braose offered 40,000 marks in settlement and to regain the king's friendship, which he could not pay.[22] Whichever version one chooses to believe, the fact is that, dispossessed of all his lands and wealth, de Braose died in French exile in 1211, and his grandsons remained in prison until 1218, two years after John's death.[23]

It is often difficult to assess the comparative reliability of the contemporary sources, but the indisputable fact is that Arthur was never seen again after his disappearance from Rouen castle. Following Angevin custom, his death brought his sister Eleanor into line for succession to the English throne. Exactly when she fell into John's clutches is not recorded, but it seems to have been *before* Arthur was captured at the Battle of Mirebeau on 1 August 1202. Being the daughter of Geoffrey, who was the fourth son of Henry II and Eleanor of Aquitaine, on the death of King John Eleanor of Brittany would have had a claim taking precedent over those of John's descendants – as would any children of hers.

Four months after the death of Arthur, on 6 December 1203 John left Normandy in a hurry, but spared the time to collect his niece Eleanor and bring her to England as his prisoner. Guarded by four knights, she was detained in several castles, where local nobility was instructed by King John to bear witness that the conditions of her confinement were not too harsh. Early in 1204 Philippe Auguste, whose vassal she was as the heiress to Brittany, demanded Eleanor's release, so that she could marry one of his sons, but John refused. Later, she was known to have been taken to Brough castle in Cumbria and placed under the control of Robert de Vipont, the very man deeply implicated in the murder of her brother. If she had heard rumours about Arthur's death, this must have been torture for her, wondering whether her uncle had sent her there, knowing her custodian would do whatever was required of him, if John wanted her dead too.

Possibly because she protested about this evil choice of custodian, John then moved her all the way back south to Corfe castle in Dorset, whose castellan was Peter de Maulay, also closely involved in the murder of her brother. As to the sort of man de Maulay was, twenty-five of the French knights taken at Mirebeau had been imprisoned there. After a bid for freedom, twenty-two of them were recaptured and starved to death in the dungeons beneath the castle's Boutavent tower. Eleanor, in contrast, was a pampered prisoner who, however, knew that she would never be released. At the time of John's death on 19 October 1216, she was 32 and still being shuttled from castle to castle, receiving at least one visit from his successor, Henry III. After thirty-nine years' detention at the whim of five English kings, she died in Bristol Castle on 10 August 1241, aged about 59. At last, John could rest easy in his tomb in Worcester cathedral, having extinguished totally the line of his brother Geoffrey.[24]

Chapter 12

Prince John

Good King Richard, Bad King John? Forget the Robin Hood films, it was by no means as clear-cut as that. When Eleanor of Aquitaine's last child by Henry II was born in Oxford on 24 December 1166 – the Feast of St John – the mewling infant was given the name of the saint. His mother was 44 years old and had been cast off by her husband because, after her approaching menopause, she would no longer serve his dynastic ambitions by producing more legitimate daughters to trade for treaties and sons to raise as warrior princes. Queen Eleanor had endured three pregnancies in her first marriage with Louis VII of France and eight in the fourteen years she had been married to Henry II. Surely that was enough fulfilment of the prime duty of a queen consort for a husband who had his mistresses for pleasure?

But she was a woman of spirit, who had been raised in liberal Aquitaine to inherit in her own right the vast and politically turbulent duchy that covered most of southwest France. Sitting quietly at home embroidering, gossiping with ladies-in-waiting and writing letters was not her style. Nor was she prepared to retire to a convent like so many other discarded wives. Being keenly aware that Henry II had obtained the throne of England largely due to her inheritance of the country of Poitou and the duchy of Aquitaine and in part due to her political acumen honed by fifteen years on the throne of France, Queen Eleanor felt cheated of the respect that was due to her.

Perhaps her dissatisfaction with her own situation as the discarded wife of the king coloured Eleanor's attitude to her latest son, who, Nature had determined, would be her last child. Whatever the reasons, she never liked John, but regarded him as the runt of the litter. Leaving England, lock, stock and barrel – it took seven cargo ships to transport all her belongings across the Channel – to return to her birthright lands of Poitou and Aquitaine soon after the birth, Eleanor left Princess

Joan and Prince John at the royal abbey of Fontevraud on the borders of Poitou and Anjou, where the twin communities of 2,000 monks and nuns were governed by an abbess according to the rule established by its founder Robert d'Arbrissel at the beginning of the twelfth century. Although referred to as an abbey, it was as large as a town and enclosed by walls, just like a town.

Why did his parents leave this son there to be brought up by religious tutors? His father dubbed him Jean sans Terre or John Lackland, the several parts of the Plantagenet Empire having already been promised to his older surviving brothers, so there was no expectation of him inheriting any territory. A remedy used as late as the nineteenth century for an excess of sons was to put one of them into the Church, which disqualified him from competing politically and militarily with the others. If the idea was to prepare Prince John for a career in the Church, as the son of Henry II he could have reached the level of archbishop, papal legate or even, maybe, pope. Today, that would sound impossible, but English-born Stephen Harding was one of the founders of the important Cistercian order and became third abbot of Cîteaux abbey; Adrian IV, who was pope 1154–59, had been born Nicholas Breakspear and schooled by the Augustinians at Merton Priory like Thomas Becket. So the papacy was certainly within the bounds of possibility for the son of an ambitious and powerful father like Henry II, if the son born just seven years after Adrian IV's death was clever enough.

If that was the plan, it misfired badly. John grew up mean and deceitful, his years of childhood acquaintance with monks and religious ritual having inculcated a disdain for everything about religion and turned him into an atheist. His only asset gained from the time at Fontevraud was an exceptional literacy in both French and Latin. He so loved books and reading that he would later have a travelling library made, in which to transport his favoured tomes wherever he went. Not only were books very expensive, but on one occasion when they had to be brought across the Channel for him, the cost was high: an outlay of 43s.10d was recorded 'for carts to carry the king's books beyond the sea'.[1] Other pleasures included gambling at backgammon – a game brought back from the East by crusaders – although he rarely won and often lost several shillings in an evening's gaming.[2] Hunting and hawking, which required royal servants to breed horses and falcons, were expensive pleasures shared with the nobility. John was fond of instrumental music, but hated the sound of singing, seemingly a legacy from obligatory daily attendance at services in the Fontevraud abbey church where the choirs sang the offices. He liked jewels – of which he had a large collection – fine clothes, wine and sex. In indulging the last pleasure, he made often inappropriate advances to ladies at court, married and unmarried. A lady-in-waiting named Suzanne and called euphemistically *domicella amica domini regis*, or lover of the king, was rewarded with new dresses.[3] In July 1797 his tomb in Worcester cathedral was opened, revealing the skeleton of a man standing about 5ft 3in tall, with the barrel chest from prolonged weapons training in youth. Two things he inherited from his father were a head of dark reddish hair and mood changes that sometimes took him from a generous geniality to the fits of rage which were said to be the legacy of their Viking ancestry.

In 1173, when John was 7 years old, Poitou and Aquitaine were riven by a rebellion of several barons against Henry II, among them the Lusignan family, whose castle twenty miles southwest of Poitiers was razed to the ground in defiance of the Peace of God, which protected the property of Hugues le Brun, a crusader prisoner of the Saracens in the Holy Land. On 6 or 7 April, while Henry's constable Earl Patrick of Salisbury was escorting Queen Eleanor near Poitiers, the Lusignans ambushed the royal party in revenge. Patrick escorted Eleanor to safety in a nearby castle while his men fought a rearguard action. Returning to the fray, Patrick was fatally stabbed in the back and his young nephew – later known as William the Marshal – severely wounded while trying to save him.[4] It was probably this event that caused Henry II to have Prince John removed from Fontevraud in case the Lusignans also defied the Peace of God and kidnapped the boy from the abbey. The first idea Henry II had to provide territory for Prince John was to betroth him to Alais, the daughter of Count Humbert III of Maurienne and Savoy, who controlled three strategically important passes through the Alps, but she died before a wedding could be arranged, leaving John once again without expectations.

After the older princes' rebellion of 1173–74, in which they were supported by Queen Eleanor, Henry II pardoned them, finding it convenient to blame her for leading them astray and placing her under house arrest in England for a decade and a half; she regained her liberty only after his death. Meantime, the settlement with the rebel princes made at Montlouis in 1174 allowed the Young King to travel almost at will with his own retinue of household knights, Poitou and Aquitaine were returned to Richard and Brittany to Geoffrey. John, who had not been party to the rebellion, was given the earldom of Cornwall and a bride. The heiress Isabel of Gloucester saw her equally entitled sisters bought out very cheaply, leaving her a very rich ward of court, betrothed to the young prince. Two years later at the Council of Oxford Prince John was made *dominus hiberniae* – Lord of Ireland. These were handsome rewards for a prince so young, and incited rampant jealousy among his brothers, convinced he was Henry II's favourite. The comings and goings of the princes can be confusing, and maybe they were to those involved: in March 1178 John's half-brother, Geoffrey the bastard bishop of Lincoln, was looking after the boy on the crossing from Southampton to Barfleur; at Henry II's Christmas court that year, John was with his legitimate brother Prince Geoffrey.[5]

With the death of the Young King at Martel in June of 1183, Henry II re-apportioned his possessions: Richard was to become king of England and duke of Normandy after his father's death; Geoffrey was to keep Brittany and John would get Anjou, Poitou and Aquitaine. *Over my dead body* was Richard's reaction: *L'Aquitaine, c'est moi!* Another internecine war erupted when Henry II ordered Geoffrey and John to take possession of Aquitaine, which they had not a hope of doing against Richard, who spend his entire adult life in warfare.

Halfway through Lent of 1185 Henry dubbed 18-year-old Prince John a knight and sent him with an army across the Irish Sea to seize and govern 'his' lands.[6] The illusion of power must have gone to his head. He pulled the beards of the Irish lords and mocked their traditional clothing. Nor did he gain allies among the Anglo-Norman landowners. Returning to England, he placed the blame for the failure of his mission on the shoulders of his viceroy Hugh de Lacy. Henry II's manipulation of his sons was epitomised in 1184 when he had John rampaging through Poitou with a force of mercenaries while Richard was laying waste parts of Brittany. With local vassals joining in to settle old scores or for loot, it was another round of pointless barbarism.[7]

And what happened when these entire armies of *routiers* were dismissed at the end of a campaign and their pay stopped? After his death, Young Henry's mercenaries raped and plundered their way north through the Berry until stopped by a band of vigilante knights and men-at-arms known as the Pacifiques, who had sworn to protect the region against their depredations. Trapped between them and the hostile people of the Limousin, no fewer than 10,500 mercenaries were slaughtered, as were 1,500 'women of ill repute' travelling with them, bedecked in jewellery looted from churches. Nor were the Young King's mercenaries the only curse on the land. Another large band of *routiers* under the Brabanter commander named Mercadier spent several months plundering their way home through the regions of Perigord and Pompadour. Etienne de Tournay, an *abbé* from Paris, was travelling through this country on a mission for Henry II shortly after he had dismissed this band, and reported, 'I saw everywhere towns consumed by fire, ruined dwellings and churches burned down and destroyed, so that places previously populated by men had become the haunt of savage beasts.'[8]

In the war 1188–89 between Henry II and Philippe Auguste, supported by Prince Richard, John changed sides when it seemed that Richard and Philippe would win. They did. Terminally ill, Henry II died on 4 July 1189, grieved to find the list of those to be pardoned for taking up arms against him headed by the name of Prince John.

After putting the Continental possessions in order, Richard arrived on 13 August in England – a country he hardly knew, having visited it only twice as an adult. His first concern was to witness personally the weighing of the treasury, which amounted to £90,000.[9] He named Prince John count of Mortain in Normandy and confirmed him in possession of large swathes of Cornwall, Devon, Somerset, Dorset and Nottingham and Derby in the North. Married to Isabel of Gloucester on 29 August, John should have been content with his lot, but had his estates placed under interdict because he and Isabel were both great-grandchildren of Henry I and therefore within the forbidden bounds of consanguinity. On 3 September Richard was crowned in Westminster abbey with all due ceremony, but he had little interest in governing his island realm, being intent on raising the colossal amount of money necessary to finance a new crusade to the Holy Land. Property, wards of court with rich dowries and offices of state and shire were all sold to the highest bidder.

Throughout Richard's absence on the Third Crusade, John was attempting to subvert or bribe major vassals, kept in check by Richard's justiciars and Queen Eleanor. When England's king failed to return after all the other surviving crusaders had come home and the news of his captivity in Austria and Germany reached England, John travelled to Paris and conspired with Philippe Auguste to pay the German emperor to keep Richard indefinitely in prison. The plot was foiled by Queen Eleanor personally supervising the collection of the ransom money and bringing Richard back to England early in 1194. While John in Normandy avoided meeting the brother he had betrayed, he was dispossessed of all his property in England by the Grand Council and abandoned by Philippe Auguste as a useless embarrassment.

Richard crossed the Channel in May with Queen Eleanor and a small army of levied knights and Welsh and Flemish mercenaries, intent on punishing his Norman vassals who had believed the rumours of his death and transferred their allegiance to Philippe Auguste. On the third or fourth night after the crossing, John begged an interview with Queen Eleanor, who spoke with Archdeacon John of Alençon, in whose house at Lisieux Richard was staying. Presumably to John's surprise and delight, Richard welcomed his weeping younger brother and forgave his treachery, saying that he had been badly advised! Before the night was out, John was riding off with a detachment of knights and mercenaries to cut Philippe's lines of communication at Evreux.

For the remaining years of Richard's reign, John supported him in the field with apparent loyalty, for which he was confirmed as count of Gloucester and count of Mortain. The dispute over the succession on Richard's death in April 1199 was due to Norman custom favouring John as the last surviving son of Henry II and Angevin custom, rooted in primogeniture, favouring Arthur as son of John's elder brother Geoffrey. Philippe Auguste supported Arthur hoping to split the Continental possessions in two. The chief justiciar Archbishop Hubert Walter and that redoubtable counsellor William the Marshal did not want a return to the struggles during Richard's absence and advised the Norman and Anglo-Norman vassals to support John, as did Queen Eleanor – not because she loved, liked or respected him, but for the sake of political stability. He was crowned at Westminster on 27 May 1199 and departed for Normandy.

For a while, it looked as though Philippe's hope was to be realised, with Arthur's army driving up the Loire towards Angers and Philippe's force driving down it towards Tours. John sought the support of the main towns, granting them charters as communes raising their own militias; on 8 July La Rochelle and St Emilion; a week later, St Jean d'Angély. On 25 July it was the turn of the Ile d'Oléron.[10] Also that summer, Arthur of Brittany was betrayed by his principal supporter William des Roches under the guise of bringing him to negotiate a treaty in Le Mans with John. Smelling a rat, Arthur's mother Constance, stole the boy away from whatever his uncle was then planning by leaving the city with him in the middle of the night.[11] That she was right to do so, was tragically born out later.

In 1200 Richard's reputedly impregnable castle Château Gaillard was still Plantagenet property. There, John welcomed his 11-year-old niece Princess Blanca of Castile, brought to France by her grandmother Eleanor of Aquitaine to marry Philippe's 14-year-old son Louis and unite the houses of Plantagenet and Capet. Instead of being celebrated with due pomp in Reims cathedral, the wedding had to take place on 22 or 23 May at the small church of Port-Mort in Norman territory near Château Gaillard because Philippe's royal domain lay under an interdict imposed by Pope Innocent III as punishment for him bigamously marrying his mistress Agnès de Méranie after putting away in a convent his second wife Ingeborg of Denmark. Thus, in Philippe's royal domain no wedding could be celebrated and even the dead could not be buried in consecrated ground. For the Capetian wedding party to be safe on Plantagenet territory at Port-Mort – they hurried away immediately after the ceremony performed by the Archbishop of Bordeaux – King John had to constitute himself a hostage on French territory for as long as the Capetians were in 'his' Normandy.

If that was an odd complication of life in thirteenth-century France, the same month had seen him sign with Philippe nearby the Treaty of Le Goulet, under which he relinquished territory in return for Philippe accepting his homage for Poitou, Aquitaine and Brittany, obliging his nephew Arthur to do homage to John as his overlord. Despite having to pay for Philippe's recognition of his overlordship of Brittany amounting to 20,000 marks, John regarded this as a political triumph, and saw nothing wrong in agreeing that he would not support the counts of Boulogne and Flanders against Philippe. Yet wool was England's main export and much of it was bought to be woven by clients in Flanders, or transited through there en route elsewhere. Others less impressed with his performance dubbed him *mollegladium* or 'softsword'.

PLANTAGENET PRINCES

He next rode south to implement the clause of the treaty requiring the counts of Angoulême and Limoges to do homage for their possessions. It was at this point that he cheated another vassal, Hugues IX of Lusignan, out of his extremely beautiful young bride-to-be Isabella d'Angoulême, the daughter of Count Aymer Taillefer of Angouleme, by the simple device of kidnapping her after sending Hugues IX and his brother into Normandy to inspect their properties there. John dumped his wife Isabel of Gloucester on the grounds of their known consanguinity so that he could marry the girl with whose body he was now besotted. That this alienated a whole family of important Poitevin nobles, he did not consider – or maybe he thought that his alliance by marriage with Isabella's father justified it. Certainly, the count was happy to be the father-in-law of the king of England. Young she was, but Isabella was also a woman of spirit. After receiving some bad news, John once shouted at her, 'You see what you have cost me?' Isabella spat back at her lord and master, 'You cost me the greatest knight in Christendom.'[12] So there!

After the capture of Mirebeau, his stock sank even lower for the manner in which he treated the captives. With Arthur dead and Eleanor of Brittany his prisoner, he retreated to England. In late 1203, John was alarmed by the tenacity and violence[13] with which Philippe Auguste was besieging Richard's allegedly impregnable castle Château Gaillard near Rouen, and launched an ambitious assault by river and on land against the besieging forces. With the tides in the river Seine badly miscalculated for whatever reason, this failed. In that hard winter, civilian dependants in the besieged fortress were expelled as 'useless mouths', but Philippe did not allow them to cross the siege lines, with the result that nearly all starved to death on the bare rock between them and the castle walls during the winter, with one woman dying in childbirth during a snowstorm. The castle fell on 6 March 1204. Angry at his failure to relieve the siege, John invaded Brittany with fire and sword, using mercenaries. Having lost his allies in Boulogne and Flanders, he had no option but to withdraw when Philippe triumphantly concluded the occupation of Normandy, Anjou and Poitou, so that the only remaining Plantagenet Continental territory was Aquitaine.

In a few short years, John had undone the empire-building work of Henry II, Queen Eleanor and Richard, earning himself the hatred of hundreds of thousands of subjects. Back in England, he pursued a very hands-on policy of delivering justice to raise funds. The tax base of the country had actually declined, the country being impoverished by the costs of Richard's crusade and his huge ransom. John raised eleven scutage taxes, some of which had no connection with any war; he imposed fines and charged reliefs for confirming inheritances – and he sold charters. One of these, sealed on 28 August 1207 created what would become the major port of Liverpool. At the time known locally as Lurpool, or 'the lower pool', it was a small hamlet, home to a handful of peasant farmers and fishermen who kept their boats in a sheltered creek. It lay in the West Derby Hundred, one of six that made up Lancashire. John was the lord of all the land between the rivers Mersey and Ribble, so he could do with it whatever he wanted.

In those days the Dee estuary, now silted up, was navigable and Chester was an important port, as it had been since Roman times, but Ranulf de Blondeville, sixth earl of Chester, was one of the barons already giving problems. If John should wish to despatch a fleet to Ireland – which was always on his mind – the earl could not be counted on to make his port available for its assembly. While recently hunting in his chase at Toxteth[14] on the right bank of the Mersey estuary, John had seen the unpretentious little fishing village with its sheltered creek, and realised that it could solve the problem of de Blondeville. On 23 August he swapped some other land with the local squire Henry fitzWarin. Five days later, the deed was done. A royal clerk sat down and wrote: *Sciatis quod concessimus omnibus fidelibus nostris qui Burgagia apud villam de Liverpool ceperint quod habeant omnes libertates ...*

> John, by the grace of God, King of England, Lord of Ireland, Duke of Normandy and Aquitaine, Count of Anjou, to all his faithful people who have desired to have Burgages in the township of Liverpool, greeting. Know ye that we have granted to all our faithful people who have taken Burgages in Liverpool that they may have all the liberties and free customs in the township of Liverpool which any Free Borough on the sea has in our land. And therefore we command you that securely and in our peace you come there to receive and inhabit our Burgages. And in witness hereof we transmit to you these our Letters Patent.

PLANTAGENET PRINCES

> Witness Simon de Pateshill at Winchester on the twenty-eighth day of August in the ninth year of our reign.[15]

This meant that the former fishing village could hold a weekly market and attract merchants and tradesmen to live there. After a second charter sealed by John's son Henry III on 24 March 1229 made Liverpool a free town, it was on its way to becoming the major port where, in the nineteenth and twentieth centuries, tens of thousands of people boarded ocean liners at the Pier Head to emigrate to the new world and the dominions.

Chapter 13

War on all sides

In 1207 John even introduced a form of income tax, justifying all this by the perceived need to defend England against a possible French invasion, which required forming a Channel fleet of more than 100 ships based on Portsmouth and the Cinque Ports. They could also be used to transport his forces for planned invasion and recovery of the lost duchy of Normandy, which in turn required raising and training two armies. Where vassals and vavasours could not pay his increasingly rapacious demands, King John confiscated their lands. For this and many other reasons, the murmurs of discontent among the earls of the realm increased to a level where even the king must have heard them, yet was deaf to their meaning.

In 1203 the Welsh were pushing into western England, where the Anglo-Norman Marcher lords engaged in sporadic raids, to push them back in mutual hatred. One of John's better ideas that year was to marry off an intelligent illegitimate daughter to the Welsh chieftain Llywelyn Fawr, prince of Gwynedd. Raised in Normandy and there called Jeanne, she became Joan in England, and took the Welsh name Siwan, acting several times as diplomatic envoy between her husband and father.[1] Another illegitimate daughter, Isabel was married to Richard fitzYves, lord of Degembris in Cornwall, and her illegitimate sibling Maude was made abbess of Barking, where she died in 1252. Because John fathered numerous other bastards both before and after being crowned, it seems to indicate that this king, who made himself so unpopular with his tenants-in-chief, had an ability to charm the ladies, although two of the leading barons in the First Barons' War cited, as their chief reasons for rebelling, allegations that he had made inappropriate sexual advances to their wives

At any rate, John did take an interest in his children born out of wedlock. In the case of the males, this often meant bestowing on them a rich heiress who had been widowed and was therefore a ward of court. On marriage, the woman's possessions became her husband's property. Richard de Warenne was named for his mother, a cousin of the king who was herself daughter of an illegitimate son of Geoffrey of Anjou. Variously referred to as Ricardus filius Regis in Latin or Richard fitzRoy or fitzJehan in Old French, his arms were the Plantagenet arms, but with two lions, not three. In 1214 King John bestowed on this royal bastard a widow named Roesia or Rohese of Dover, a great-great-granddaughter of Henry II's justiciar Richard de Luci. Richard the royal bastard was also given the barony of Chilham and its castle in Kent – an imposing fortress with three baileys and a barbican[2] – after which, he called himself 'Richard of Chilham'. He fathered several children by Rohese. In 1215, a year after his very advantageous marriage, he was knighted and fought for the king in the First Barons' War and, after the death of John, for his half-brother Henry III.[3] He had every reason to be loyal to his father and half-brother, who excused him several debts to the Exchequer and bailed him out of other debts. He was, to put it mildly, a spoiled and feckless husband.

The position of a royal bastard in society could lead to fame and fortune, but unfortunately we rarely know the name of the mother who became King John's mistress for a time; some produced more than one child by the king. An exception named Oliver was born to a noble lady called Hawise, and had his moment of fame in 1216 while defending Wolvesey castle in Winchester for Bishop Peter des Roches during the First Barons' Revolt. Rewarded with lands confiscated from the rebellious Peter fitzHerbert, Oliver threw this good fortune away by travelling with papal legate Pelagius to the Fifth Crusade and died from causes unknown at Damietta in the Nile delta. Other royal bastards attested in various sources include a cleric in London named John, a friar named Bartholomew and a knight called Osbert, who held lands in Oxfordshire, Essex, Sussex and Suffolk. Another bastard named Philip took a wife named Lavinia in Surrey and had at least one son by her. The oddest reference in the list of John's purported bastards is to a Henry, who claimed to be a son of the king but, so John said, was actually his nephew. Fathered by whom? one wonders. Not Richard, but possibly Guillaume Longuespée, a bastard son of Henry II.

In 1203 King John unwittingly did a favour for the author by commanding the construction of two castles at Rauzan and

Eleanor of Aquitaine (above, left) married Henry II, said to resemble his father Count Geoffroi d'Anjou (above, right). Of their five sons, William died young, but Young Henry, Richard, Geoffrey and John lived to experience all the highs and lows of medieval royalty. The genealogical detail below is from a contemporary charter.

Chivalry did not then exist. Although the knight at Angoulême cathedral (above) is slaying a dragon to save a maiden and the knight at Melle church (below) is portrayed like Christ, reality was different.

At the battle of Bouvines in 1214 fully armoured knights confronted each other (below). But most medieval war involved laying waste the enemy's land. At Fontenay a duke of Aquitaine, probably Prince Richard, is depicted riding down a poor peasant (right).

Henry II arranged the match of Young Henry to Marguerite, daughter of King Louis VII. They were a handsome and popular couple (above at the church of Condes St Martin). But Henry II was more interested in the bride's dowry, the castle at Gisors (below).

To assure the succession, Henry II had Prince Henry crowned as the 'Young King' (above) and served him at the table during the feast, only to be insulted by his son (below). It was a bad beginning.

Louis VII never wanted to be king of France. His seal (above) is most unmartial, whereas Henry II's (below) shows him as a knight riding into battle.

After Henry II's death at Chinon castle (above), Prince Richard (his seal below) became king. Having spent his whole adult life in warfare, he taxed the dual realm heavily to finance an army for the Third Crusade.

This fanciful nineteenth century steel engraving (above) shows Richard as a battling crusader. After arrival at the besieged port-city of Acre (below) he besieged the Saracen besiegers.

War in the Holy Land was mostly skirmishes (above) and sieges (below). Thousands died, more from disease than combat. Tens of thousands of Muslim, Christian and Jewish civilians were killed.

Returning from the failed crusade, Richard was taken prisoner for ransom and reduced to kissing the feet of German Emperor Heinrich VI in token of submission. (above). Back in France, he was killed when trying to steal a treasure from the castle of Châlus (left).

He was entombed at the abbey of Fontevraud (above) beside the father he hated. His reputedly impregnable castle at Les Andelys was besieged and taken by the French five years later (below).

He was succeeded by Prince John (head of effigy in Worcester cathedral left). He was no warrior, despite the image on his seal (below), and lost most of the Plantagenet possessions in France.

John's son Henry III (above) inherited a war with his barons. His own brother Richard of Cornwall sided with them before being crowned king of Germany (below).

Edward I (left) was called 'the hammer of the Scots'. He also invaded Wales, building a ring of castles like the one that still frowns down at Conway (below) to convince the Welsh he was their king too.

Edward II was not interested in his queen Isabelle of France (right). After his lover Piers Gaveston was killed by the barons, his new lover Hugh Despenser was publicly castrated and disembowelled (below).

The eldest son of Edward III, known as the Black Prince (effigy in Canterbury cathedral above), died before his father. His ~~younger brother~~, crowned as ~~Richard III~~ (left) ~~was the last Plantagenet king~~. He died in prison, probably killed by order of his cousin, the usurper Henry Bolingbroke.

SON RICHARD II

RICHARD III LAST PLANTAGENET KING KILLED IN BATTLE 1485. AT BOSWORTH FIELD

Pujols – the latter being Occitan for 'the little hill' – in the modern French *département* of Gironde. The latter was built to serve as the strongpoint of a *castelnau* new town. The *castelnaux* were designed to make possible the settlement of empty territory that produced no tax. Unwalled settlements were set up adjacent to castles that had a levelled bailey inside their curtain walls large enough for the locals to drive their livestock inside and stay there with it until the raiding band outside had moved on elsewhere. Both of these castles still stand, that at Pujols serving the author as the local post office and accommodating the meetings of the commune's council in its ample main hall.

In 1205 John's only significant move towards regaining the lost provinces in France was despatching a small force under Guillaume Longuespée, third earl of Salisbury *iure uxoris*, to Poitou and northern Aquitaine. It was on this enterprise that another of John's bastards named Geoffrey was killed in Poitou. John also headed there himself in the following year, but had to turn south into Gascony, to counter an invasion by Alfonso VIII of Castile. Alfonso was attempting to take possession of Gascony in the belief that it was the dowry promised by his father-in-law Henry II when he married his daughter Princess Eleanor to Alfonso. Thanks to Eleanor of Aquitaine, who arranged the wedding of Alfonso's daughter Blanca – her own granddaughter – to Philippe Auguste, the Castilian king was an ally by marriage of the French king.[4]

In July 1205, after the death of Archbishop and Chancellor Hubert Walter, John sought to appoint Bishop John de Gray of Norwich to the see of Canterbury. In what was termed the investiture contest, many monarchs insisted that they had the right to appoint bishops and archbishops in their realms, but the papacy did not agree. The situation in this instance was complicated by the monks of the cathedral chapter electing their own sub-prior, named Reginald, and by Pope Innocent III refusing both candidates, investing the English-born Roman cardinal Stephen Langton as successor to Hubert Walter. After Innocent III ruled that the new incumbent of the see of Canterbury must be approved by him, John immediately banned Langton from returning to England[5] and seized the lands and possessions of the cathedral.

John's spiteful punishment of priests obeying Rome's instructions caused him to be excommunicated by Innocent in November 1209, with the realm of England placed under interdict. The political-religious *bras de fer* continued until, at Dover's Templar church in May 1213 papal legate Pandulf agreed a settlement: John declared that his kingdom was a fief of the papacy and agreed to pay 1,000 marks – or £666 – each year to Rome, although only two of these annual payments were actually made. Whoever thought up this plan, it was a very astute way of converting the interdict into papal protection, under which an invasion by Philippe Auguste would constitute an attack on the papacy. In July Stephen Langton travelled to England with his exiled supporters and all appeared settled.

However, during and after a two-year truce with Philippe Auguste for the years 1206–08, John's obsession with tightening the fiscal screws on his English subjects of all classes to raise funds for the reconquest of Normandy and the other lost French provinces was a form of what in military psychology is called 'mission fulfilment' when a commander become obsessed with his allotted task, despite repeatedly incurring heavy casualties without taking the objective. This obsession permitted Scotland's King William the Lion to flex his muscles on the northern border. In 1209 rumours that he was going to revive the 'auld alliance' with France, incited John to make a small-scale invasion of Scotland, ending in a treaty agreed on 6 August at the border castle of Norham overlooking the river Tweed, which required William to pay £10,000 and hand over his two eldest daughters as wards of John. So weak did this leave William politically in Scotland that John had to intervene militarily on his behalf in 1212!

Isabella of Angoulême giving birth to a male heir for John at Winchester on 1 October 1207 did nothing to mellow his mood. Nor did her second child, another son born in January 1209.

Ireland was another problem throughout John's reign. Although given the title Lord of Ireland by his father, his influence extended only into the occupied eastern counties, and even there the various Anglo-Norman settlers rebelled against rule from London, seeing John's weakness vis-à-vis the Anglo-Norman lords who had been absolved by Pope Innocent III from their oaths of loyalty to him.

Still, it seems, desirous of increasing the tax base for his wars in France, John took a considerable army of knights and thousands of men-at-arms and mercenaries to Ireland in June 1210. The campaign lasted sixty-three days. Whether John's outlay for hire of 700 ships and payment to all the mercenaries made a profit, is debatable. Never one to stint on celebrations, John conducted his Christmas court in York, resplendent in fine robes and jewels while planning an invasion of north Wales to put down a rebellion by Llywelwyn ap Iorwerth, the lord of Gwynedd. The first invasion in May was a failure as the Welsh retreated into the mountains, disappearing like snow on the water while John's forces starved in a land that had no food for them.

John narrowly missed betrayal and probable death in 1212 by calling off an invasion of Wales after being warned by his daughter Siwan of a conspiracy between some of his barons and the Welsh to isolate and kill him in the field.[6] More paranoid than ever, he never went anywhere without a strong bodyguard and demanded two relatives from each baron to serve as hostages for proof of their loyalty. Robert fitzWalter was a baron from Little Dunmow in Essex who was the constable of Baynard's Castle, one of the fortresses built within the Roman walls of the capital after the Conquest. Refusing to comply, he fled to France, his lands being confiscated by the king, who seized a niece as hostage and destroyed Baynard's castle in January 1213. On 13 May, as a condition of his reconciliation with Pope Innocent, John restored fitzWalter's lands, allowed him to return to England and paid a small compensation.[7]

With all this trouble 'at home' John had less time and money to spare for affairs across the Channel, and attempted to establish something like peace in England by issuing safe conducts for the barons who had fled abroad although a chance encounter on 30-31 May 1213 did destroy Philippe Auguste's invasion fleet. Guillaume Longuespée, commanding the English fleet sent to support the count of Flanders discovered that the 400 ships in the harbour at Damme, near Bruges, were not Flemish, but French, commanded by Savaric de Mauléon, who had been fighting for John and would change sides again later. Most of the crews being ashore, Longuespée's men took as prizes 300 ships loaded with wine and food, weapons and treasure for the invasion of England – and set fire to another 100 vessels that had been beached for repairs. Papal legate Pandulph arranged a truce with the Welsh and, on 9 July, Archbishop Stephen Langton returned to Britain, formally cancelling John's excommunication two weeks later at Winchester, and enjoining the barons to respect their allegiance to the king but leaving the interdict on England in place for the time being while negotiations in Rome dragged on.

PLANTAGENET PRINCES

The year 1214 was a fateful one for John's rule. Just when England needed a strong and just king on the throne, in February he departed for Poitou in what would turn out to be an expensive nine-month campaign with a scratch army. Many otherwise loyal Anglo-Norman knights argued that their feudal obligations covered supporting their king in England, but not abroad, and were replaced by mercenaries. Initially, all seemed well, with John driving back Philippe's forces in Anjou while Guillaume Longuespée pushed into Normandy with a force of German, Portuguese, Flemish and Boulonnais mercenaries. Then, at the battle of Bouvines in Flanders on 27 July this coalition fell apart, giving Philippe a crushing victory and forcing John to agree the terms of a humiliating treaty sealed at Chinon – the formerly mighty Plantagenet treasure castle – two months later. He acknowledged the loss of Normandy, Maine, Anjou, Touraine and Brittany, and had to pay £60,000 reparations to Philippe. For the barons of England, whose taxes had largely financed his failed campaign, this was the last straw.[8] In many parts of the country cities and whole shires refused to pay their dues. Ignoring John's stratagem of swearing an oath to depart on crusade, which placed him under the direct protection of the pope as a crusader, the rebels gathered with 2,000 knights and men-at-arms on 13 April 1215 at Stamford in Lincolnshire. When the barons formally declared *diffidatio*, despite pressure from Innocent III, Archbishop Stephen Langton refused to excommunicate them.

The leading baron Robert Fitzwalter had formerly been loyal to King John and was taken prisoner when fighting for him in France. Elected 'Marshal of the Army of God and Holy Church', on 15 June he met John and some barons who remained loyal at Windsor, moving in the afternoon to the neutral ground of Runnymede, where John was forced to accept the list of demands of the barons. Their main point was the creation of a grand council of twenty-five nobles led by fitzWalter and Eustace de Vesci which might apply the process called 'distraint' to prevent the king, if necessary by force, from taking actions contrary to their agreement. It was agreed that they would keep control of the city of London until August but, so mistrustful of their king were they, that the venue for an important tournament at the end of June was moved from Stamford to Hounslow Heath, so they would be close to London, if John tried to take the city by force.[9] The royal chancery having produced the formal document, referred to as *Magna Carta*, or the Great Charter, on 15 July, John's Great Seal was affixed. On 19 July the barons conditionally renewed their oaths of loyalty.[10] On 24 August John's technical overlord Pope Innocent III declared the charter invalid and excommunicated thirty of the prime movers in the rebellion, whose names had been forwarded by their king.[11]

On 15 July John failed to attend a pre-arranged meeting, instead pressuring Archbishop Langton to implement the excommunications. Whatever the details of legality, John was now effectively at war with his own vassals. Thanks to fitzWalter's influence in London, the city sided with the barons, although the garrison of the Tower stayed loyal to the king. Sending Isabella and their children to the safety of Corfe castle, he sailed to Dover in expectation of the arrival of a mixed mercenary force from Poitou, Gascony and Flanders to put down the rebellion, but their vessels were scattered in a gale on 26 September. Many sank, drowning knights and men-at-arms and sending treasure to the bottom of the Channel. With no further reason to delay at Dover, John was in Canterbury when he heard that a baronial force was advancing down the old Roman road towards him and was already a short day's ride to the west. He hastily returned to the safety of Dover castle. The barons in turn halted outside King Stephen's intended capital of Faversham and retreated to Rochester castle. Besieging the castle, commanded by the rebel leader Robert d'Aubigny, from 11 October John provisioned his hastily summoned forces, sending out foraging parties in all directions, to plunder or steal by force what they needed from the local population. This was now open war. To prevent the arrival of reinforcements for the garrison, John used fire ships to destroy the Medway bridge they would have to use. D'Aubigny made a sortie and reached the bridge to prevent this, but was beaten back with losses.

John's siege of Rochester castle, was a model of the genre. His treatment of the neighbouring cathedral was simple spite, using it as a stable for his horses and stealing everything of value. Five siege engines were set up and sappers undermined the castle's outer wall, causing a breach that enabled John's men to enter and occupy the bailey, where they proceeded to undermine also the southeast tower of the keep. The roof of the cavity under the tower was propped up with stout oak beams and a mass of flammable brushwood and pig carcasses lit, burning through the props and causing the masonry to collapse into the hole. With this corner of the keep reduced to a pile of rubble, the defenders retreated behind the cross-wall, but refused to surrender, having seen the treatment meted out to a few comrades who had left: their hands and feet were amputated by sword blows. Like so many other besieged castles, Rochester fell due to starvation, not combat, on 30 November. Ordering a massive gallows set up, on which to hang the survivors, John was dissuaded by Savaric de Mauléon telling him that it would serve as precedent for the same treatment of him, if he were ever taken prisoner.

Splitting his forces, he sent Guillaume Longuespée to blockade the many rebels in London and take East Anglia, while he drove north, taking Nottingham on the way to lay waste the fiefs of the Northern dissidents. In January 1216, he continued northwards as far as Edinburgh after repelling Scottish King Alexander II's invasion of Northumberland. On turning south, John learned that, although fitzWalter was no great soldier, he had asked the French King Philippe Auguste for help. Philippe refused because he had signed a five-year truce with John after Bouvines and did not wish to break it.[12] Nor would he risk alienating the pope by attacking his English fief at this time of weakness, but his frustrated 27-year-old son Prince Louis, who had been dubbed a knight in 1209 but denied any important role since then, agreed to plan an invasion of the troubled island realm to take place in May 1216 in support of the barons' revolt. The rebel barons wanted a semblance of legitimacy, and found it in Louis' wife Blanche being a granddaughter of Henry II, which made Prince Louis a grandson-in-law. If John could be ousted and Louis put on the throne with his wife Blanche of Castile as consort – or so the argument went – that would have sufficient air of legitimacy. Assembling a flotilla of vessels on the south coast to repel the French ships before they could make landfall, John's plan came to naught when winter storms scattered the English vessels and sank many of them.

As an earnest of his intentions, Louis had already sent a small force of between 120 and 140 knights from the Artois district centred on Arras, who landed at the mouth of the river Orwell in Suffolk with a contingent of foot-soldiers. His plan, shared with Blanche, was for a full-scale invasion of England in May 1216, led by himself, which would inevitably result in his excommunication, since it was now papal territory and John had sworn to take the Cross, which made him personally protected by the Church as a crusader – although he had no intention of actually going on crusade. Despite pressure from Papal legate Gualo Bicchieri, Louis continued preparations.[13]

Using the money collected to pay for the drowned mercenaries, John's winter campaign was comparatively successful, laying waste the rebels' lands as far north as Nottingham by Christmas. He then continued to the Scottish border at Berwick, returning to confront the anticipated French invasion after reducing twenty more rebel strongholds. As during King Stephen's war against Empress Matilda, his Flemish mercenaries robbed and raped as they went, while in the south and east, another loyalist army blockaded the city of London, held by the rebels, and attacked the barons' fiefs with fire and sword, cutting down orchards and burning crops and homes. This civil war was followed with interest by Prince Louis who, with Queen Blanche's active help, was assembling a fleet of 800 ships of all sizes to transport an army of 1,200 knights, their mounts and servants and several thousand men-at-arms to England.

On the night of 17 May Louis set sail in a storm that made any interception by English ships unlikely, to land at Stonar on the Isle of Thanet with just seven vessels, the others having turned back or been blown off-course. Crossing the Wantsum channel, which then separated Thanet from the mainland, on the following day he entered the port of Sandwich as the rest of the French fleet arrived – some 600 vessels transporting reinforcements and eighty cogs carrying supplies.[14] King John rode towards Sandwich but failed to attack during the chaos of disembarcation and unloading of supplies and weapons, uncertain how far he could rely on his vassals who also held fiefs in France, and chose instead to flee westwards to the ancient West Saxon capital of Winchester. Finding that the only real resistance in Kent was from irregular bowmen hiding in the forests under the command of a royal bailiff named William of Cassingham – now Kensham – but popularly known as Willikin of the Weald, Louis marched his men westward through Canterbury to Rochester, where they were welcomed by some of the rebels who swore fealty to him in the castle restored to Archbishop Stephen Langton by Magna Carta.

The knowledge of the country enabled Willikin's men repeatedly to ambush the French force causing many casualties.[15] On 2 June Louis rode into London, where the mayor, fitzWalter and the citizenry proclaimed him the uncrowned king of England although he could not formally be crowned because Westminster abbey refused him entrance as an excommunicate. The commandant of the Tower similarly did not permit him entrance until 6 November.[16] Louis swore an oath that he would restore the ancient rights in accordance with Magna Carta, and split his forces in two: half to subdue John's supporters in the eastern counties and half to ride out of the city with him on 6 June in pursuit of John. They took the castles at Reigate, Farnham and Guildford, reaching Winchester on 14 June. John had fled, leaving the garrison demoralised, surrendering after a ten-day siege. Soon Louis and the rebels controlled one-third of the kingdom, with John's loyalists holding out in the west and north. Exactly how Philippe Auguste was kept up to date with developments in England is not known, but his criticism of his son's failure to reduce the strategic castle at Dover resulted in a belated siege of it by Louis' forces beginning on 19 July. The high ground north of the castle was occupied, the besiegers undermining the barbican and attempting to do the same to the fortified castle gateway.

After Innocent III died in Perugia on 16 July, Philippe Auguste was thanked by his successor Honorius III for remaining neutral in the civil war across the Channel. The only good news for Louis was the arrival in Kent of King Alexander II of Scotland in September 1216 after leading his army south in a forced march of over 400 miles. To show his appreciation, Louis rode west to welcome him at Canterbury, where Alexander swore fealty to him as 'the king of the English' for his own fiefs south of the border. A few short miles away at Dover, the castle was still holding out on 14 October, when Louis agreed a truce and headed back to London. King John was in East Anglia at the port of Bishop's Lynn – now King's Lynn – on 11 October, when he fell ill with dysentery. Perhaps his judgement was affected by sickness because it was said that he panicked, left a small garrison in the town and took a short cut across the Wash, during which the tide changed. Quicksands claimed many victims and were said to have swallowed up John's treasury.

John arrived in agony, unable to ride a horse and carried on a litter, at Newark castle. There, after dictating a testament in the first person, not using the royal 'we', he died during the stormy night of 18-19 October, two months short of his fiftieth birthday. But, is the story of the quicksands of the Wash credible, for the royal cavalcade would have had local guides who would be aware of the tides? A monk called Jean de Savigny arrived in Newark on the morning after John's death and found the servants of the royal household pouring out of the castle laden with all manner of goods and other moveable loot. Reporting this, historian J.C. Holt surmises that the story of everything being swallowed up in quicksands was invented by them as a plausible explanation why so much property was missing.[17] The monk stood vigil and celebrated a Mass for the king. Also present was the abbot of Croxton, who had cut out John's heart, to keep in his abbey. The rest of the body was taken to Worcester cathedral, escorted by a guard of mercenaries, and still lies there entombed, despite the abbot of the Cistercian abbey at Beaulieu, founded by John, claiming rights to it. The effigy on the tomb is unusual in that the king in his coronation robes has his sword drawn, not sheathed as was usual in English kings' effigies. The significance is emphasised by the lion beneath his feet twisting round to seize the sword in its teeth and, presumably, bend it – a symbol of rebellion against the monarch.[18]

Chapter 14

Henry III

Prince Louis rejoiced at the news of John's death, believing that he could immediately step into the dead king's shoes until it became apparent that many barons who had rebelled against John for personal reasons considered that his 9-year-old son Prince Henry would now be a more pliable successor than the son of Philippe Auguste, who had fought Henry II and Richard and driven John out of Normandy. Almost overnight, Louis' support base was whittled away.

John's successor Prince Henry had been born on 1 October 1207 in Winchester castle and was sometimes known as 'Henry of Winchester'. Cared for by his wet-nurse named Ellen and apparently close to his mother, Queen Isabella, he had just one younger brother and three sisters – a modest household for a father with all King John's bastards. At the age of 5, Henry was removed from all family – and especially maternal – influence and entrusted to the care of Peter des Roches, bishop of Winchester. It is unlikely that he was a kindly guardian, for his friends joked that his French name, Pierre des Roches, meant a 'stone among rocks'. After his father's death, Henry could not be crowned in London or Westminster because Louis and the rebels refused to leave the city and Westminster Abbey was too close to it, to take the risk of bringing him there. Escorted to Devizes and thence to Gloucester, the boy prince was knighted there by William Marshal and hastily crowned by Peter des Roches in the presence of papal legate Guala Bicchieri, to whom Prince Henry did homage for the throne of England and the lordship of Ireland in recognition of his father having made the realm a vassal state of the papacy.

He was named King Henry III on 28 October 1216. So swiftly was this done that there was no time to make the ceremonial robes and old ones had to be cut down to fit him. With the real crown inaccessible in Westminster, a makeshift had to be fashioned, using a golden necklace belonging to his mother. This was not quite as inappropriate as what happened after his father's death and the similar treatment meted out to his grandfather Henry II's body after his death at Chinon in July 1189, when servants stole all the dead king's belongings and a fake crown had to be fashioned for the corpse from the golden tassels of a woman's dress, but it was hardly a favourable augury. The ceremony of consecration was omitted, to be performed later by Archbishop of Canterbury Stephen Langton, who was in Rome at the time.[1]

The kingdom this prince was inheriting was in great chaos: roughly half of England was occupied by hostile forces continuing the civil war, there was no organised government, no county sheriffs collecting taxes, no Exchequer, no royal seal even, with which to validate any charters issued in his name.[2] Having a 9-year-old boy on the throne was fraught with problems for his guardians. His mother Queen Isabella could reasonably have expected to rule as regent in his name, but the barons who had charge of her son rejected her as a foreigner and cast around for a powerful regent from among their own number. The first choice was William the Marshal. He had served Henry II, Richard and John loyally and was almost universally respected, but he was 70 years old – an age that few men and even fewer warriors then attained. Fearing that personal enemies would accuse him of being greedy for power, William reluctantly accepted the role after being approved by both Guala and Ranulf de Blondeville, the powerful earl of Chester. It was decided that the safest place in the unsettled realm for the boy-king to hold his court was Bristol, the current castellan of which castle was that ageing survivor Savaric de Mauléon. There, Magna Carta of 1215, which had been disapproved by Honorius III, was revised on 11-12 November, with nineteen clauses removed.[2] William as *rector* and Cardinal Guala affixed their seals to a version naming Hubert de Burgh as regent. The Latin term *rector* means a ruler or governor, but also a guide or steersman of a boat, so it was an appropriate title for William the Marshal. By the time the pope's approval to all this reached England through Guala, many of the rebel barons had already changed sides. Indeed, Guala ordered letters to be sent to sheriffs and castellans all over England, ordering them to do homage to their new monarch.

On 6 December 1216 Prince Louis took Hertford castle, allowing the defenders to march out with personal weapons and their horses, as he did at Berkhamstead too later that month. If he thought this would win him supporters, he was wrong: the political tide was against him. Casualties and defections having taken their toll on his forces, early in the New Year he decided to return to France for reinforcements, but had to fight his way back to the south coast through territory that had been for him and was now hostile. Nearing Lewes, an ambush by William of Cassingham's irregulars cost him many more casualties, the survivors taking refuge at Winchelsea – a former Saxon fishing village on the coast – where the arrival of ships sent by Blanche with supplies saved them from having to choose between starvation and surrender. Louis returned to England in May 1217 to find William of Cassingham and one of John's bastards named Oliver attacking and burning the hutments of the French siege camp outside the walls of Dover castle. Landing at the neighbouring port of Sandwich and marching back to Dover, he was in the wrong place at the wrong time. Almost 100 miles away, forces under William the Marshal and Foulkes de Bréauté attacked and roundly defeated a coalition of the rebellious Anglo-Norman barons besieging Lincoln castle on 20 May. Commanding the loyal troops inside the castle was one of those great female warriors of the Middle Ages. Lady Nicolaa de la Haye was the hereditary castellan of Lincoln castle, who had offered the keys of the fortress to King John because she felt too old in her mid-sixties for such a responsibility. He refused, ordering her to stay at her post and making her sheriff of Lincolnshire. She had held the castle for three months against the rebels when the Marshal's force appeared and Foulkes de Bréauté secretly led a small detachment of crossbowmen into the castle, where they could fire down on the besieging rebels attempting to prevent Ranulf of Chester attacking the north gate. At the east gate, the Marshal led an attack without waiting for reinforcements. For several hours close-quarters combat continued until the town was taken and he departed for Nottingham, to inform the boy-king of the victory. Less than 200 rebel knights made it back to London. In William's absence, the royalist force turned to plunder and the slaughter of civilians who resisted. The valiant Lady Nicolaa was turfed out of the castle, her offices of sheriff and castellan given to the earl of Salisbury, although she later put her case to the new king, whose advisers reinstated her as castellan and lady of the town.[4]

Nine months after John's death, the widowed Queen Isabella finally realised that she was politically a non-person, debarred not only from power, but even contact with her elder son, whom William the

Marshal kept away from her in the charge of the bishop of Winchester. She decided to returned to southwest France, where, since 1202, she was *suo iure* countess of Angoulême. Her blonde-haired, blue-eyed looks still turning heads wherever she went, in the spring of 1220 she married Hugues X de Lusignan, the son of Hugues IX, to whom she had been betrothed before John stole her away twenty years earlier. Isabella's daughter Joan was already present in Hugues X's household, having been betrothed to him by King John, but Hugues preferred the sexually available and fertile mother to her pre-pubescent daughter, and married her instead! Here a mysterious figure enters the story. Philippe de Faulconbridge, reputedly the only child fathered by Richard the Lionheart, was given by his father the heiress Amélie de Jarnac, who owned property in Cognac, Merpin and Archiac, and took the name Philippe de Cognac.[5] When he died at an unknown date early in the thirteenth century, these lands reverted to the English Crown and were given to Isabella d'Angoulême by Henry III.

As a widowed queen of England, Isabella should have asked the consent of the English *curia regis* before re-marrying. Because she did not, in the name of her son King Henry her dower lands – intended to support her in the event of widowhood – were confiscated and her pension stopped. Isabella and Hugues X retaliated by threatening to keep Princess Joan, who had meantime been promised by the regency council in marriage to the king of Scotland. After several exchanges of letters, a deal was worked out, under which Joan was sent back to England and Isabella was granted the revenues for four years from the city of Aylesbury and from Ashburton, Chagford and Tavistock, three prosperous stannary towns in Devon. She was also paid £3,000 arrears previously withheld from her pension. As payouts went, it was a good one – perhaps too good, for Isabella could never accept that she was no longer the queen of England, and behaved towards the Capetian royal family with an arrogance that got her into trouble later.

On the Ile de la Cité nearly 300 miles to the north of Angoulême, in audience with Philippe Auguste, Prince Louis' wife Blanche accused her father-in-law of failing in his paternal duty to his own heir apparent, who might die in England for lack of reinforcements and money. Unwilling to openly defy the pope, when she walked out of the audience, Philippe Auguste called her back and promised funds, with which she could do as she willed.[6] Using them to raise a new force of knights, mounted men-at-arms and foot-soldiers, in early August 1217 she had assembled at Calais a fleet of eighty vessels including seven large warships carrying some 120 knights and their horses and many smaller vessels laden with the supplies and treasure that Louis' force urgently needed. But the royalist forces were not sleeping: skirmishes took place at Winchelsea and Dover. On one occasion an English raid on the port of Calais provoked the French to sally out and apparently capture 140 vessels of various sizes, the crews fleeing in the lighter boats towed behind them. The French fleet set sail and was already off Dover when a terrible storm drove them back to Boulogne and Flanders.

Blanche's fleet finally set sail on the night of 23 August under the command of Robert de Courtenay, whose deputy was a notorious pirate named Eustace the Monk. Early on the following morning, as they neared the English coast and sailed past the port of Sandwich, heading for the Thames estuary, a flotilla of forty English ships of various size sailed out to engage them. These ships had been summoned by William the Marshal largely from the Cinque Ports, but were under the command of Hubert de Burgh. One of the ships was captained by King John's illegitimate son Richard fitzRoy. The Cinque ports were completely disenchanted with both John and his son, but were won over by the Marshal restoring to them their lost privileges and promising them they could keep all the salvage and spoils from the coming battle.[7]

Seeing the English ships emerge from Sandwich on a collision course, the advice of that hardened sailor Eustace the Monk was to flee with a following wind, but the gung-ho land-lubber de Courtenay insisted on engaging the English vessels, which rode higher in the water, since they were not carrying all the knights, foot soldiers, horses and supplies loaded on the French vessels. De Courtenay's ship was carrying several horses for Prince Louis and a large trebuchet siege engine. At a critical moment, the wind changed in favour of the English. Sea battles then being fought as on land, the English archers aboard de Burgh's ships, having the advantage of height, rained arrows and crossbow bolts down on the French sailors and passengers. They also catapulted at the enemy large terracotta pots, which broke on landing, releasing blinding clouds of eye-stinging quicklime. The largest English ship and that of Richard fitzRoy grappled Eustace the Monk's on both sides, their soldiers taking prisoner all thirty-six ransomable French knights on board and slitting the throats of the sailors and men-at-arms before throwing their bodies overboard. It was particularly hard on Eustace, whose experience had told him the French ships could not win, to be dragged from a hiding place below decks. He offered 10,000 marks as ransom, if his captors would spare his life. Because he had previously been in King John's service, fitzRoy and the other English captains regarded him as a traitor. He was tied down on the deck and beheaded with an axe[8], his head stuck on a lance and exhibited as a trophy, the headless corpse being thrown overboard. Later, the impaled head was paraded in a primitive ritual through the streets of Canterbury.

The now leaderless French ships came about, attempting to sail back to Calais, pursued by the English, attacking them with iron rams on their prows and grappling irons and cutting their rigging to bring down the masts. Only fifteen of the larger vessels made it back to France, and that was due to their pursuers turning aside to take the smaller ships as prizes, to be plundered for the provisions and arms they carried. Most of the French sailors and men-at-arms aboard were murdered or simply thrown overboard to drown – few people could swim in those days – with a couple of men from each ship allowed 'to live and tell the tale' when they eventually got home. The spoils of the battle of Sandwich were divided among the commanders, sailors and soldiers with money put aside for one charitable work. Since the sea battle had taken place on St Bartholomew's Day, a pilgrim hospital bearing the saint's name was built in Sandwich, near the cattle market. It later became almshouses and St Bart's chapel still stands on the Dover Road.

The French defeat brought to naught all Princess Blanche's efforts to support Prince Louis.[9] Cut off from further reinforcements, supplies and funds, Prince Louis found nearly all his Anglo-Norman allies abandoning him and seeking an amnesty for their treason. Peace was agreed in principle two weeks later at Lambeth Palace, the London residence of the archbishop of Canterbury, but the treaty eventually sealed was known as the Treaty of Kingston, to distinguish it from the Treaty of Lambeth sealed on 4 May 1212 by King John and several Continental counts, forming a coalition against Philippe Auguste. There are no known extant copies of the Treaty of Kingston, finally ratified on 20 September after Cardinal Gulala sought to humiliate Prince Louis by insisted that he appear before him as a penitent, barefoot and clad only in a simple woollen gown. To save face, Louis was at the last moment allowed to cover the gown with a more princely garment when he was absolved for his sin in invading England.

Many Anglo-Norman barons who had stayed loyal to the Crown wished to impose punitive terms on him and the rebel barons, but William Marshal made a statesmanlike decision: in return for Louis abandoning any claim on the throne of England, he was free to go. The only punishment meted out was an order to the rebels who had fought for him to raise 10,000 marks to cover his costs in repatriating his French knights – which also bought an amnesty for the rebels. Louis evacuated London and departed from Dover harbour on the 28 September, Alexander's army marching back to Scotland. On Sunday 29 October young Henry and his court rode into the capital, to be greeted by almost universal acclamation from its citizens. Despite lingering discontent in some quarters – the loyal barons wanted a reward for their loyalty during the civil war, which was not forthcoming – the 18-month conflict was over. Ironically for William the Marshal, who had amassed a fortune in ransoms won at tournaments on the continent, in October 1217 he banned them in England for the same reason Henry II had done: to prevent a gathering of several thousand knights masking the start of another rebellion.

Guala obtained the approval of Pope Honorius III to the terms agreed and, when the legate left England in November 1218, peace had been made with the Welsh, a truce agreed with Scotland, the Exchequer was reopened, a great seal had been made for Henry III and the administration was gradually returning to normal.[10] A relatively minor effect was that the *Iles normandes* or Channel Islands, which had been occupied by brothers of Eustace the Monk, were given up by them and became English again. Another revision of Magna Carta was published, also the Forest Charter, which had far greater effect for free citizens living in or near the forests, permitting them limited, but important, rights, like pasturing their pigs on the acorns. The death penalty for poaching deer, imposed by King Richard, was replaced by a substantial fine. Historian Matthew Lewis commented that the Forest Charter was the longest-standing statute in English law, remaining in force until 1971.

Also in 1218 many participants in the Barons' War thought it prudent to go on crusade until things quietened down. With them, excommunicated by Cardinal Gualo Bicchieri, was a chaplain in the household of the prominent baron Earl Robert fitzWalter, lord of Dunmow in Essex.[11] Also called Robert, the chaplain travelled with his master via Genoa, arriving safely enough in Acre but there fell foul of the ordinances of the Templars through his penchant for drink and gambling, and was cast out of the crusader community. Doubly exiled, so to speak, he stayed alive by his wits and an astonishing talent for languages. Already having French and Latin, he taught himself Arabic and the Mongol tongue, somehow making his way through enemy territory via the Black and Aral seas and north of Lake Baikal on a journey of 3,000 miles to Karakorum, capital of Genghis Khan's empire, where his potential usefulness as an envoy in the planned invasion of eastern and Central Europe by Batu Khan was immediately appreciated. Teaching himself Hungarian, ex-chaplain Robert travelled back to Europe and played his part in the subjugation of Hungary, Poland and Russia,[12] which was to be dominated by the 'Tatar-Mongol yoke' for two and a half centuries.

On 2 February 1219 William the Marshal fell ill in Marlbrough. In considerable pain, he travelled back to London and took quarters in the Tower with his wife, continuing to exercise his duties. Five weeks later he took a barge up the Thames to his manor at Caversham, wishing to die there in peace. The royal court moved to Reading, just across the Thames, to receive his last counsel, which was to chide Peter des Roches for his naked ambition to replace William. In the Marshal's opinion, such an appointment could provoke another civil war, between des Roches' supporters and those of Hubert de Burgh. Fortunately, the presence of the new legate Cardinal Pandulf kept des Roches in check. Buried in London's Temple church, where his remains still lie, on 20 May 1219, William was hailed by Archbishop Stephen Langton as 'the greatest knight of all the world'. It was a fitting tribute.

In an attempt to quieten the northern border, Henry's sister Joan was, after her return to England, married to Alexander II of Scotland. On 25 June 1221, the day of their wedding in York Minster, she was nearly 11 and her bridegroom 23. Her dowry was Northumberland, always coveted by the Scots as a buffer against incursions from England. In the Scottish court dominated by Alexander's mother, the dowager queen Ermengarde de Beaumont, Joan's life was a misery.

With the pope's blessing, on 17 May 1220 Henry III was crowned again in Edward the Confessor's abbey at Westminster in an appropriately magnificent ceremony, to compensate for the hurried coronation at Gloucester. Archbishop Stephen Langton got rid of the new papal legate, Pandulf, claiming that he alone was *legatus natus* – the righful legate. In 1221 Hubert de Burgh accused Peter des Roches of treason and he, to save himself, departed on crusade. Not all the barons accepted the king's peace until 1224 when de Burgh and Henry III – now 17 – besieged their last strongpoint at Bedford castle for two whole months, and showed no grace when it fell, executing all the surrendered garrison with the exception of ransomable knights.

After considerable inroads made by the French into Poitou and Aquitaine under Louis VIII – his father had died in July 1223 and Prince Louis was crowned on 6 August – in early 1225 the Great Council approved a tax to raise £40,000 for Henry III to send an army to southwest France, where it recovered part of Aquitaine from Bordeaux south to the Pyrenees. Henry formally assumed full powers in 1227, richly rewarding de Burgh and making him earl of Kent and justiciar for life. One great failing Henry III had inherited from his father was an obsession with recovering the Continental possessions lost by John. Since the money to do this had to come from taxes in England, this alienated many of his Anglo-Norman vassals who might otherwise have been his supporters. It was perhaps a desire to acquire an energetic earl who would never desert him that caused Henry to knight his very positive younger brother Richard on 2 February 1225. It must have been quite a spectacle: the 17-year-old king knighting his 16-year-old brother. Eleven days later, Richard was created earl of Cornwall, and seemingly near this time he was also made count of Poitou. Being thus launched on the world stage, he departed four weeks later with a small army for Gascony, the expedition being halted before it was properly under way by Pope Honorius calling a truce on the grounds that Louis VIII was a crusader charged with the extermination of the Cathar heretics in the south of France. Attacking his lands was therefore punishable by excommunication. In August, Henry decided to ignore the pope and renew the offensive under his brother, which was swiftly crowned with success, La Réole, the last rebel town being taken before the end of November.

Chapter 15

King v. barons, round 2

Henry III's obsession blinded him to the alienation of his barons, who refused to pay another scutage and also resented his elevation to positions of power of Poitevins and other foreigners from Aquitaine. Departing at the end of April 1230 for Brittany and Anjou, he had to return to England with Richard as both were ill. As far as the barons were concerned, the campaign was just another expensive waste of their taxes. Just over a year later, on 4 July 1231 another truce was sealed with Louis VIII, leaving Henry blaming Hubert de Burgh for this latest failure. In 1231, after Peter des Roches returned to England arguing that de Burgh had abused his powers, Henry had his justiciar imprisoned in the Tower of London. But des Roches' corruption and hostility to the barons led in turn to a kind of civil war, pitting his supporters against barons led by the late William the Marshal's son Richard, who at one point had to ally himself with the Welsh prince Llewelyn against des Roches and the king! The year 1233 saw a disastrous famine in England that caused widespread deaths among the common people. In May 1234 Stephen Langton's successor Edmund Rich intervened to persuade Henry III to dismiss des Roches and make peace with his vassals. At this low point in his reign, Henry learned that the expiration of the truce he had made with Louis IX had brought another French invasion of Brittany, which he could do little to combat.

Unlike his father, Henry III seems to have fathered no illegitimate offspring – possibly because he recalled an unhappy childhood sharing his own father's royal household with many of the bastard half-brothers and sisters. Nor did he marry until he was 28 in 1236 when an alliance with Count Ramón Berenguer IV of Provence and Fourcalquier seemed a way to take a small step against Louis IX by marrying one of the count's four daughters by Beatrice of Savoy, all of whom made politically successful marriages.[1] The problem for their parents was to find all the necessary dowries, which were never completely paid. Nevertheless these young women were extraordinary. In May 1234 Marguerite married Louis IX of France; in 1236 Eleanor, with whom Marguerite remained close all her life, married Henry III of England; in 1243 Sancha married Henry III's brother Richard of Cornwall, who became king of Germany in 1257; in 1246, Béatrice married Louis IX's brother Charles d'Anjou, who became King of Sicily and King of Naples.

Henry III's 12-year-old bride, Eleanor of Provence was exceptionally well educated, literate and cultured. Married in Canterbury cathedral shortly after arriving in England, she was crowned queen at Westminster abbey in a sumptuous ceremony staged by Henry, who enjoyed ceremonial and spent considerable time and expense making sure her quarters were as she wished. Before puberty, she was supposed to remain a virgin, but presented him with a son in London on 17 June 1239 when she was only 15. The child was named Edward, after Henry's favourite saint, the Confessor. The happy event was somewhat marred when Henry's avarice was made clear: he returned many of the gifts received on the grounds that the donors had the means to send something more valuable. The popular joke had it that 'God sent us this child, but the king sells him to us.' In the following year, Eleanor produced a daughter christened Margaret. Two years later, while accompanying her husband on another ineffectual intervention in Poitou, Eleanor gave birth to a second daughter, named for Beatrice of Savoy. Another son, Edmund, arrived in 1245, being named for the Christian king of Wessex martyred by pagan Vikings in or about 869. A third daughter was born handicapped and unable to speak in 1253 and lived only three years, her death greatly affecting her parents although infant and child mortality was common in those times.

A rebellion against Louis IX occurred in 1241 when the Poitevin nobility under Hugues X de Lusignan assumed they could count on Henry III to support them in the field. It took him nearly a year to raise £80,000 and arrive in southwest France, where his performance was so lamentable that Hugues secured an amnesty and changed sides. On 20 May 1242 the remnants of Henry's army was surrounded at Taillebourg and only managed to escape to Bordeaux thanks to his brother Richard of Cornwall and Simon de Montfort fighting a rearguard action to cover the retreat, after which Henry agreed a four-year truce with Louis IX, having achieved nothing except to enrage his barons in England with this latest waste of their money. His only positive action was to have his mother's remains removed from her penitential grave *outside* the abbey at Fontevraud and re-buried inside the abbey, after which Henry took ship for England with Eleanor and his new daughter Beatrice.

Despite all her childbearing, Eleanor of Provence was a forthright and outspoken woman, who stiffened Henry's frequent lack of resolve although, like other foreign-born brides, she failed to win the hearts of Henry's subjects. A powerful reason was the 170 or so relatives, known collectively as 'the Savoyards', who followed her to England and settled on the road from the city to Westminster in the area still occupied by the Savoy hotel. Her uncle Boniface became archbishop of Canterbury in 1241 in succession to the later canonised Edmund Rich. Presumably due to pressure from Eleanor, Henry III employed in his household and arranged marriages to rich wards of court for many of the Savoyards, which angered the Anglo-Norman barons who, or whose sons, had been expecting to marry them. A letter from Hugues de Lusignan promised Henry that, with enough money, he could raise all the nobility of Poitou and Aquitaine to shrug off the French yoke, but when Henry called a council to discuss the necessary tax, he was met with a refusal either to join his expedition to southwest France or to provide him with *any* money. Since he had been enjoying the revenue of the vacant sees of Canterbury and Winchester, the council considered that he should have enough money of his own for an expedition unlikely to be successful. Where had all the money gone? Apparently, into the new shrine Henry had commissioned for Edward the Confessor in Westminster abbey, fashioned in pure gold and decorated with costly jewels.[1]

His brother Richard of Cornwall returning from crusade may have played a part in the king's decision to head again to Poitou with him, although Richard thought it an ill-considered idea. They departed on 15 May 1242 with seven earls of the realm and 300 knights, leaving England under Archbishop Walter de Grey as justiciar. Richard had been right in estimating that the invasion was yet another waste of money. After the failure of that campaign in France, Henry III also encouraged about 100 relatives of his step-father Hugues X to travel to England, where he granted them incomes and fiefs. If he thought they would later aid him in the obsession to recover Poitou and Anjou, he was wrong. In addition, even the Savoyards resented another foreign influx into the kingdom and Simon de Montfort was outspoken and far from alone in declaring his king a poor warrior and generally unfit to reign.

About this time, the discovery of tin in Germany caused something of a depression in England. Until then it was thought that the mineral existed only in Cornwall. Suddenly cheaper German tin was, if not flooding the market, certainly undercutting the prices the Cornish tin brokers had previously been able to demand. During the regency, Henry's sister Joan had been used to obtain a truce with Alexander II of Scotland. In 1244 Henry sacrificed a daughter in the same cause, betrothing 3-year-old Princess Margaret to Alexander's son by his second wife Marie de Coucy. After Alexander II's death in July 1249, his 7-year-old son became Alexander III. Two years later Princess Margaret, aged 11, was married to Scotland's boy-king at York, as her aunt had been. Henry III's love of ceremonial – and a desire to impress the Scottish regents – caused her wedding and the wedding feast to be a time of unrivalled luxury and feasting,[2] as proven by a comprehensive record of the preparations preserved in the archives of York Minster.[3] Margaret's life was to be tragic. Kept apart from her young husband – the only person in Scotland whom she knew – by the regents for four years, she fell into a profound depression. Even after the young couple were allowed to cohabit, they were taken prisoner by the clan of Comyn in a bid to oust the regents, and had to be rescued from Edinburgh castle by her father's intervention. Tragedy stalked Margaret, who died in 1275, all three of her children by Alexander III also dying within eight years.

In 1245 one dream of Henry III was to re-build in the new Gothic style his abbey at Westminster. He despatched his favourite mason/architect Henri de Reynes to France, where he visited and sketched several of the new cathedrals at Bourges, Reims, Chartres, Amiens as well as the Sainte Chapelle in Paris. On his return began the ambitious project of replacing Edward the Confessor's Saxon abbey with essentially the building one sees today. All that survives of the Confessor's building are the foundations and undercroft. The construction cost about £45,000 or enough for a war, but for once the barons could not complain too loudly. Henry said this tax was for God, although some wagging tongues alleged the abbey was being re-built to satisfy his ego, so that he would be remembered as a builder long after people forgot his reign. The abbey was still incomplete when consecrated in October 1269, as it was when Henry III died on 16 November 1272. Since then, about 4,000 other burials in and near to the abbey have taken place. On his death, all work stopped for many years, probably in consequence of climate change, which caused disastrous harvests and consequent famines in 1272, 1277, 1283, 1292 and 1311. Given the small yield of medieval grain species, it took several years to recover from each one.[4]

His attitude to the Jews in England, who came directly under him because they fitted nowhere else in feudal society, was ambiguous. In the first years of his reign, they prospered under the regency because William the Marshal ignored instructions from Rome to implement the anti-Semitic provisions of the Fourth Lateran Council. With usury forbidden to Christians, England's Jews were widely regarded as valuable sources of loans. True, the rates of interest were high, but so also was the default rate on debts due for repayment. In 1239, as Henry became more religious, he turned against the community, imprisoning its leaders and exempting their debtors from repayment. In 1244 he imposed a collective fine of £40,000 on the Jews, which was not popular with his vassals, because this money could have been loaned to them. That the fine also made some moneylenders insist on earlier repayments in order to pay the king's tax, made it an even more unpopular measure.

In 1253 Henry introduced the Statute of Jewry, which forbade the construction of synagogues and required the Jews to wear distinguishing badges. This was also the time of the Blood Libel – the allegation that Jews seen by Christian servants enjoying *borscht* beetroot soup were actually drinking the blood of Christian babies. Pressure on Jews to convert to Christianity forced one in ten to seek a way out of their misery by becoming converts, some coming to live in the *domus conversorum* built as sheltered accommodation for them in London. Ninety-one other Jews were sent to the Tower and eighteen of them executed so that the Crown could expropriate their property and take over debts owing to them in 1255. The western border with Wales was in intermittent turmoil and the regions of Ireland held as fiefs by Anglo-Norman nobles received no help from Henry III in return for the taxes they paid. In 1254 Henry III made his son Edward lord of Ireland, much as Henry II had named John Lackland lord of the emerald isle. Henry III eventually had to accept that he would not regain the Continental possessions of his grandparents. France was, of course, weakened by Louis IX departing on the costly and abortive Seventh Crusade, but the country he left was protected by the papacy in his absence. So Henry III declared that he too would depart on crusade but the funds he raised were spent instead on yet another campaign in Gascony, where Simon V de Montfort's aggressive senechalship had provoked the local barons into another rebellion. Influenced by the Lusignans, Henry III supported the Gascons, while Queen Eleanor blamed de Montfort's harsh measures. This difference of opinion caused a rift that lasted a year, during which Henry left England in the hands of Queen Eleanor[5] with Archbishop Walter de Grey and Richard of Cornwall as regents, sailing again for Poitou and Gascony on 6 August 1253, restoring order at great expense and arranging a truce with King Alfonso X of Castile, who had taken advantage of the unrest to invade in the hope of validating his claim to Gascony. The key to the treaty with Alfonso signed in 1254 was, once again, a betrothal – of Prince Edward to Alfonso's half-sister Eleanor.

Travelling back from southwest France, Henry III met Louis IX face-to-face for the first time, the meeting being arranged by two of the Provençal sisters, Queen Eleanor of England and Queen Marguerite of France, who had corresponded more or less regularly during the years their husbands waged war. Louis can hardly have been impressed by this brother-in-law who had repeatedly failed to recover territory in France – and who was now deeply in debt. About this time, encouraged and subsidised by Pope Innocent IV, Henry became fixated on winning the Norman kingdom of Sicily for his second son Edmund. When Innocent died in December 1254, his successor Alexander IV took a more sanguine view of the Sicilian situation, withdrew any further financial support and demanded that Henry III repay £90,000 advanced by Innocent. Henry had to ask his barons for help, but they – including Richard of Cornwall – were not interested in his latest pipe-dream, correctly concluding that he was out of his depth. In 1257 – a year of climate change due to an enormous volcanic eruption in the East Indies with a hard winter and very wet spring that spoiled such crops as were growing – Pope Alexander threatened to excommunicate Henry if he did not immediately send an army to Sicily *and* repay the money. Flailing around desperately for funds, Henry blackmailed senior churchmen into buying charters that raised less than half of his shortfall.

Whilst the king sought money to repay his debts, England was in the grip of famine. Another rebellion of the barons was looming, supported by the English Church. In April 1258 seven barons – Simon V de Montfort, Roger and Hugh Bigod, John fitzGeoffrey, Peter de Montfort, Peter de Savoy and Richard de Clare – decided that the king was exceeding by far his functions according to Magna Carta and marched into his bedroom in full armour, although with their swords left outside. Henry was at first terrified, thinking that they had come to kill him. He then asked whether he was their prisoner, which they denied while pointing out that they could have come armed. Instead, they forced him to abandon rule by proclamation and accept a council of twenty-four senior vassals, lay and religious. However, the twelve nominees of the king were mainly Poitevins installed in England, which was unacceptable to the faction of de Montfort, who was both a brother-in-law of the king, having married his sister Eleanor, and also a godfather to Prince Edward – the other was the prince's uncle Richard of Cornwall.

In June, the 'mad parliament' forced Henry III to accept the Provisions of Oxford, which created a different council of fifteen members, all chosen by the barons. Many of the king's Poitevin supporters were exiled, their property in England forfeited. So far, so good. But differences of policy within the council of fifteen soon became apparent. Some, led by the Bigods, wanted to keep things as they were and just muzzle the king; others under de Montfort wanted more widespread reform, reducing the power of the senior barons, as well as the king, and keeping in check the voracious royal officials. For this reason, Simon de Montfort has been considered by some as the father of parliamentary rule. It seems strange that Prince Edward allied himself with the reformers, leading to the radical Provisions of Westminster in 1259. At the end of the year, Henry III and Eleanor of Provence travelled to Paris, escorted by de Montfort and other barons, to sign a peace treaty with Louis IX. In return for abandoning any claims to Normandy and the northern French counties, Henry was recognised as ruler of Gascony and did homage to Louis for it.

After his barons returned to England, Henry III cheated on his undertaking to accept the guidance of the council of fifteen, issuing charters without consulting them. He returned to England in April, when disagreements between the traditionalist barons and the reformers under de Montfort and Prince Edward came to a head. What promised to be a three-way civil war was de-fused by Richard of Cornwall, de Montfort was put on trial and Prince Edward was reconciled with his

PLANTAGENET PRINCES

father. But the king was unable to stabilise the situation; in October de Montfort and de Clare resolved their differences and Prince Louis rejoined the coalition. The country slipped further into chaos as Henry purged the ranks of his officials and paid foreign mercenaries to shore up his power.

In May 1261 Pope Alexander IV died after sending Henry III a letter absolving him from his oath to abide by the Provisions of Oxford, which rather went to Henry's head. Louis promised him a cost-free army for seven years to enforce his will. Prince Edward abandoned de Montfort's faction, returning to his father. Having told the barons that he had no money, Henry ransacked the treasury of the Tower, using the valuables to reinforce the building and change the locks on the city's gates. With several of the barons bringing their knights to the capital, to find themselves locked out, many people feared another civil war. In 1262, sniffing the winds of change, 22-year-old Prince Edward returned to the de Montfort camp. In January 1263 the king agreed to abide by the Provisions of Oxford, the Welsh were pushing in against the Marcher lands and the citizens of London rose in a revolt whose main victims were the Jews, some 500 being murdered, usually by their debtors. The king and queen were in the Tower when Simon de Montfort brought a considerable force inside the walls. Queen Eleanor attempted to escape up-river to the protection of an army under Prince Edward at Windsor, but was prevented by the Londoners, who rained filth down on her barge from a bridge.

After Simon V de Montfort took the royal couple prisoner, Richard of Cornwall, who was respected by both sides, tried to restore peace. A process of arbitration in early 1264 by Louis IX, influenced by Queen Eleanor, her sister Queen Marguerite and the pope in favour of Henry III, and known as the Mise of Amiens, led nowhere. Henry's return from the French court to England on 8 February 1264 was not popular and by April the civil war people had been fearing was a reality after the barons declared *diffidatio*. At the battle of Lewes on 14 May tens of thousands of men clashed – the exact numbers are disputed. Henry III's numerically superior force was defeated with the usual bloodshed thinning the ranks of his mercenaries. The king, Richard of Cornwall and Prince Edward were prisoners of Simon de Montfort, the king being forced to pardon the rebels and reinstate the Provisions of Oxford. The parliament of 1265, known as de Montfort's Parliament, was the first to have elected representatives – and the last until Cromwell's time.

KING V. BARONS, ROUND 2

But the war was not over. Prince Edward escaped in May and gathered a new royal army, trapping de Montfort at Evesham, where his prisoner Henry III, wearing borrowed armour, was nearly killed by Edward's troops before being recognised and escorted to safety. After the royalist victory, the corpses of Simon de Montfort and his son were castrated and the father's corpse beheaded. With an important group of rebels holding out under siege at Kenilworth castle, a parliament held nearby during the siege was persuaded by papal legate Ottobuono dei Fieschi to make it possible for the rebels to re-purchase their confiscated lands on payment of fines and this was provided for in the Dictum of Kenilworth, published on 31 October 1266. In June 1267 the earl of Gloucester argued that the disinherited barons could not pay their fines before a conditional restoration of their lands enabled them to raise the necessary money and the Dictum was amended to that effect.

The rest of Henry III's reign was marked by a decline in the royal power as he retreated into the comfort of a covey of cronies, concentrating on re-building palaces and castles to the extent that he is mainly remembered as a builder. That he was devout, attending Mass every day, is partly due to his liking for richly appointed ceremonial. Charitable works included feeding 500 paupers a day and making pilgrimages – some of which were thought to be an alibi for avoiding confrontations and difficult decisions.

Henry III died on 16 November 1172, having achieved little in his long reign except to further weaken the monarchy. It is sometimes said that Magna Carta was the forerunner of democracy when, in fact, it strengthened the aristocracy in parliament, not the common people. For nearly two years after Henry's death, England was without a king, since his successor, Prince Edward, showed no haste in returning to the island realm to wear the crown and take up his responsibilities. In England, the war with the barons dragged on until the final rebel stronghold on the Isle of Ely was taken in July 1276.

Chapter 16

Richard of Cornwall

King John's second legitimate son Richard was born on 5 January 1209 at Winchester castle and therefore known initially as Richard of Winchester. He collected other titles quite young, being named High Sheriff of Berkshire when only eight. Aged 16, he was made count of Poitou, but handed the title to that restive county back eighteen years later. His brother King Henry also named him High Sheriff of Cornwall, thus making him one of the wealthiest men in Europe, thanks in part to the tin mines in that county, which had already been exploited for more than two thousand years. That same year – 1225 – saw him apparently trying to curry favour with the Cornish people, who had their own language and customs,[1] by swapping some land at Merthen for the site of Tintagel castle, revered by the natives as having belonged to their great mythological hero King Arthur. The castle Prince Richard built there was – to use a later term – a folly, deliberately constructed in a rather primitive style to make it look more ancient. It was so well done that even today some historians believe it could have been the Dark Ages fortress of the mythical king. Actually living in Cornwall meant that Richard was too far from the court, where his brother needed his support frequently, so in 1225 the king granted to him the castle of Berkhamsted, thirty miles from London. Enlarged and embellished when Becket was tenant before his disgrace, the castle thus became the administrative headquarters of the earldom of Cornwall, which became the Duchy of Cornwall a century later. A constant stream of bailiffs and other officials shuttled between the castle and Richard's estates in far-distant Cornwall.

In 1231, at the age of 22, Richard married Isabel of Pembroke, the wealthy widow of Gilbert de Clare, fourth earl of Hertford and fifth earl of Gloucester. Ten years older than her new husband, Isabel was a daughter of William the Marshal, with whose family Henry III was often at odds, possibly because of the dominant role William had played during Henry's minority. Richard became stepfather to the six children of Isabel's first marriage. As a new family home, he acquired Wallingford castle in Berkshire,[2] where he and Isabel were to have four children of their own, only one son named Edmund surviving childhood.

Though he campaigned on King Henry's behalf in Poitou and Brittany, and served as regent three times when Henry was in Poitou, relations were often strained between the two brothers. Richard actually rebelled against Henry III three times, each time returning to the fold after receiving expensive bribes.

In 1234 Pope Gregory IX issued the bull *Rachel suum videns* calling for a new crusade in anticipation of the end of the ten-year truce agreed by German Emperor Frederik II and the Egyptian sultan al-Kamil at the end of the Sixth Crusade in February 1229, which had given the Christians control of Judean Bethlehem,[3] Jaffa, Jerusalem, Nazareth and Sidon. Seeking adventure – he was one of the richest men in Europe and hardly needed to acquire any fief in the Holy Land – in 1238 Richard of Cornwall left England on what was known as 'the barons' crusade'. The English army with two commanders – him and Simon V de Montfort – arrived at the crusader port of Acre early in 1239, where any illusions Richard may have had of a great Christian host, fired with religious inspiration, fighting heroic battles to 'liberate' the Holy City of Jerusalem, swiftly died. They constituted the second wave of this crusade, the first having been commanded by Count Theobald of Champagne, better known as King Teobaldo I de Navarra, or simply 'Teobaldo el trovador'. He had just reduced the Christian forces in-country by leaving with his army a few weeks earlier, although some hundreds of French and other European knights still remained in-country. What exactly his crusade achieved is hard to say, although he justified his nickname 'the troubadour' by writing love songs for his far-distant wife Marguerite de Bourbon, while living in reasonable style in Acre. Far from celebrating the derring-do in the Holy Land, these songs expressed a most unmilitary longing to be at home with her. One includes these lines:

> *Dame, de cui est ma granx desiree*
> *salus vos mant d'outre la mer sale*
> *comme a celi ou je pans main et soir*
> *n'autres pansers ne me fai joie avoir*

> Lady, for whom I have such great desire,
> I send you greetings from over the salt sea.
> You are the one of whom I dream day and night –
> the only thought that gives me joy.[4]

In another poem to Marguerite, he commits what was surely blasphemy, even if many other disillusioned crusaders shared the same thought:

> *Pour quoi fu la terre d'outremer*
> *qui tant amant avra fait dessevrer*
> *dont puis ne fu l'amours reconfortee*
> *ne ne por la joie remenbrer*

> Why ever does this land of Outremer exist?
> It will have separated so many lovers
> whose lost feelings never could be reborn
> and who never could rekindle their love.[5]

Theobald was a passionate man. Although he had a couple of illegitimate children and one by a previous marriage, it was with Marguerite that he fathered six legitimate children.

To complicate things further for the Barons' Crusade, Pope Gregory IX split the available forces by re-directing a French army under Baudouin de Courtenay – the heir to the Latin Kingdom of Constantinople – to head for that city instead of the Holy Land. The idea was to save the Latin king of Constantinople Jehan de Brienne from attack by Orthodox Christian forces of John III Vatatzes of Nicea and Ivan Asen II of Bulgaria. No one was able to persuade Gregory that dividing the available crusade in two halves was a bad idea.

On 10 June 1240 Richard of Cornwall left England with a dozen barons and several hundred knights including his illegitimate uncle William II Longuespée, who later travelled east again for Louis IX's abortive Seventh Crusade, and was killed at the battle of al-Mansurah in February 1250. Richard's army reached Marseille in mid-September, took ship soon after and and landed at Acre on 8 October – three weeks after Theobald's host had left. This was surely the record for speed of any crusader army. Simon V de Montfort travelled separately, accompanied by Richard's sister Eleanor as far as Brindisi.[6] Richard's crusading host saw no combat, but they did complete the negotiations for a truce by pitting the Egyptian Ayyubid leaders against the rival Ayyubids from Damascus. In fact, Richard never fought a battle in the Holy Land and spent much time in protracted negotiations for the release of Christian prisoners. Released on 23 April 1241, these included Amaury de Montfort, older brother of Simon, who had been held by the Muslims for seventeen months after the defeat at Gaza of a crusader raiding force, preying on peaceful caravans of Muslim merchants, killing them and stealing their animals and merchandise against the orders of Theobald and Duke Peter of Brittany and the counsel of the leaders of all three military orders. Like so many confrontations during the crusades, their bloody marauding expedition was not just pointless, but counter-productive. The breakaway column of knights found themselves on 13 November 1239 facing a superior Egyptian force and were catastrophically defeated before Theobald's main force could arrive to reinforce them.

About a month after the battle at Gaza, the sultan An-Nasir Dawud, whose caravan they had plundered, marched on largely unprotected Jerusalem, driving the inadequate force of defenders into the ancient citadel known as the Tower of David. After a month-long siege, the garrison surrendered to Dawud on 7 December, accepting his offer for safe passage to Acre and leaving Jerusalem in Muslim hands for the first time since 1229.[7] Anticipating a split between the Egyptian and Syrian Ayyubids, the crusaders accepted an invitation from a dissident emir to join him at a place known as 'the pilgrims' mountain' near Tripoli. It was a waste of time. After some months enjoying the hospitality of the Latin King Bohemund V of Antioch, the crusaders abandoned the expedition and headed back to Acre.[8]

In addition to arranging the prisoner swap at Gaza, Richard also arranged for the re-burial of the remains of hundreds of Christian knights and foot-soldiers from that battle in a Christian cemetery at Ashkelon and oversaw some of the rebuilding of the derelict fortress there, which he later handed over, significantly, to an agent of German Emperor Frederik II and not to the Latin king of Jerusalem. This earned him the enmity of the in-country nobility, but he still had his sights set on richer pickings. He departed from Acre on 3 May 1241, leaving the Latin Kingdom larger than it had been since 1187. It all came to nothing three years later, when, on 15 July 1244 Jerusalem was taken by the Muslims and sacked, burned to the ground and reduced to ruins, its Christian residents massacred by the Syrian Ayyubids. This setback was redoubled on 17-18 October when a Christian force of 1,000 knights and 6,000 foot-soldiers with Ayyubid allies from Damascus, Homs and Kerak suffered more than 5,000 dead and 800 knights taken prisoner by an Egyptian Ayyubid army commanded by the Mameluke Baibars,[9] reinforced by Khwarezmian mercenaries at the battle of La Forbie, near Gaza. Emir al-Mansur of Homs advised the Christians to fortify their camp and wait until the undisciplined Khwarezmians lost interest and abandoned Baibars' army, but Walter IV de Brienne, the gung-ho commander, ignored that good advice, attacked at the wrong time and ended up one of 800 crusader prisoners. In effect, all Pope Gregory had achieved with his call to crusade answered by Richard and Simon de Montfort was to demonstrate that there was no longer a unified Christian sense of religious purpose in Europe.[10]

On his return to Europe, Richard visited his sister Isabella, married to the Emperor Frederik II, as an excuse for spying out the political land in the German, or Holy Roman, Empire. On 17 January 1240 his wife Isabel of Pembroke had died in childbirth, aged 39. Just before expiring, she asked to be buried beside her first husband at Beaulieu abbey, leaving one to reflect on the lives of medieval noblewomen, obliged to remarry and bear children for their new husbands although, as in her case, still emotionally tied to the deceased previous spouse. Taking only token notice of her wishes, after his return to England Richard had her interred in Tewkesbury abbey, sending her heart alone to be buried in Beaulieu.

Richard accompanied Henry III to Poitou in 1242, an ill-thought-out initiative that would have ended with the king in captivity, had not Richard persuaded him to retreat after losing the battle of Saintes and then negotiated their escape from Taillebourg. In England, after the birth of Prince Edward, there was some unease about the succession, should Henry III die, given the power that had accrued to the Savoyards. It seems to have been Queen Eleanor who found the ideal way of solving any hostility on the part of her widowed brother-in-law by proposing that he marry her younger sister Sancha. Not only would the two brothers married to two sisters form a sort of political 'happy family' but with the two other Provençal sisters married to Louis IX of France and his brother Charles, an optimist might have thought that the long hostilities between the English and French Crowns would be brought to an end – which, for a while, they were. On the way to the Holy Land, Richard had been given hospitality by Count Ramón Berengar IV of

Provence and there met Sancha, whom he married on 23 November 1243 in Westminster abbey. A special tax on the Jews was levied for the wedding feast, celebrated on a lavish scale that included purchase of 3,000 plates.

In the following month Richard of Cornwall renounced his fragile title as count of Poitou, leaving that rebellious county to Louis' brother Alphonse. In 1246 Sancha bore him a son, also called Richard, who died after a few days. Another son named Edmund was born in 1249 and a third, also given the name Richard, in 1252.

While acting regent of England 1253–54 during another expedition to Poitou by Henry III, Richard summoned knights to represent all the shires at the critical Easter Parliament of 1254. Politically speaking, his eyes were set on wider horizons than just the earldom of Cornwall. In 1256 he was chosen as the new king of Germany by four of the seven electoral princes but Ottakar II of Bohemia later changed his mind and voted for the competing candidate Alfonso X of Castile. Bribing Alfonso's supporters cost Richard 28,000 marks, which must have seemed cheap at the price on 27 May 1257, when Richard was crowned in Aachen as 'King of the Romans' by Archbishop Konrad von Hochstaden of Cologne. That the German empire was known as 'the Holy Roman Empire' seems curious today, the title owing its origin to Charlemagne being invested on Christmas Day of the year 800 by Pope Leo III as ruler of the *sacrum imperium romanum*. When Richard of Cornwall was elected at Aachen, the empire consisted of the kingdoms of Germany, Italy, Bohemia and Burgundy. This was later regarded as the first German empire, the second dating from the unification of the hotch-potch of German-speaking principalities and kingdoms united by Bismarck in 1871 and ending with the German defeat in 1918. The third German empire, of course, was the infamous Nazi Third Reich.

However, if Richard of Cornwall thought that acquiring the German crown meant that he was shortly going to be elected Holy Roman emperor, he was wrong. In the twelve years following his coronation, he made only four brief visits to Germany although usually travelling with a small body of courtiers, who resented the way their king was treated in England as just another vassal of his brother, albeit a very important one. With many Anglo-Norman barons resenting the way so many of Eleanor of Provence's Savoyard relatives had followed her to the English court, her uncle Boniface becoming archbishop of Canterbury, when Henry III invited also Poitevin half-brothers from his mother's second marriage to Hugues X de Lusignan and rewarded them with large estates, this was naturally resented by the English barons. From 1236 to 1258, Henry III listened to far too much conflicting advice from the Savoyards and Lusignans, which did nothing for his reputation, already sullied by his constant demands for extra taxes, his weak government and the widespread famine that afflicted his realm.

Richard of Cornwall supported the king in the Second Barons' Revolt against the rebels under Simon V de Montfort, a brother-in-law of both the king and Richard of Cornwall since he had married their sister Eleanor, youngest child of King John. Therein lies a scandal: she had been previously married on 24 April 1224 to the son of William the Marshal, he 34 years old and she 9. When he died just before their seventh wedding anniversary, she swore an oath of chastity before Archbishop Edmund Rich. Although theoretically entitled as a widow to one third of the joint estate, her fortune was drastically reduced by Richard of Cornwall seizing much of it to repay her late husband's debts. Seven years later, she met and secretly married Simon V de Montfort on 7 January 1238 in, of all places, the king's chapel in Westminster palace. This angered Henry III, worried about that vow of chastity. So Eleanor's new husband travelled all the way to Rome, to free her from the oath she had sworn. The couple went on to have seven children, but ended up on opposing sides in the Second Barons' War.

When the royalists were defeated at the battle of Lewes on 14 May 1264, Richard hid in a windmill, but was dragged out and mockingly called 'the Miller'. Imprisoned for sixteen months by the rebels, he was released in September 1265 after the battle of Evesham on 4 August 1265 was won by royalist forces. Henry III, present at Evesham as a prisoner of the barons, had been dressed in armour belonging to Simon V and was nearly killed by his own men in the *mêlée* before being recognised, rescued and led to safety. Hearing of the death and dismemberment of her husband and eldest son, de Montfort's wife Eleanor fled to France, perhaps fearing violence against herself. She need not have been afraid because Henry III bore her no malice and indeed supported her protracted legal battles to recover her English inheritance. She became a nun at Montargis abbey, where a sister-in-law was the abbess, and died there in 1275.

After the parliament held at Winchester that September when all the noble rebels were disinherited, hard-liners held out inside the reputedly impregnable Kenilworth castle, besieged in the summer of 1266. When in October the Dictum of Kenilworth allowed all former rebels to buy back their lands, those in Kenilworth at first turned down this peace offer but by 14 December conditions inside the walls had become so intolerable that they chose to surrender, rather than starve.

The last rebels to submit having retreated to the Isle of Ely, Prince Edward went there in force in summer 1267 and settled the terms with them,[11] after which England was for the moment at peace.

Richard of Cornwall's second wife Sancha having died in 1261, he sought to increase the likelihood of election as German emperor by marrying on 16 June 1969 the beautiful Beatrice of Valkenburg, daughter of his supporter Count Dietrich I of Valkenburg. She was 15 years old and he, 61. There was no issue. In December 1271 he suffered a stroke, which left him paralysed down the right side of his body and unable to speak. He died four months later in April 1272 at Berkhamsted castle, and was buried at Hailes abbey in the Cotswolds, a Cistercian community he had founded, where many pilgrims came to revere a wondrous phial of Christ's blood, which was as genuine as the counterfeit phials of Becket's blood sold at Canterbury, in which the red liquid was dilute fruit juice. After the Reformation, the Hailes phial was found to be filled with dilute honey coloured with saffron. Richard's body was placed next to the grave of his second wife, Sancha of Provence, who had died in 1261. Beside them lay the remains of Henry of Almain,[12] Richard's last surviving son by Isabel Marshal, murdered one year earlier on 13 March 1271 by his cousins, Guy and Simon the Younger de Montfort while attending Mass at the Chiesa del Gesù in Viterbo, in revenge for the way their father's and elder brother's bodies had been mutilated after death at the battle of Evesham.

In Cornwall, Richard was succeeded by his second son by Sancha, Edmund of Cornwall. In his three marriages, he fathered six legitimate children, none of whom had issue, but he did have illegitimate progeny. They were John of Cornwall, who was born in January 1232, died the same year and was buried at Reading abbey; Isabel of Cornwall was born in September 1233 and died a year later, also buried at Reading abbey; Henry, born in November 1235; and Nicholas of Cornwall, who died shortly after birth in January 1240 and was buried at Beaulieu abbey with his mother. By Sancha of Provence Richard had two more sons, one of whom died in infancy.

Chapter 17

Edward I

In adult life, Henry III's eldest son Prince Edward was bold, decisive and seemingly determined from the moment he became king not to waste energy, lives and finance on the Continental possessions lost by his grandfather, but to expand the island realm to the north with Scotland – he was known as *malleus scottorum* or 'the hammer of the Scots' – and to the west in Wales and Ireland. Although he had been a sickly child, narrowly escaping death three times, he grew very tall for the time, reaching 6 feet 2 inches. Well meriting the epithet 'Longshanks', his stature, allied with his quick temper, made him an imposing character. He inherited a drooping eyelid from his father and had a slight speech impediment.[1] His long reach made him a formidable swordsman. Blond when young, his curly hair darkened as he grew up and turned nearly white in old age.

At the age of 15, Prince Edward was used as a pawn to deflect Castilian threats against Gascony and married on 1 November 1254 at the abbey of Santa Maria la Real de las Huelgas outside Burgos to 13-year-old Leonor, half-sister of King Alfonso X of Castile. This was a rare medieval marriage, enriched by fidelity and mutual respect, that lasted until her death. Henry III was so keen to extinguish the Castilian claims on Gascony that he cancelled elaborate preparations for dubbing Prince Edward a knight in England and asked Alfonso X to knight his son in Burgos before the wedding. The ceremony was set for 13 October, but Edward was detained in Aquitaine by business of state connected with his vague status as *dominus aquitaniae* and did not arrive in Burgos until 18 October, when Alfonso knighted both the prince and several of his companions, 15-year-old Edward standing head and shoulders above the other candidates.

After the wedding, the young couple travelled north into Gascony, where Prince Edward had to borrow money repeatedly, whether to pay the troops left there to garrison this English territory or for his own expenses. Although on parchment he was lord of Ireland, and owned much land in Wales and England, including the important earldom of Chester, his father kept political and fiscal control, leaving Edward little power or income.[2] The young couple was still in southwest France when Leonor gave birth before or just after her fourteenth birthday. The child was a daughter, who died shortly after birth. Following her recovery, Leonor was despatched to England in the late summer of 1255. Reaching London on 17 October, her first acquaintance with the city was its stink, wafted towards the new arrivals on the prevailing westerly wind, from the foul effluent of all kinds floating down the network of open watercourses leading to the Thames,[3] where the incoming tide would hold it for hours before it was carried away seawards. Her official welcome was one of the impressive ceremonials which Henry III adored. He came out to greet her in company with the mayor of London and other VIPs, to the sound of the choirs of St Paul's and Westminster Abbey. The citizens' welcome was, however, frigid because they regarded Leonor's numerous Castilian retinue as yet another influx of foreigners to be fed, clothed and accommodated at their expense.[4] The young wife of Prince Edward was also criticised for her Castilian fashions until she was persuaded to adopt English dress; she persisted, however in arranging Spanish gardens and importing carpets, regarded as a 'foreign luxury' by Henry III's subjects.

In the palace of Westminster, Eleanor – as Leonor became in England – found her quarters thoughtfully redecorated by the king in Castilian style. For six weeks she was at a loose end, until Prince Edward finally reached London on 29 November, in direct defiance of an order from his father to go instead to Ireland. Princess Eleanor's relationship with her mother-in-law was frigid, Queen Eleanor not concealing her expectation that she would again control her son after his long absence from England, during which he had become accustomed to making his own decisions. This was not at all the way Eleanor of Castile saw things.

The citizens of the capital regarded Prince Edward as too much influenced by his mother's Savoyard relatives, but after 1257 he identified more with the Poitevin half-brothers of his father and angered Henry III by taking sides in Poitevin squabbles. The Provisions of Oxford in May 1258 saw him standing by the Poitevins, against whom the Provisions were largely directed, but in March 1259, he allied himself with the reforming Earl Richard de Clare of Gloucester and, by that October was supporting the restless barons under Simon de Montfort. His father's departure for France in November, which Edward judged ill-timed, given the unrest in England, emboldened him sufficiently to declare openly his sympathy with the rebels, to the extent of holding a parliament in the king's absence. Suspecting him of planning a coup d'état, Henry III wrote from Normandy to Archbishop Boniface of Canterbury and several important vassals on 19 February 1260, refusing the very idea of a parliament in his absence. On his return to England, he showed his sense of having been betrayed by Prince Edward in refusing to meet him until after mediation by Richard of Cornwall and Boniface.[5]

Tension there still was between father and son, leading to Edward being sent abroad in November. In 1262 he was back in England and given command of an army to put down a rebellion by the important Welsh prince Llywelyn ap Gruffudd. With Simon de Montfort fomenting unrest among the barons, it was at this point that Edward decided to side with his father, supporting him in what became the Second Barons' War. After battles at Gloucester and Northampton, with de Montfort controlling most of southeastern England, Prince Edward and Henry of Almain were defeated and taken prisoner at the battle of Lewes on 14 May 1264. With Henry III and his consort Queen Eleanor trapped in the Tower of London and both Prince Edward and Henry of Almain taken hostage, de Montfort was the *de facto* ruler of England. Considering Eleanor of Castile, commanding the castle of Windsor, used as a prison for captured rebels, too dangerous to be left at liberty, he had her confined in the palace of Westminster, and called a parliament from 12 January to mid-March 1265 against the wishes of the king. Because de Montfort summoned burgesses from the major cities in addition to barons and knights from the shires, this has been seen by some historians as a precursor of a modern parliament.

On 28 May Edward managed to escape his captors and led the royalist forces to victory in the battle of Evesham, when the bodies of de Montfort and his son were mutilated on the field.[6] Princess Eleanor was now the consort of a proven warrior prince, and frequently appeared at his side on public occasions, with no longer the stigma of being 'just a foreign princess'. In the spring of 1268, after producing three daughters, all of whom had died young, Eleanor gave birth to a healthy son christened John. He was followed by another son named Henry in 1268 and a daughter who survived in June 1269, named Eleanor after her mother. Two years later, with England relatively calm, Prince Edward decided it was time for him to embark on the great adventure of the Eighth Crusade with Louis IX. Preparations for a crusade took even the Pisan, Venetian and Genoese between eighteen months and three years. In addition, Edward's problem was that he had no funds and crusading was an expensive luxury that required him to borrow money from all and sundry, even mortgaging Gascony to King Louis for 17,500 *livres tournois*, to be repaid from the revenues of Gascony over twelve years.[7] In addition, parliament sanctioned a tax of a twentieth of all incomes after Henry III consented to confirm Magna Carta and impose restrictions on Jewish money-lenders.[8]

Together with his brother Edmund and Henry of Almain, Prince Edward took the cross in a grand ceremony on 24 June 1268. Also planning to depart on the crusade were some of the barons he had recently been fighting, who now became his brothers-in-arms in the relatively small English contingent, numbering about 225 knights and less than 1,000 foot-soldiers, that eventually set sail from Dover on 20 August 1270. The numbers were greater than this suggests because each knight came with a squire, a groom and two or three foot-servants. On the land journey, he would ride a palfrey, as would the groom, who also led one or two destriers – war-horses that were far too valuable to be ridden for long, and which carried only their own tack and maybe some provisions – and a couple of sumpter horses carrying the bulk of the luggage. Horses also need rest days – at least one in six unless they are to suffer saddle sores and damage to feet and legs.[9] Multiply that typical troop by 225 and add the wheeled transports carrying heavier loads, and the logistics of even a small crusade become apparent.[10] The logistics of a long sea voyage were complicated and costly with regular station-keeping among ships of different speeds, assistance to vessels in distress and, of course, adequate provisioning.[11] Horses need fresh water – about 8 gallons or 36 litres a day – and water on a slow sailing ship goes brackish very quickly. Since horses cannot vomit, they become very ill in bad weather. Even confined in their stalls in calm weather, they suffer 'Monday morning sickness' after a few days and need the transport ships to put into land so they may move about and graze;

typically on the crossing from Sicily to Acre, landfall would be made at Rhodes and Cyprus.

Prince Edward's household during his absence from England was to be administered by one of those extraordinary royal servants who enabled their masters to confidently leave everything in their hands. This was Robert Burnell, an unconventional ex-chancery clerk who kept a mistress, to whom he was faithful and who reputedly bore him four sons and several daughters. Edward esteemed Burnell so highly that he attempted to have him elected to the see of Canterbury, but the community there elected its prior instead. Disapproving Burnell's family life, Pope Gregory X refused both candidates and appointed his own man. A second attempt by Edward to gain Canterbury for Burnell in 1278 likewise failed when Pope Nicholas II refused him. Among many improvements to the administration introduced by Burnell were locating the chancery permanently in London, instead of travelling everywhere with the court, and improving the remuneration of the clerks.

Princess Eleanor had grown up with the males of her family fighting their crusade against the Moors in Spain and decided to accompany Edward on this crusade, copying her grandmother Eleanor of Aquitaine, who had insisted on joining her first husband Louis VII on the Second Crusade in defiance of the papal ban on women accompanying their menfolk. The original purpose of this new crusade, to relieve the long siege of Acre, had been shelved, Louis IX having been erroneously informed by his brother Charles of Anjou, then king of Sicily, that Tunis would be a softer target because its emir wanted only the excuse of *force majeur* to surrender to the Christians. He set sail for the North African littoral with his own fleet of twenty-five galleys and thirteen smaller vessels transporting 500 cavalry and 1,000 longbowmen,[12] whose weapons were not adapted to the dry climate on arrival, and tended to break in use. The real enemy at Tunis, however, was not the Muslims but plague, which first claimed the life of Louis' son Jean Tristan and also of his father on 25 August. One day after Prince Edward's English flotilla arrived off Tunis, Charles abandoned Tunis and set sail for Sicily, the English contingent following.

With the health of Henry III becoming precarious and discontent among the barons growing again, he wrote to Edward, telling him to return to England. Intent on the great adventure, Edward did not comply. A terrible storm off the west coast of Sicily scattered the French and

English ships, wrecking several. This was the final straw for Charles of Anjou and Louis IX' successor Philippe III, who refused to countenance any further thought of going on to the Holy Land. While Prince Edward and Princess Eleanor spent the winter of 1270-71 on Sicily as guests of Charles d'Anjou she gave birth to another daughter, which died before being christened, and was pregnant yet again before they resumed the journey to the Holy Land in spring.

Edward had a fleet of eight sailing ships and thirty galleys – the latter could go faster, especially in calm weather, but the more rowers on board for faster speeds, the more nourishing food *and water* was required. Edward arrived on 9 May 1271 at the Templars' besieged fortress-port of Acre – the most important city of the Latin Kingdom, Jerusalem having fallen in 1244. And Acre was no haven of Christian peace. Divided into quarters occupied by Pisan, Venetian, Genoese and other nationalities, it saw many periods of armed struggle between them.[13] As Edward was to discover, getting his fleet and army to the Holy Land was only the prelude of an impossible dream. Despite calling in loans from all and sundry and levying all the taxes his English and Gascon vassals and the Church could bear, the costs of his crusade mounted higher and higher, reaching an estimated £100,000 – an astronomical sum for the time that would cripple him financially for years to come.

On the principle that my enemy's enemy is my friend, the Christians formed an alliance of sorts with the Mongol invaders to the east and north of the Holy Land, but this achieved little apart from raiding and skirmishing, an attack on Nazareth concluding with the massacre of all the inhabitants. The Egyptian armies under Baibars were withdrawn after a ten-year peace treaty was agreed in May 1272 with Hugues III of Cyprus, who was nominally also king of Jerusalem. There were many assassinations and attempted assassinations in the Latin Kingdom, riven by internecine struggles among the Christians and frequent outbursts of violence between them and various Muslim factions. In one such attack in the month following the treaty, Edward was wounded by an assailant's dagger, said to have been poisoned, but possibly just dirty. He might have lost the use of the injured and inflamed arm, had not a surgeon cut away much necrotised flesh before the inflamation had spread. Later versions of the event described Eleanor sucking the poison out of her husband's wound to save his life, but this was poetic embellishment to illustrate the depth of their attachment for one another.

PLANTAGENET PRINCES

Weakened by the complications of his wounding, on 24 September 1272 Edward left Acre. Arriving in Sicily, he was met with the news that his son John was dead. His father had also died, making him king of England. The political situation in England was stable after the mid-century upheavals, the country being governed by a council of four regents led by Robert Burnell, Edward's very competent chancellor. Placing complete trust in him, the still convalescent uncrowned king of England pursued a leisurely journey overland, due partly to his poor health. In Italy during early spring 1273, he spent two months at Orvieto with the court of Pope Gregory X, seeking and obtaining the excommunication of Guy de Montfort, then crossed the Alps to visit Savoy as grandson of Beatrice, where he studied at length the latest castle-building techniques. Travelling on into Aquitaine, he sorted out some unruly vassals there, before staying with King Philippe III, known as Philippe the Bold, in Paris for ten days, during which he did homage for Aquitaine. He even took part in a tournament at Châlons, where he narrowly avoided being taken hostage. Why do that, when he was, as all returning crusading kings were, no matter how little they accomplished, a hero of all Christendom simply for having actually been to the Holy Land? In June 1273 Henry of Almain crossed the Channel to urge Edward's return, but he still did not hurry back to his island realm. Eleanor meanwhile was in Aquitaine, pregnant again, and gave birth on 24 November to a boy named Alphonse after her half-brother Alfonso X of Castile.

In June and July of 1274 Eleanor and Edward were in Ponthieu, for them to cast an eye over this northern French county of which Eleanor was now the heiress, since her brother Alfonso had died. There, Joan of Acre, now approaching 3 years old, was left with her grandmother when her parents departed. On 2 August 1274, they stepped ashore at Dover and met the dowager queen Eleanor of Provence at Canterbury with the surviving children who had been left behind in England: 6-year-old Prince Henry and 4-year-old Princess Eleanor. The joint coronation of Edward and Eleanor took place immediately after their return to Westminster on 19 August 1274, nearly two years after the death of Henry III. King Edward appointed the faithful Burnell Lord Chancellor and gave him the see of Bath and Wells in January of the following year.

EDWARD I

Just two months after his parents' return, Prince Henry died after a long illness in the care of his grandmother Eleanor of Provence, this death presenting King Edward with the problem of no longer having a son and heir. Unrest on the western frontier included treachery among the Welsh princes and two of them defecting to the English in 1274.[14] Determined to end the 'Welsh problem', Edward, who had lived on borrowed funds for years, placed a permanent tax on wool, England's most valuable export and set out with Burnell to improve many aspects of the royal administration and other legal areas like criminal and property law. Edward's favourite bishop was also sent abroad on diplomatic missions and for a time governed the troublesome province of Gascony. A permanent parliament was also established, providing a functional legislature and a system for raising taxes, nevertheless resented by the barons, the Church and the increasingly important burgesses of the cities. These measures were largely pushed through by Burnell, while increasingly the king's time was taken up with warfare, both the Scots and the Welsh taking advantage of rising discontent in England. Since there was no salary as such for the chancellor, it was taken for granted that he would enrich himself by other means.

To put down the rebellion of Llywelyn ap Gruffudd in July 1277 Edward invaded Wales with an 'English' army 15,500-strong – of whom more than half were Welsh, from principalities hostile to Llywelyn.[15] The prolonged campaign ended in a surrender of the Welsh insurgents after a series of minor English victories. This was followed by a declared war of total conquest in 1282–83. It started with a rebellion by former Welsh allies who were discontented with the reward they had received for supporting Edward in 1277. Llywelyn and other Welsh princes joined in when they understood what Edward had in mind, defeating the English in June at Llandeilo Fawr. A pontoon bridge had been built from the mainland to Anglesey, but shortly after Edward's force crossed it, an ambush cost them heavy losses at Moel y Don, casualties including a brother of Burnell. Then, on 11 December, Llywelyn was lured into a trap and killed at Orewin bridge. Not until June 1283 was the Welsh leader taken prisoner and executed in Shrewsbury a few months later.

Permanently to subjugate the Welsh, Edward built a series of state-of-the-art castles from Conwy and Rhuddlan in the north to

Builth Wells in the south, a number of them being the work of a master-builder named Jacques de St-George, whom he had met in Savoy on his slow journey back from the crusade. To provide the extra money needed for this, Queen Eleanor was reduced to selling off some of her jewellery, while Edward mortgaged her dower possessions and borrowed on a colossal scale from a consortium of Italian bankers. Their terms were roughly 15 per cent per annum, but the accounts were adjusted to conceal the fact that the king of England was involved in usury condemned by the Church. When Edward refused to repay the loans from the Frescobaldi banking family of Florence, they went bankrupt with him owing them the equivalent of £417 million in today's values. It was a bad time for Italian bankers: Philippe IV also confiscated the wealth in France of the Ricciardi banking family. Inevitably the Jews also suffered. In 1279 Edward executed 300 Jewish moneylenders to avoid loan repayments,[16] and later followed this up with the Edict of Expulsion in 1290, driving the entire community out of England for three and a half centuries until Oliver Cromwell brought them back.

It was in the partly constructed castle at Caernarvon that Queen Eleanor gave birth on 25 April 1284 to another son named Edward and known initially as 'Edward of Caernarvon'. Using the model of the fortified *bastides* towns in Gascony, his father also built walled towns at Flint, Aberystwyth and Rhuddlan, settling them with English in-comers – much as Oliver Cromwell later did disastrously in northern Ireland. Meriting his nickname *malleus scottorum* – the hammer of the Scots – he then decided to conquer Scotland too, in a long, intermittent war that continued even after his death. Jacques de St-George served him there too, building Linlithgow castle and modifying the castle at Stirling.

Edward was still talking about making another crusade, but fate had other plans. In 1290 Eleanor of Castile was suffering from some debilitating disease, thought possibly to have been an opportunistic infection due to attacks of malaria having weakened her. In the summer, the royal couple took a leisurely tour of Eleanor's estates in northern England. At the beginning of August in Silverstone, with her too ill to attend Mass in her own chapel, Edward summoned his autumn parliament to Clipstone in Nottinghamshire, since he did not want to leave her for long enough to travel to London and back. Queen Eleanor's last weeks saw the daily itinerary of the court reduced by her worsening health to eight miles a day until it reached the village of Harby in Nottinghamshire, which she was never to leave alive. With Edward by her side, she died in the evening of 28 November 1290, aged 49. Stunned by her loss, for three days he was incapable of any kingly action. Edward had been faithful to her throughout their married lives lasting thirty-six years, which was rare among monarchs of the time. He displayed his deep grief by erecting twelve stone crosses bearing her likeness, one at each place where the sorrowful funeral cortège stopped for the night on its way back to London. Although eroded, three of these still stand.

Taking advantage of Edward's attention thus being elsewhere, in 1294 Philippe IV confiscated Gascony, the last remaining Continental possession of the Crown, after Edward refused to apologise for English privateers or pirates capturing several French ships and a combined English-Gascon force sacking the port-city of La Rochelle in Poitou.

Before long, his counsellors advised that he should marry again, to beget more sons, in case Edward of Caernarvon should die and leave the kingdom prey to a power struggle between the husbands of his sisters. Eventually accepting this argument, Edward I agreed in 1294 to marry Philippe IV's half-sister Marguerite, but various complications including war delayed the wedding until 1299, when he was 60 and she 20 years old. She bore him two sons who reached adult age and a daughter christened Eleanor in memory of his first wife, but who died aged 5. The succession was secure as it could be, but it was in fact Eleanor of Castile's last-born son who came to the throne as Edward II in 1307 after Edward I died at Burgh by Sands, near Carlisle, while on the way to invade Scotland. His body was kept at Waltham abbey for several months before being transported to Westminster abbey, where Edward II had a simple marble tomb carved for it. Queen Marguerite never re-married, declaring, 'When King Edward died, all men died for me.'

Chapter 18

Edward II

When Edward II was enthroned in 1307 aged 23, he was, although ceremonially knighted the previous year, a son totally unlike his bellicose father. Born in Caernarvon castle on 25 April 1284, only a few months after Edward I had 'pacified' north Wales, he was initially known as 'Edward of Caernarvon'. Whether the place of birth was chosen to make him literally 'the prince of Wales' or whether Eleanor of Castile just happened to be there with Edward I when she gave birth, we cannot say.

The little prince was less than four months old when his 10-year-old brother Prince Alphonse died in Windsor castle on 19 August, making him heir to the throne. Prince Edward seems to have had little contact with his mother, who was always travelling with her husband in England and Gascony. Whether that played some part in his character development, we cannot know. Cared for by a wet-nurse named Mariota or Mary Maunsel for a few months until she fell ill, he was then given into the care of Alice de Leygrave. A household staff was created for the new baby, under the direction firstly of a Flemish clerk, Giles of Oudenaerde,[1] succeeded in 1293 by William of Blyborough. It is thought that Eleanor of Castile had him educated in religion by Dominican friars and otherwise by a learned member of her household, Guy Ferre, who supervised the young prince's education in riding and military skills among other subjects.[2]

The young prince liked horses and dogs, although not for hunting, which was a widely enjoyed sport among noble males. Falconry too, failed to interest him, but he did adore music, poetry and play-acting, also tournaments as a spectator only – possibly because he had been forbidden to participate to avoid injury or death for the heir to the throne. Popular with his household staff, Prince Edward grew up tall and well-built, enjoying rowing and – strangely for a prince –contact with the lower classes like farm labourers, which drew criticism from the nobility, but indicates that he could speak Anglo-Saxon as well as the Norman French of the upper classes.

He was betrothed when 6 years old in 1290 to Margaret of Norway, a potential claimant to the Scottish throne, but she died within the year – as did his mother Eleanor of Castile, on 29 November, followed by Edward's grandmother Eleanor of Provence in June of the following year, which caused Prince Edward to inherit the county of Ponthieu, making him a vassal of the French King Philippe IV.[3] That may have been embarrassing in 1297 and 1298 when Prince Edward was made regent – with powerful counsellors, of course – whilst his father campaigned in Flanders against Philippe IV, who was its overlord, as revenge for the French occupying part of Gascony. That prolonged spat was ended by the peace treaty under which King Edward married Philippe's 20-year-old sister Marguerite as his second wife and betrothed Prince Edward to Philippe's 2-year-old daughter Isabelle. The hope was that, if the young couple's betrothal bore fruit, the disputed county of Gascony could one day be inherited by a descendant of both kings, ending the long-running dispute over its ownership.[4] Prince Edward seems to have adjusted well to his young stepmother and liked his two half-brothers whom she bore to Edward I in 1300 and 1301.

When King Edward resumed his conflict with Scotland in 1300, he chose to make Prince Edward a subsidiary commander under experienced knights, to train him for kingship. In the following year, he rewarded his son with the official title 'Prince of Wales' with various grants of land in north Wales as well as the wealthy earldom of Chester. After accepting the homage of his Welsh vassals, Prince Edward travelled north with a cohort of 300 men to join his father in Scotland, capturing Turnberry castle on Scotland's west coast, later destroyed by Robert the Bruce to deny it to the English. Edward's education in kingship continued with his father entrusting him with peace negotiations with the Scottish lords in the spring of 1304. When these failed, he joined his father at the siege of the strategically important castle at Stirling, where the king employed seventeen siege engines, causing significant damage to the buildings.

The first real quarrel between the two Edwards came in 1305 after the prince accused Bishop Walter Langton, the royal treasurer, of failing to accord him an appropriate share of the household's money.

Taking the treasurer's side, Edward I banished his son and a clique of his friends from court without any subsidy. Negotiations by relatives and friends achieved a reconciliation, which led to King Edward, grown weary with the passage of years and his many wars, deputing command of the next invasion of Scotland in 1306 to Prince Edward after knighting him and a number of other young men in an impressive ceremony in Westminster abbey followed by a great feast in the neighbouring palace.

During another round of pointless slaughter in the north – Robert the Bruce was now the unyielding king of Scotland – two of the author's ancestors paid a cruel price for their allegiance to the Bruce. Sir Robert de Boyt was taken prisoner and Duncan Boyd was hanged, presumably because he had no ransomable value.[5] It is doubtful whether Edward II gave much thought to the hanged man or the noble prisoner languishing in an English prison. Nor, probably, was he thinking much about his betrothed because he had fallen in love with a handsome Gascon knight in the king's household named Piers Gaveston, who had been among the young squires knighted with Prince Edward. After he learned that his son planned to give the county of Ponthieu to Gaveston, the king was so furious that he attacked Prince Edward physically and exiled Gaveston to break up the relationship. Another invasion of Scotland in 1307 was called off after Edward I died on the journey north at Burgh by Sands near Carlisle on 7 July. Immediately he heard the news, Prince Edward rode there, to take command, and was proclaimed king two weeks after the old king's death. Leaving Burgh by Sands, Edward II led the army into Scotland, accepting his vassals' homage at Dumfries, but then did an about-turn and headed south. One of his first actions was to recall Gaveston to court, where he was given the prestigious earldom of Cornwall – and a wealthy heiress, 14-year-old Margaret de Clare, as wife. To celebrate his new affluence, Gaveston held an expensive tournament at Wallingford castle. Bishop Langton was among those members of the royal household who were sacked by their new master. In Langton's case, the young king's spite had him thrown into prison.

In January 1308 Edward II crossed the Channel to Paris to finalise his marriage to Philippe IV's daughter Isabelle, scandalising the Anglo-Norman nobility by making Gaveston his regent with unprecedented powers during his absence. King Philippe disliked England's new monarch and refused to give way to Edward II's demands, forcing him to do homage for Aquitaine and to define and guarantee Isabelle's dower lands in England. The wedding took place on 25 January, after which the young couple took ship for England. Arrangements for the coronation banquet had been in the hands of Gaveston, and included building forty ovens and a fountain, from different spouts of which came jets of fine wine and spiced wine. The double coronation took place on 25 February in conditions of profound disapproval by the barons of Edward II's repeated reliance on Gaveston's advice instead of listening to his counsellors, and bestowing on his favourite some of Isabelle's jewellery. The barons knew that the counts of Lincoln and Warwick and the future count of Pembroke had been expressly charged by Edward I on his deathbed with guiding his son and preventing the return of Gaveston,[6] but here was the exile lording it over them all.

Among the courtiers accompanying Isabelle from Paris were her uncles Charles de Valois and Louis d'Evreux. The dowager queen of England was an aunt of hers, two of Edward's half-brothers were her cousins and England's most powerful baron, Count Thomas of Lancaster, was her uncle. So one would think she was well placed to insist on her rights. But even the ceremony did not begin well. The royal couple walked from the palace of Westminster to the neighbouring abbey on a woollen carpet strewn with flowers under an embroidered canopy carried aloft on decorated poles by the barons of the Cinque Ports. Ahead of them, carrying regalia for the coronation, walked the earls of Lancaster, Warwick, Lincoln and Hereford, but it was Gaveston, dressed even more sumptuously than the king in a robe of imperial purple silk embroidered with pearls, who insisted on carrying St Edward the Confessor's sacred crown. In a magnificient and costly coronation dress, Isabelle was radiant, but Edward could not take his eyes off Gaveston during the ceremony conducted by Bishop Henry Woodlock of Winchester, causing one of the nobles present to declare that he only restrained himself from attacking Gaveston physically out of respect for the young queen and the sanctity of the abbey.[7]

Edward swore to uphold 'the rightful laws and customs which the community of the realm shall have chosen'. Depending whether the wording was his or not, this could either mean that he was being forced to comply with future legislation by the parliament, or was possibly an attempt by him to ingratiate himself with the barons, who were well aware that the kingdom he had inherited was badly in debt, to the tune of £200,000 from borrowings to finance Edward I's wars.

When the king and Queen Isabelle moved back to the palace, the festive arrangements made by Gaveston turned out to be awful. The banquet was served late and was poorly cooked, despite all those ovens. The final insult to Isabelle was her husband choosing to sit with Gaveston instead of beside her. Behind the two men hung tapestries depicting their personal arms, and not the arms of King Edward and his queen.

After the departure of her scandalised French uncles, Edward's teenage queen had to navigate a careful path between the courtiers who hated Gaveston and those who sought to curry favour with him in order to reach the king's ear. She played a waiting game, not confronting Edward and not associating herself with any baronial faction, but it was a lonely existence. Isabelle's best ally at court was Thomas of Lancaster. She did try to create a positive relationship with Gaveston, which cannot have been easy, given his often criticised arrogance and his excessive influence over the king, summed up by one chronicler writing that there were 'two kings reigning in one kingdom, the one in name and the other in deed'.[8]

In the parliament of February 1308, the barons insisted that the problem of Gaveston be settled. Hoping to avoid bloodshed, Earl Henry de Lacy of Lincoln had the question postponed until April, when the barons with the backing of Queen Isabelle and Philippe IV in Paris arranged for him to be sent back to Aquitaine, on pain of excommunication by Archbishop Walter Reynolds of Canterbury should he return. Somehow, Edward wriggled out of this by 'exiling' Gaveston in June to the richly remunerated position of the Lord of Ireland.[9]

The Christmas court was held at Windsor without him. A century before, England had been ruled by Richard I, whose known sexual preferences did not diminish his reputation because he 'took the man's part' with his male partners, but Edward II, it seems, did not.[10] Some historians have believed that Edward II and Gaveston were 'just good friends' – exactly the same euphemism used for unmarried couples in the less-permissive early-to-mid twentieth century. An anonymous annalist of the small Cistercian foundation of Newenham abbey in Devon actually referred to 'the king and his husband' and the reverberations of Edward II's relationship with Gaveston were still echoing nearly six centuries later in 1872 when Marcus Stone RA painted a garden scene in which Edward and Gaveston were being physically affectionate while a group of courtiers looked on disapprovingly.

EDWARD II

Edward II was still seeking to facilitate the return of his favourite to court in April 1309 by persuading Pope Clement V to annul the archbishop's threat of excommunication. The troublesome Gascon returned to England in June, to Edward's obvious delight. Nobody else was pleased to see him back and hear him openly insult the great barons of the realm who used Edward's inability to control him to force the formation of a board of twenty-one Ordainers to effect widespread reforms. Borrowing £22,000 from Italian bankers, Edward departed with an army of 4,500 men and Gaveston in joint command to subdue Scotland. King Robert the Bruce showed what he thought of this initiative by refusing to stand and fight. Edward and Gaveston moved the army inconsequentially from place to place until the borrowed funds were exhausted in 1311.

Back at court, Edward found that the Ordainers had been busy and formally required him to strip Gaveston of all his titles and exile him, to live nowhere in England, Ireland or Gascony. With no choice in the matter, Gaveston departed and Edward left court in a sulk, retiring to his estates at Windsor and elsewhere. There, he revoked the Ordinances and summoned Gaveston back once again. They met at York in January, to the fury of the barons led by Thomas of Lancaster. Archbishop Reynolds confirmed his threat of excommunication of Gaveston. Making a strange household, Edward, Isabelle and Gaveston fled towards Newcastle, pursued by the barons. To escape, they took ship to the south, landing at Scarborough, where Gaveston remained while the royal couple hurried back to York. Besieged at Scarborough, Gaveston surrendered on 19 May to Aymer de Valence, count of Pembroke, after being assured he would not be harmed. In his possession was a hoard of gold, silver and gems, and several very valuable horses – all of which he was later accused of having stolen from the king, but which may have been simply given to him by Edward along with other treasure.[11]

Because the barons had every reason to suspect that Edward II would again cheat them of revenge, an initial meeting was held with the king in York while Gaveston was left in the custody of Pembroke. On 9 June, Pembroke departed to visit his wife, leaving the prisoner under guard at Deddington rectory in Oxfordshire. Since he must have known the immediate plan of his allies, this sudden absence seems like his way of establishing an alibi that would enable him to tell the king that he was not present when Gaveston was killed. On the following morning Warwick arrived at the rectory, took Gaveston captive and brought him back to the castle at Warwick for trial. According to the chronicle of Trokelowe, Lancaster warned the other barons – Warwick, Hereford and Arundel – that, so long as Gaveston was alive, Edward II would insist on protecting and restoring his favourite. So Gaveston was not even allowed to speak at the trial. On the other hand, the canon of Bridlington claimed that two royal justices, William Inge and Henry Spigurnel, were summoned to examine the evidence against him, to give a semblance of legal process. After being condemned to die for violating the terms of the Ordinances, on 19 June Gaveston was taken out along the road towards Kenilworth onto land belonging to Lancaster at Blacklow Hill, where two Welsh mercenaries stabbed him to death and beheaded the body, to give a semblance of judicial execution.

Gaveston having died excommunicate, could not be buried in consecrated ground, so the body was left there, but later transported to Oxford by some monks, Edward II, presumably grieved and certainly furious at what had happened. swore a terrible revenge on the barons involved. Given the intense feelings on both sides, another barons' war appeared likely until the Earl of Pembroke, who had not partipated in the trial or the murder, tried to negotiate a peace treaty between the two sides in December: pardon in exchange for the barons' support in yet another invasion of Scotland. Such was the depth of the barons' feelings that what they had done was right, even if not legal, that negotiations dragged on into 1313. Pembroke further demonstrated his renewed allegiance to the king by negotiating with Philippe IV for a settlement of the dispute over Gascony. To confirm this, Edward and Isabelle travelled to Paris, where they were lavishly entertained and Philippe compromised with Edward over Gascony. The new friendship was cemented by both kings swearing to go on crusade together, with their wives.

Back in England, an intervention by the earl of Gloucester and others not involved in the murder of Gaveston at last produced a settlement on 14 October 1313, under which the barons involved were pardoned and the horses, gold, silver and jewels taken with Gaveston were returned to the king. Parliament sanctioned the raising of taxes, the pope made a loan of £25,000, Philippe extended another of £33,000 and Edward's new Italian banker Antonio Pessagno arranged still further loans. For the first time Edward II was well-funded in the short term, although heavily in debt.

EDWARD II

Edward secured a papal annulment of the excommunication so that Gaveston's body could be buried in consecrated ground on 2 January 1315 at the Dominican foundation of King's Langley priory. Despite the pardon, Edward's burning hatred of Thomas of Lancaster continued until 1322, when Lancaster was defeated at the battle of Boroughbridge and executed. With the poor harvests all over Europe between 1315 and 1319, most people had more pressing problems than commemorating Isabelle's unpopular uncle. Lack of sun and warmth prevented the evaporation of salt, the most important medium for preserving meat – not that many animals survived in parts of England, due to lack of pasture. It was said that the poor people resorted to cannibalism, in some cases of their own dead children.[12] Not until 1823 was a memorial cross erected at Blacklow Hill by the local squire. It bears the following strange wording:

> In the hollow of this stone was beheaded on the (indistinct) day of July (sic) 1312 by Barons lawless as himself PIERS GAVESTON, Earl of Cornwall, the minion of a hateful king, in Life as in Death, a memorable instance of Misrule.

Although 'minion' may now mean just a humble subordinate – which certainly does not accord with Gaveston's constant overweening arrogance – the above usage is Victorian prudery, using the word in its original French meaning – *mignon,* a favourite, sweetheart or lover. The most famous *mignons* in the history of France were '*les mignons de Monsieur*' a stable of pretty boys kept for his pleasure by the perfumed, bewigged, bejewelled and exquisitely dressed transvestite Philippe d'Orléans, younger brother of Louis XIV.

Queen Isabelle, it seems, put her memories of Gaveston behind her. Whatever other sexual relief Edward may have had, she bore him three children in the coming years in addition to the future Edward III, born in November 1312. In August 1316 their son known as John of Eltham was born, but would die twenty years later, leaving no issue. In June 1318 Eleanor of Woodstock was born; she likewise left no issue when she died in 1355. Edward's last child by Isabelle, a daughter known as Joan of the Tower, did marry David II of Scots when he was 4 and she 7, but likewise left no issue when she died in 1362, despite her on-off marriage having lasted thirty-four years in all. Before Queen Isabelle came of age, which would have been about 1310 – records of her birth date are vague – it seems that Edward also fathered a bastard known as Adam Fitzroy in or about 1307. So in today's language, he was not exclusively gay, but bisexual – as were his two favourites.

Beginning with prolonged torrential rain in 1314, followed by very low winter temperatures and a very wet spring, Europe's climate degenerated, producing very poor harvests in England for the following seven years. Not only grain supplies, but meat farming too, suffered greatly, producing a great famine. Trade too suffered, with customs duties for the Exchequer on exported wool severely reduced. With little possibility of importing grain, food prices rose uncontrollably. The requisitioning of provisions for the court during this time saw society splitting apart, threatening yet another civil war.

To make matters worse, by 1314 Robert the Bruce had recaptured most of the Scottish castles captured by the English, and was raiding northern England as far south as Carlisle. Edward used his borrowed wealth to muster an army of 15,000 or more and marched north with Lancaster and the barons, to relieve the siege of Stirling castle, whose commander had undertaken to surrender, should the English army not arrive by 24 June. Open hostilities began on the preceding day with skirmishing at the Bannock Burn, where a stream with a single bridge was surrounded by marshland. Having wrongly deployed his forces, and with no chance of redeploying on the surrounding marshland, Edward had to be dragged away from the fray by the earl of Pembroke. After he fled, Stirling castle surrendered and the English never recovered it, losing thousands of casualties for no gain. The English defeat at Bannock Burn was followed by the Bruce raiding further and further south, reaching Lancashire and Yorkshire at the same time as his brother Edward Bruce invaded Ireland after declaring himself its king. Edward II's attempts to drive the Scots back northwards were hampered by the famine, which made feeding his army all but impossible, and requisitions provoked rebellion in Lancashire and Bristol. One bright moment came when the severed head of Edward Bruce was sent to London by the justiciar of Ireland after the battle of Faughart in 1318. When the barons demanded restoration of the Ordinances of 1311, open hostility between Edward and Lancaster's supporters had caused parliament's suspension for two years, but Pembroke again brokered a truce between the two parties, which was sealed at the Treaty of Leake in August 1318.[13]

EDWARD II

In Oxford, a madman claimed he was the real king, having been exchanged with Edward I's son in infancy and the general dissatisfaction with Edward II and his new favourites – two household knights, to whom he gave the vast de Clare inheritance – made many people believe such stories. Possibly, the two knights were just being generously rewarded for fidelity, but rumour said that one of the new favourites was more than just a friend. This was his chamberlain, Hugh Despenser the Younger, an extremely acquisitive and unpopular noble, whom one chronicler noted that Edward 'loved ... dearly with all his heart and mind'.[14] In 1326, the year before Edward II's death, Bishop Adam Orleton of Hereford made a number of public allegations that Edward and Despenser were sodomites. The chronicle of the abbey of Meaux, written by its aged abbot Thomas Burton in retirement at Fountains Abbey, simply noted that Edward 'gave himself too much to the vice of sodomy'.[15] How much was too much? Was this a distinction between male sex partners who 'took the man's part' and those who did not?

In 1321 the tension between the barons and the court dominated by the Despensers father and son became open conflict in May. Edward hoped that Pembroke would once again save his skin, but he did not. Despenser lands were seized by other Marcher lords they had wronged and dispossessed. In June Lancaster assembled many lords spiritual and temporal to condemn the younger Despenser for having contravened the Ordinances. In July, Edward was forced to exile both Despensers and pardon their many enemies. The country was again riven, with Lancaster and the barons holding the north and Edward the southeast, giving him the confidence to recall and pardon the Despensers.

After Boroughbridge, Edward thought he had decapitated the barons' movement by chopping off Lancaster's head and set up courts to try his followers, imposing execution and confiscation of property, redistributed to the king's favourites. Even Pembroke had to pledge all his possessions as a proof of loyalty. Edward's share of the confiscations made him reckless; at York in March 1322 the Ordinances were revoked and fresh taxes agreed for yet another campaign against the Scots. Despite, or because of, the royal army of more than 23,000 men, it was another failure. The Bruce retreated, drawing the English further and further into land where there was no sustenance for them and no way of re-supplying so many hungry bellies, forcing their reteat, pursued by the Scots. Among the casualties was Edward's 15-year-old bastard

Adam fitzRoy. In Tynemouth, Queen Isabelle fled before the Scottish advance, taking ship to the south. Seeking someone to blame, Edward selected Andrew Harclay, the man who had won him victory in 1321, for taking the most intelligent step of negotiating a peace treaty with Robert the Bruce, and had him executed.

That Harclay had been right to seek peace on the northern frontier was proven in 1325 when Isabelle's brother in Paris, crowned King Charles IV in 1322, demanded that Edward II, as duke of Aquitaine, pay homage. Edward sent Pembroke to negotiate a settlement, but that much abused supporter died en route and King Charles invaded the duchy. In England, the Despensers were running amok, using their positions to exploit the widespread unrest and acquire by threat, theft and fraud more and more possessions. When Charles IV suggested that Isabelle should come to Paris with Prince Edward, who could swear homage, Edward was advised to send Isabelle alone. It was a fatal error. Negotiations dragged on until her 10-year-old son was indeed despatched as titular duke of Aquitaine to swear fealty to King Charles in September.

Afterwards, Isabelle showed no sign of returning. Apart from Edward's extramarital activities, she detested Hugh Depenser and felt ashamed of her husband having to flee Scottish incursions for the third time. He had confiscated her dower properties, placed her children in the care of Hugh Despenser's wife and made her the censor of Isabelle's correspondence with France. It was all too much for the queen to bear. She turned to the exiled Marcher Lord Roger Mortimer, forming with him a nub of revanchist exiles in Paris hostile to the Despensers. This worried King Edward to the point of fortifying the south coast against a possible French invasion. South of the Channel, Isabelle and Mortimer formed an alliance with Count William of Hainault, who promised them eight vessels of war and 132 transport ships for an invasion. Relations were cemented in the usual way, by betrothing Prince Edward to Count William's daughter Philippa of Hainault.

Edward II appealed to his subjects to defend the realm, but so low had his prestige declined that few answered the call; at one muster, out of 2,000 men summoned, only fifty-five turned up, so that the landing in the estuary of the river Orwell in Suffolk of Isabelle, Mortimer, Prince Edward and Edward's half-brother Edmund of Woodstock was unopposed, and rapidly attracted barons and clergy, who came with their supporters. King Edward fled the security of the Tower of London on 2 October with the

Despensers, heading west. Behind them, the city fell into anarchy with mobs releasing the prisoners in the Tower and assassinating officers of the king. The fugitive king and his lover reached Gloucester in the second week of October and crossed into Wales hotly pursued by Mortimer and Isabelle, whose following grew as Edward's diminished.

He and the younger Despenser took ship from Chepstow and sailed down the river Wye to the Severn estuary, perhaps with the intention of raising an army in Ireland. Bad weather forced them back to land, where they retreated to Caerphilly castle, property of Eleanor de Clare, Despenser's wife. A few miles to the east, Isabella's supporters surrounded Bristol, where the elder Despenser surrendered and was summarily executed. Learning this, Edward and Hugh the Younger departed from Caerphilly castle on 2 November – in such haste that they left behind their jewellery, the king's treasury totalling £13,000, of which Queen Isabelle took charge, to use as she pleased, and most of their provisions. Two weeks later the fugitives were betrayed and tracked down thirty miles away at Neath abbey, the siege of Caerphilly by Isabelle's forces continuing until April 1327. Meanwhile Edward was taken back to English soil and held in Lancaster's castle at Kenilworth while Isabelle, Mortimer and their barons pondered what to do with him.

There was no such problem with Hugh the Younger, who was summarily judged for high treason and castrated, disembowelled and quartered on 24 November, apparently while tied to a high ladder so that the large crowd assembled for the spectacle could see all the gory details of his dying,[16] after which his head was taken to London for display, impaled on a pike at London Bridge. Edward's chancellor Robert Baldock was allowed to die in the Fleet prison; the earl of Arundel was among those beheaded. Bishop Orleton was far from alone in decrying Edward's deplorable kingship; all the citizens of London echoed his sentiments. A parliament was called to discuss the matter of de-throning the king, but Edward refused to attend. On 12 January, it was generally agreed that he should be replaced by his son Prince Edward.

But if Edward II was allowed to live, there was a possibility of his supporters rescuing him and using him as figurehead for another bloody civil war. The death of William Rufus, deniably killed by bowshot while hunting in August 1100, had put Henry I on the throne, but it was hardly a useful precedent. Edward II would not have gone hunting even if free. In a secure cell, what 'accident' could befall him?

Two bishops visited him in Kenilworth castle with Lancaster, urging him to renounce the crown in favour of Prince Edward, promising him fair treatment if he did so, otherwise the people would repudiate him *and his sons*, ending the dynasty. The king was then led out, weeping and half-fainting, before the main delegation, and accepted the ultimatum. On 21 January 1327 one knight representing the whole kingdom formally withdrew his homage and officially ended Edward's reign. A proclamation was sent to London, announcing that he, to be known just as Edward of Caernarvon, had freely resigned his kingdom and that Prince Edward would succeed him.

Some desperate supporters, who had everything to lose with a change of regime, broke into Edward's quarters in Berkeley castle in Gloucestershire on 21 September 1327 and rode off with him. Swiftly reapprehended, the late king was returned to Berkeley, with the ringleader imprisoned to die without trial, but Mortimer feared a better organised rescue might succeed. One further attempt did get as far as breaking into the prison within the castle. As a result of these threats, Edward was moved around to other locations in secret for a period, before returning to permanent custody at the castle in the late summer of 1327.

On 23 September Prince Edward was informed that his father had died at Berkeley Castle during the night of 21 September, which was very convenient for Mortimer and Isabelle. The most probable cause was death by suffocation, which left no traces that could be discerned at the time. The three knights who most probably performed the deed had rid the country of a useless monarch. Later historians have imputed a strengthening of parliament to him, but this took place despite him. The three knights were tried for his murder three years later, but allowed to escape to France, one of them afterwards having his estates quietly restored after his return to England and sitting in parliament for more than two decades.

Later, it was rumoured that Edward II was held down by his killers, a pierced horn inserted into his anus to prevent any superficial scarring and a red-hot poker thrust deeply through it as fitting punishment for sodomy. Whatever people had really thought about him as king, his effigy on the marble tomb in Gloucester abbey was carved in alabaster, chosen for its luminance suggestive of saintliness. The tomb became a pilgrimage site credited with miraculous cures engineered by the abbey's community to attract donations from thousands of pilgrims.

Chapter 19

Edward III

During January 1327 at Westminster, Parliament debated the future of this king who refused to plead before it, even to save his life. A few miles down-river in London, the citizens were declaring that Isabelle's younger son John of Eltham was the true lord of the capital and that his 14-year-old brother Prince Edward should replace his father on the throne of England, with the deposed king incarcerated for life.

The way was clear for Prince Edward – who had been given the title Earl of Chester when only twelve days old – to be crowned as King Edward III in Westminster abbey on 1 February by Archbishop of Canterbury Walter Reynolds. With Isabelle his guardian until he came of age, not everyone was happy, for she had secured the restoration of her dower estates, their value increasing from an annual value of £4,400 to £13,333, which revived her reputation for avarice.[1] Mortimer too was unpopular for using his position to enrich himself and acquire property and titles. It was a slap in the face for him to be excluded from the council of regency headed by Lancaster.

Deciding it was time for the young king to be married to his betrothed, Isabelle sent the bishop of Coventry to France in October to marry Philippa of Hainault as Edward's proxy in Valenciennes. She cannot have had any idea that she had set in motion a chain of events that would have tragic consequences. With Edward III's fifteenth birthday approaching, Isabelle and Mortimer knew their guardianship of him had just over three years to run. Henry of Lancaster, who had succeeded with some difficulty to the titles and lands of his executed brother Thomas disapproved of Isabelle's and Mortimer's recent conduct, and he was far from being alone. By October 1328 the country was again in a state approaching civil war. In command of the royal forces, Mortimer took the fortresses of Lancaster, Leicester and Bedford with Isabelle appearing on horseback wearing armour at his side, to show

PLANTAGENET PRINCES

that Edward II's widow was truly a military commander. This was not necessarily because she intended to place herself in physical danger from armed combat, but because this specifically masculine medieval costume was the perfect mode of cross-dressing for women wishing to switch genders in the social sphere: the armour, by completely concealing the form of the female body, made her to medieval eyes an, albeit temporary, male leader of men.[2] The same device was more famously associated with the great French heroine of the following century Joan of Arc, whose statue in armour stands in many French churches still today.

Perhaps the first nail in the coffin of Roger Mortimer was his performance in the battle of Stanhope Park. A part-mercenary English army[3] set out from York on 1 July 1327 to drive back a Scottish invasion. On 15 July, approaching Durham, they saw smoke from burning farms on the horizon and realised that the Scots were nearby. The phrase 'smoke from burning farms' gives a glimpse into the misery that the long drawn-out cross-border warfare imposed on the civilians living in the north of England and south of Scotland. After much manoeuvring to and fro by the English had failed to make contact with the enemy, Mortimer decided to position his army to cut the Scots off from a retreat to the north. Crossing the river Tyne, he made camp on the far side and waited a week for the Scots to arrive without success.

Sending out search parties, he marched his army southward. On 30 July one of its scouts named Thomas Rokesby returned after being captured by the Scots and released on condition he led Mortimer's army to them. Contact was made at last near Stanhope in County Durham. The Scots occupied a strong defensive position near the river Wear. Mortimer took a position on level ground, hoping to lure the Scots forward by skirmishing and withdrawing. It did not work. The Scottish commander Lord James Douglas sent a message, saying his army would stay where it was. This was perhaps deliberate disinformation because on the night of 2-3 August he moved into Stanhope Park, causing Mortimer to shift camp to be nearer. It was a bad move. The following night, Douglas led an attack on the poorly guarded English camp, in which several hundred defenders were killed and Douglas himself penetrated as far as Edward III's tent. The guy ropes having been slashed, it had collapsed with the young king inside, but Douglas was driven back before the English king could be taken prisoner.

In the night of 6-7 August the Scots withdrew to the north without pursuit.[4] This minor war had cost £70,000.

The manner of Edward II's death was no secret among the nobility and the youthful king certainly blamed Mortimer for it, with dire results as time would tell. On 24 January 1328 the wedding of Edward and Philippa was celebrated in person at York Minster[5] and their new queen was swiftly taken to their hearts by the nobility of England, so different was Philippa's gentle character and generous nature to that of the assertive and acquisitive dowager queen Isabelle, most people seemingly forgetting the ample causes Edward II had given her to take care of herself in the face of his neglect and insults. Philippa, in contrast, seemed the embodiment of the passive feminine virtues of humility, obedience, modesty, piety and chastity. In the medieval work *speculum dominarum* – the mirror for princesses – which was written for Jeanne de Navarre by her confessor Durand de Champagne about this time, the role of a queen is expressed almost entirely in terms of charitable acts. It reads, in part, 'her reputation for mercy should make her visits a welcome solace to the poor, the oppressed, and the unfortunate', epitomising the queen's 'virtuous love of God, relatives, neighbors, fellow Christians, husband, and children'.[6] Philippa personified all these medieval feminine virtues.

Isabelle negotiated a peace treaty to end the warfare on the northern border that had continued since 1296 in the form of raids, skirmishes and cattle-rustling. The treaty was sealed by Robert the Bruce in Edinburgh on 17 March 1328 and ratified by the English parliament sitting at Nottingham on 1 May. The final ignominy for Mortimer was the acknowledgement in the treaty that all English claims of hegemony over Scotland were dropped. A betrothal and marriage being the conventional way of sealing the new alliance, Isabelle's daughter Joan of the Tower was married in York Minster on 17 July 1328 to Robert the Bruce's son David. She was 7 years old and her groom even younger. One year later, after the death of his father on 7 June 1329, 5-year-old David Bruce became king of Scotland, although not formally crowned at Scone Abbey until November 1331. The death of King Robert at the manor of Cardross near Dumbarton, one month before his fifty-fifth birthday, was a mystery. Scandalous English rumours that he had suffered from leprosy, syphilis and other unpleasant diseases can be discounted; the theory of his Milanese physician Maino de Maineri was that the Bruce, who ate well, had been killed by eating a large meal of partially cooked eels, whose blood is poisonous to humans, but this sounds like a re-run of the death of Henry I after eating a surfeit of lampreys.

On 15 June 1330 Edward III and Philippa had a son. Possibly, this had something to do with a decision he took four months later. On 19 October he decided to take direct action against Mortimer, who was staying with Isabelle at Nottingham castle. A band of twenty-three armed men commanded by Edward and his associate William Montagu entered the castle by a secret passage and took Mortimer by surprise. He had been planning to arrest Montagu, but had missed his chance. There was a brief but bloody passage of arms before Mortimer was overpowered. Fearing that he would be slain on the spot, Isabelle threw herself on the floor in front of Edward, crying, 'Fair son, have pity on gentle Mortimer!'[7]

To complete the operation, Henry of Lancaster's troops rapidly took control of the whole castle, blocking any chance of Mortimer's escape or rescue. He was tried in the following month and found guilty on fourteen charges of treason, including the murder of Edward II. The accusation covered most of the long-term political grievances against Isabelle as regent, all now blamed on her 'partner in crime'. Sentenced by parliament to be drawn and hanged as a traitor, Mortimer was hanged at Tyburn on 29 November but, by the clemency of Edward III, not subjected to the tortures and indignities often imposed on executed traitors. Although confined in Windsor castle for several months until escorted to her own property at Castle Rising in Norfolk, Isabelle was never accused of any wrongdoing during the regency. True, her immense riches accumulated during that period had to be returned to the state, but she was given the generous allowance of £3,000 per annum by Edward III,[8] which made her appropriately rich for England's dowager queen.

With Mortimer's death and his mother's internal exile at Castle Rising, Edward III could at last feel that he was truly king. In 1332 Edward Balliol had seized the throne of Scotland with the support of Edward III, but then been driven out of Scotland. Edward III decided to take this as a challenge and besiege the border town of Berwick-on-Tweed. A small holding force laid siege in March 1333, joined in May by Edward at the head of an English army. Philippa travelled with him, but was left safely in Bamburgh castle, twenty miles to the south, while the army took up a position on Halidon Hill, a commanding site two miles to the southwest of Berwick. To confirm a truce, Edward took hostages including the son of Sir Alexander Seton, the Scottish commander of Berwick. Considering that Seton was not abiding by the terms of the truce, he announced that he would hang two of the hostages on each day the town continued to hold out. One of the first two hanged in sight of the walls was Thomas, Seton's own son.

A large Scottish army advanced to lift the siege, to avoid Seton having shortly to surrender the town. Attacking the English on Halidon Hill on 19 July, the Scots suffered so bad a defeat that Berwick surrendered the next day. Balliol was reinstalled as king of Scotland after ceding a large part of southern Scotland to Edward III and agreeing to do homage for the rest of his kingdom. To safeguard the lives of the two children David Bruce and Joan of the Tower, they were sent into the care of King Philippe VI de Valois in Paris, the Scots and French being longtime allies. During their absence from Britain, David's cause attracted more support in Scotland, so that he and Joan were able to return home when, aged 17, he could rule in his own right. The cross-border warfare continuing, he was taken prisoner in County Durham in October 1346, and remained in English captivity for eleven years, during which Edward III allowed his sister Joan to visit her husband confined in the Tower of London. If Edward's purpose was to get Joan pregnant – perhaps to keep hostage a child of David by her – it failed, despite a number of conjugal visits. Whether or not this weighed on Philippa's mind as tarnishing her husband's soul, we cannot know.

Although Isabelle never regained political power in England, she did serve her son the king in France, agreeing on his behalf with Charles IV a settlement of the quarrel over Gascony that upped a previous offer for the territory of £60,000 by a further 50,000 marks, with an amnesty for the Gascon rebels who had been fighting the French king, except for eight named knights who were banished and their castles destroyed. Pushing her luck in France, when her brother Charles IV died in February 1328 leaving no male heir, Isabelle slightly bent the rules of feudal succession with the argument that, since her son Edward III was a nephew of the dead French king and his closest male relative, being a descendant in direct line through her of Philippe IV, he should therefore inherit the throne of France. The claim did not succeed.

In 1337 Philippe VI seized Edward III's Continental territories of Gascony and Ponthieu. Instead of seeking a peaceful resolution to the conflict by paying homage to the French king as his father had done, Edward reiterated his claim to the French crown as the grandson of Charles IV, but this failed and the Hundred Years' War exploded with a resounding English victory at Sluys near Bruges on 24 June 1340. The French had been attacking English shipping in the wine trade with Gascony and the wool trade with Flanders, and also raiding south and east coast towns, Portsmouth, Southampton and Hastings among them, while the English raided Boulogne, Dieppe, Le Tréport and Mers. With no fleet of his own, at the time Edward had only one warship, two others having been captured earlier. To compensate for the lack of a professional navy, English ship-owners had their vessels pressed into service, for which they were to be paid *post bellum*, but Edward underpaid and paid late, so those ship-owners who could fail to answer his summons, did so, with the result that he had only at most 150 ships. Partly for this reason, he was in a foul mood before the battle even began.

The majority of these pressed ships were cogs: high-freeboard, round-hulled merchant vessels with one mast bearing a square-rigged sail. At the assembly point on the river Orwell, the horses originally loaded for the landing of an English army had to be off-loaded and put ashore while fore- and after-castles fitted to the transports as well as crows' nests atop the masts, turning them into temporary warships for an attack on the French fleet. It consisted of 213 ships chained together in threes to make wider fighting platforms, all lined up blocking the inlet at Sluys from bank to bank. Aboard were 20,000 soldiers tasked by Philippe VI to interdict a landing by the English, as he seems to have been unaware that Edward's plan had changed. In addition. there were six Genoese galleys commanded by the Mediterranean pirate Egidio Boccanegra – the remnant of a Genoese flotilla that had mainly deserted because unpaid, whether cheated by their own captains or simply not paid by Charles VII. Being more experienced than either of the aristocratic French commanders, Boccanegra told them their tactics were all wrong, but they did not listen to him because he was not of noble blood.

After sending three knights ashore to effect a reconnaissance of the French position and tactics, in mid-afternoon with the wind and tide in his favour, Edward sailed in to the attack, his longbowmen having a dual advantage over the Genoese crossbowmen in the galleys: they outranged them by 300 yards against the crossbows' 200 yards and each longbowman could loose several arrows in the time it took to fire and re-load a crossbow. In addition, the cogs rode high in the water, so that the English men-at-arms were firing down at the men on the decks of the French ships and catapulting heavy stones onto them.

At the last moment, the French commanders realised that roping and chaining their ships together made it impossible to manoeuvre them and the prevailing wind was driving them ashore in a great confusion. Edward sent his ships into the attack in units of three – two ships full of archers flanking one carrying men-at-arms. The ships with archers came at a French vessel from both sides while raining arrows down on its decks. Once the ships had grappled, combat continued as on land. No firearms yet being available, fighting was by brute force with daggers, swords and cudgels, both the dead and wounded casually heaved overboard on the spot. When both the French commanders had been taken prisoner, one was beheaded and the other hanged from the yardarm of his own ship.

The wind changing direction, an allied Flemish fleet came out to assist the English, provoking panic that apparently caused many French soldiers to throw themselves overboard in desperation. A conservative estimate of the casualties was that 15,000-20,000 men died of wounds or drowning with 170 French ships sunk or taken prizes. The violence of the fighting is illustrated by the fact that only half of the very experienced Genoese galley force managed to escape under Boccanegra.[9] Inhabitants of English coastal towns thought this was the end of French raids, but later that year the reconstituted French fleet raided Portland, Teignmouth, Plymouth, the Channel Islands and the Isle of Wight.

In July 1346 Edward 'took the war to the enemy' by invading Normandy with an army of 15,000 men that sacked the city of Caen and marched across northern France to rendezvous with allied forces in Flanders. On 26 August at Crécy, north of the Somme, he decided to halt and fight off the much larger French army following in pursuit. The resulting English victory was largely attributed to Edward's longbowmen, who fired, not individual aimed shots but barrages that came down near-vertically on the French cavalry, killing both knights and their mounts and causing panic when wounded horses reared and plunged, breaking up the French charges. After the battle, the walled town of Calais was ordered by Philippe VI of France not to surrender to the victorious English. An 11-month siege ensued.

Philippe VI called on Scotland under the 'auld alliance', persuading King David II that, with Edward and his army laying siege to the strategic Channel port and city of Calais with an army of 35,000 men, northern England would be wide open for a diversionary invasion. The siege of Calais had begun on 4 September 1346, but things did not work out as Philippe had foreseen. David invaded in early October, sacking Lanercost and Hexham abbeys. By 17 October he was approaching Durham, still anticipating little resistance. On the following day, the 12,000 invading Scots found themselves at Neville's Cross, an Anglo-Saxon monument outside Durham city, facing an English army of half that size drawn from the counties north of the river Trent under the command of the Wardens of the Marches in the persons of Lord Ralph Neville and Lord Henry Percy.

By the end of the day, the Scots were beaten, King David was wounded and a prisoner. Percy invaded Scotland and conquered much of the south and centre of the country. David was confined for eleven years in the Tower, Windsor, Odiham and other castles – to be released following the Treaty of Berwick in 1357 against a ransom of 100,000 marks, only a fifth of which was ever paid by his bankrupt realm.

With the Scottish border secure, Edward was free to continue the siege of Calais, where the population had been ordered by Philippe VI not to yield. After eleven months, starvation forced a surrender on 3 August 1347. In such circumstances, it was not unusual for the town to be sacked with considerable bloodshed. With an eye to the future strategic value of Calais as a foothold in France – which it was to remain until January 1558 – Edward promised to spare the other citizens if six burghers volunteered to pay the price of this obstinate resistance. He demanded they walk out wearing nooses around their necks in preparation for hanging, carrying the keys to the city and castle to give to him. When the six volunteers emerged, prepared to be hanged, they found an unexpected advocate in Queen Philippa of Hainault, who pleaded with her husband to pardon them, as reported by the French chronicler Froissart. She persuaded Edward III to exercise clemency by claiming that their deaths would cast guilt on the child she was carrying. Sadly, the child Thomas of Windsor survived for only a year.

In 1884 the town of Calais commissioned Auguste Rodin to depict this event in bronze slightly larger than life-size. Installed in 1889, with twelve original copies across the world – one in stunning position on the roof of the Metropolitan Museum of New York – it stands as a fitting memorial Queen Philippa. At the time, public opinion found Rodin's composition lacking in the expected pomp for its initial high pedestal. Later moved to a lower position, it shows his representation of heroic self-sacrifice.

Edward III had set out to repair all the damage caused by his father's reign, both internally in the administration and externally against Scotland and France – and succeeded very largely. However, a new enemy had invaded Europe and was shortly to reach England. There had been many plagues before during recorded history and doubtless also before writing enabled records to be kept, but this one – the Black Death or bubonic plague, associated with a pneumonic plague at the same time – was to kill a third of the population of Europe. Its first recorded appearance in *c.* 542 ravaged the Roman empire of Justinian, and is sometimes called Justinian's plague. Its medieval manifestation began *c.* 1347 in Byzantium and spread clockwise around the Mediterranean littoral, reaching London at the end of 1348 and continuing to Russia by the end of 1350, leaving millions of dead in its path. For whatever reason, there were a few pockets which it missed: the county of Béarn in the Pyrenees was one and most of Poland too. But this disgusting epidemic was still lurking in western Europe in 1665, when it was labelled the Great Plague of London, and it reappeared in China and India, where it killed 6 million or more, as late as 1892–96. Nor was that its final fling. For some reason it struck again in Suffolk in 1910, but rapidly died out,[10] as happened also in New York City in the early 2000s!

One result of the plague in fourteenth-century England was a critical shortage of farm labour. Landowners had to increase wages until parliament introduced the Ordinance of Labourers in 1349 and the Statute of Labourers in 1351 but even these measures could not offset the ravages of the plague, which killed the high-born as cruelly as the labourer and serf. Certainly tax-collectors suffered, being sent into plague areas to collect the king's dues, and often finding no one left alive in small villages and few survivors in the towns. Edward III was reduced to exempting whole areas of the country from previous fiscal obligations because lack of labourers caused a total lack of money. A royal declaration of 1352 stated

> Since the greater part of the said population died while the plague was raging, now, through the dearth of servants and labourers, the inhabitants are oppressed and daily are falling most miserably into greater poverty.[11]

Across the Channel, the situation was equally grim, although France with a population many times greater than England could better afford the plague's cull. One unfortunate victim was Edward III's daughter Princess Joan, who died in 1348 at Bordeaux on her journey to Castile, where she was to be married to the king's son.[12] In the north of France, Gilles le Musis wrote,

> It is almost impossible to credit the mortality throughout the whole country. Travellers, merchants, pilgrims and others who have passed through it declare thay have found cattle roaming without herdsmen in the fields, towns and wastelands, that they have seen barns and wine-cellars standing wide open, houses empty and few people to be found anywhere and, in many areas, both lands and fields are lying uncultivated.[13]

In summer 1349 the plague reached Le Musis' own city of Tournai, where he reported a widespread belief that immoral conduct was to blame. Unmarried couples were forced to marry or separate; swearing, playing at dice and working on the Sabbath were prohibited. New, larger graveyards were opened outside the city walls and the dead, never mind how rich or important they had been in life, were thrown in with the poor. When the flagellants came to the city on their 'crusade', they were numbered at 3,500. Some cities knew far larger flagellant inflows; others closed the gates to forbid them entrance. In 1346 Edward III barred lepers from entering the city of London in deference to the widespread belief that their proximity or breath, or sexual congress with whores in brothels, would contaminate the healthy citizens. Bishop William Edendon of Winchester left a bizarre memorial of the ravages of plague. Having demolished the twin towers of the west end of the Norman cathedral, prior to reconstructing the nave in the Decorated style to his own greater glory, he found neither labourers nor masons to erect the new towers and resorted to erecting two more modest 'temporary' towers that have stood for six centuries.[14]

There were some in London who quite logically connected with the sickness of the inhabitants the practice of throwing excrement, offal, slaughterhouse refuse and putrescent food into the streets of the capital for the rain to wash away. A royal proclamation read the air in the city is very much corrupted and infected, whence abominable and most filthy stinks proceed [and] sicknesses and many other evils have happened to such as have abode in the said city, or have resorted to it, and great dangers are feared to fall out for the time to come unless remedy be presently made against it ...[15]

The proclamation merely moved the problem. For a while, the streets were cleaner, but Edward III later complained of the dumps of 'dung, lay-stalls and other filth' that lined the banks of the Thames, distressing his nostrils as he passed by in the royal barge. The Black Death also made street-cleaning less efficient: there were fewer surviving sweepers and those that still worked were required to transport the thousands of bodies to the cemeteries outside the walls as the first priority.

Although Edward survived, many of his closest associates did not. One by one, his original supporters – can one talk of friends of a king? – were dying off. William Montagu, perhaps the closest of that band of brothers to the king, died in 1344. William de Clinton, who had also stolen into Nottingham castle with him on the fateful night in 1330, died in 1354. William de Bohun, one of the new earls the king had created, died in 1360. The plague did not just come once and die out. It reappeared in England in 1361-2 and claimed the life of Henry de Grosmont, a coeval second cousin of Edward III who had gained important victories for him in Gascony. A patron of learning, he founded Corpus Christi College Cambridge in 1352 and was made the second member of the new Order of the Garter.

Something had happened to Edward III that took the fire out of this king whose early years had promised so much. Since medieval man thought of misfortune as the punishment for disobeying God's will, did he believe that he was somehow to blame for all the deaths? In modern terms, that would be called post-traumatic stress. This king died at the age of 65 after a long illness ended by a stroke in the palace of Sheen on 21 June 1377. Since he had been ill for some years – and Prince Edward was already dead – many of the powers and duties of kingship had in the meantime had been assumed by John of Gaunt. However, by right of primogeniture, succession passed to Edward's son, Prince Richard, who was crowned as Richard II.

Chapter 20

Edward, the Black Prince

The eldest son of Edward III was born in the palace of Woodstock in Oxfordshire on 15 June 1330 and therefore known initially as Edward of Woodstock. A few weeks after his birth, Edward III proposed to betroth his infant son to a daughter of Philippe VI. Whether this might have effected a peaceful rapprochement of the houses of Plantagenet and Valois, we cannot know, but nothing came of it. In his lifetime, Prince Edward was regarded as the epitome of knightly courage and martial enterprise. Although later known to history as the Black Prince, opinions differ as to whether this title came from wearing dark armour in the field or from his ruthless methods in warfare, black being the colour of evil.[1] Since he fought in the main against the possessions of the French kings, this prince is known in Aquitaine as a hero and called in Occitan *lo princi neguer*.

While still three months short of his third birthday, his father gave this first legitimate son the rich earldom and county of Chester to provide funds for the expenses of his household. Two years later, with Edward III convinced that the French were about to invade, Philippa and the children were moved to Nottingham in the north of England[2] and on 9 February 1337 Prince Edward was created duke, the considerable wealth of his duchy of Cornwall being administered by his mother Queen Philippa for bringing up this son and his sisters, the princesses Isabella and Joanna of the Tower.

Edward III began very early this son's education for the kingship that was never to be attained. Towards the end of 1337 the young prince is reputed to have ceremonially welcomed two cardinals to London and conducted them into his father's presence. In July 1338 Edward III appointed him 'guardian of the kingdom' during his absence in Flanders, and later sought to betroth him to a daughter of the duke of Brabant for the sake of an alliance. He entrusted the prince with the same office again in 1340 and 1342. Not too much should be read into this, since the boy prince had little real power, which lay with the Grand Council, but he was getting the feel of state matters. At Westminster on 12 May 1343 Edward III gave the young prince the title Prince of Wales. It was obvious to his contemporaries that the king intended a great future for this son.

At the beginning of August 1345 Henry of Lancaster landed an army of 500 men-at-arms, 1,000 archers and 500 Welsh foot-soldiers in Bordeaux and took the city of Bergerac by the end of the month. The campaign was made profitable by the ransoms for several hundred prisoners. Joined by another English army led by Henry de Grosmont, earl of Derby, he besieged Perigueux with a force of 2,000 men-at-arms and 5,000 archers and foot-soldiers. A French army of 3,000 men-at-arms and 6,000 foot-soldiers was sent to relieve the city but stopped eleven miles away to besiege the castle of Auberoche. There, on 21 October Henry of Lancaster took it by surprise and defeated it, gaining more ransoms to fill his coffers. He continued to reduce one *bastide* or walled town after another until all the territory between the tidal reaches of the Garonne and the Dordogne[3] had been conquered with the exception of La Réole, which yielded on 8 November with the exception of the citadel. It surrendered five weeks later.

Philippe IV's eldest son Prince Jean, duke of Normandy, seemed unable to outwit or outfight the Anglo-Gascon troops, which caused numerous Gascon lords and bishops to transfer their allegiance back to Edward III as duke of Aquitaine. So, while French revenues from the southwest declined catastrophically, Edward III found himself the richer by £70,000 from all the ransoms. To raise another army, King Philippe borrowed from Italian bankers and even the pope, sending Duke Jean south again in the spring of 1346 to reverse his losses with an army of something like 15,000 men including mercenaries, among them 1,400 Genoese crossbowmen. In the north Edward III knighted 16-year-old Prince Edward soon after landing in France. To prove his worth as a warrior prince, Edward then led a raid down the whole length of the Cotentin peninsula, leaving devastation and thousands of starving civilians behind him before taking the city of Caen.

Also in spring 1346 Duke Jean travelled south to lay siege to Angoulême and nearby Aiguillon with an army variously estimated as high as 15,000 men including the 1,400 Genoese crossbowmen.

He succeeded in taking Angoulême but found the tables turned with his army in the centre of a wide zone of scorched earth, in which there was neither food for men nor fodder for horses. So, he had to abandon the plan to besiege Aiguillon at the end of August, and headed north, summoned by Philippe VI to repel Edward III's invasion of Normandy.

At the battle of Crécy on 26 August 1346, Prince Edward was given command of the English right wing at the head of some 4,000 men, and was for a time in real danger due to his youthful impetuosity. Although begged by the prince's companions to send help, on learning that he was not wounded Edward III refused. The prince was unhorsed and could have been killed, had not he been rescued by his standard bearer, who beat back the immediate attackers and gave his master the respite to regain his feet. When father met son after the battle, they embraced: each had conducted himself as was proper. Among the French casualties was King Johannes of Bohemia, whose emblem had been three ostrich feathers and the motto *Ich dien* – I serve. As a token of respect to the fallen monarch, Prince Edward adopted these as his own emblem and they continue to be the arms of the princes of Wales up to the present. Prince Edward returned to England with his father on 12 October 1347, indulging in tournaments and other courtly activities and being invested with the new Order of the Garter, a privilege that had been conferred on few. With the advent of *mors atra* – the Black Death – mortalities in Edward III's family included Princess Joan and the princes Thomas and William.

At the end of 1349 Prince Edward took part in his father's capture of Calais, famously leading his household knights in serving the meat course to his father and the VIP prisoners at the top table before sitting down at a less prestigious table with his knights.[4] If that seemed like princely gallantry at the time, the true face of medieval war was his laying waste of the city's hinterland within a radius of thirty miles, leaving the adult inhabitants to starve and watch their children and old folk die. The return of the plague caused a halt in campaigning, but in the following year Prince Edward's younger brother John of Gaunt also had to win his spurs. On 28 August 1350 the two princes embarked at Winchelsea with Edward III, but in a separate vessel, to drive off the Castilian fleet of Carlos de la Cerda blockading English ports on behalf of France. When battle was joined, the princes' ship was grappled by a much larger Castilian vessel, which proved to be good luck, as their overloaded vessel was sinking, many of its hull timbers being rotten. Thus saved from drowning, their second piece of luck was to find the Castilian ship attacked from its other side by Henry of Grosmont. The Castilians either killed or thrown overboard, the encounter was a timely victory for England, allowing the crew of the princes' ship to leap aboard as their vessel was untied and sank out of sight.[5]

On the death of Philippe VI, his son Jean II de Valois, known as Jean le Bon, was crowned in Reims cathedral on 26 September 1350, just four days after his father's death. He inherited a kingdom with very similar problems to those of England: the plague, a consequent shortage of agricultural labour and difficulties in collecting taxes with so many subjects of all classes dead, plus other economic problems. Although he liked to hunt, the new French king was of fragile health and avoided tournaments, preferring books, paintings and music. His was not the personality of a successful medieval king, and his consequent unpopularity was increased by a tendency to shut himself away with a few familiars, instead of holding spectacular tournaments or parliaments. As though all this was not enough, across the Channel Edward III disputed his title to the throne of France and, to the south of disaffected Gascony, King Charles of Navarre also contended for the throne.

Life for a prince between wars was not all play. In 1353 Prince Edward as earl of Chester rode with Henry de Grosmont, duke of Lancaster, to the neighbourhood of Chester, where

> the Cheshire Men having committed Insolence or Riot against the Servants of the Prince of Wales ... the King was much incensed against them and resolved to make them submit to the Law or the Sword, sent ... two of his Justices itinerant to sit in Eyre upon them and, at the same time, ordered sufficient Forces under the leading of his son the Prince of Wales ... to go thither to prevent any Violence or Insurrection. But the Cheshire Men, knowing themselves at Fault, compounded with the Prince of Wales their Lord for five Thousand and sixty Marks, to be paid within four Years and gave such Security as the Prince desired, on Condition that the Justices should no longer continue the Circuit of Eyre upon them.[6]

The Law always has another trick up its sleeve. Just when the Cheshire Men thought they had arranged everything, the justices opened an inquisition of trailbaston, or pursuit of brigands, and imposed large fines, seizing offenders' houses and land for the prince, who salved his conscience, if he had one, by giving a tenth of the proceeds to rebuild the neglected abbey church in Vale Royal on his way home.[7]

Deciding in 1355 to reactivate the war against France, Edward III ordered Prince Edward to 'restore order' in Aquitaine while he and the king of Navarre attacked Normandy and Duke Henry of Lancaster invaded Brittany. Many of the Aquitaine vassals agreed to support Edward, not from loyalty but a greed for plunder. Given the newly created title Prince of Aquitaine,[8] Edward prepared to depart at the end of June, but was detained by contrary winds until 8 September – rather late in the year to start a war. With him sailed about 300 ships carrying four earls of the realm, 1,000 men-at-arms, 2,000 archers and 'a large body' of Welsh infantry. With the Gascon lords assembled at Bordeaux eager to make a short campaign before winter set in, on 10 October Edward set off with a considerable force: his 2,000 archers, 3,000 infantry and 1,500 mounted men-at-arms. Although presented as an attack on territory of the French Crown, the *chevauchée* was nothing short of a raid to the east of Aquitaine, penetrating right through the county of Toulouse, laying waste the fields and orchards and killing entire peasant families, to reach the Mediterranean at Narbonne. Plundering as they went, the small but fast-moving army ignored well-defended cities and left alone others that could afford to buy it off. When a papal envoy caught up with him, pleading for an end to the slaughter, Prince Edward pretended that he could not stop the marauding before he received 'his father's instructions'. It was the onset of winter that ended the two-month march with the return to Bordeaux, laden with booty.

After some respite, at the beginning of next July Prince Edward rode out from Bordeaux heading northward with the aim of rampaging through the heart of France and joining up with his father's current ally Charles II of Navarre in Normandy. As on the previous expedition, he laid waste a vast swathe of the land through which he travelled in Auvergne, the Limousin and Berry. Having failed to take the city of Bourges in the very centre of France, he headed west, leaving a trail of bloodshed, before learning that he could not cross the river Loire, well defended by the French troops of King Jean II. By the second week of September, the English-Welsh-Gascon army was being pursued through Berry by Jean II. Then suddenly the French were ahead, between Edward and the city of Poitiers. On Sunday 18 September Cardinal Talleyrand of Périgord intervened. Edward was prepared to give up the fortresses and cities he had taken, release his prisoners and agree a truce of seven years with Jean II. But the French king, whose vassal he technically was, insisted on the surrender of Edward and 100 of his knights, to pay for their treason in attacking him. To this, Edward would not agree.

The next day, battle was joined outside Poitiers, ending in mid-afternoon with 11,000 French dead and 100 counts and barons taken prisoner with Jean II and his youngest son Prince Philippe. Coming after Sluys, Crécy and Calais, the English victory at Poitiers was bad news indeed for the French. After the battle Edward earned a reputation for chivalry by insisting on serving King Jean and his nobles at table, no one present caring too much about the 2,500 French dead and nearly 2,000 prisoners taken by Edward at the battle.

France was in chaos with its king a prisoner of the English. The states general even considered putting Charles of Navarre on the throne, only being thwarted by the dauphin, future Charles V, taking power as regent. First held at Bordeaux, which Prince Edward's triumphant army reached on 2 October to the acclamations of the population, the French king had to twiddle his thumbs while Edward's men spent on festivities much of the booty they had accumulated. On 23 March 1357 the prince concluded a two years' truce so that he could return to England, leaving the duchy under the control of four Gascon lords. So great was their anger at his intention to take Jean II with him that he had to buy their compliance with 100,000 crowns. The prince and his prisoner landed at Plymouth on 4 May and reached London on 24 May, King Jean II riding a costly white horse, while he rode a very ordinary black palfrey, presumably to show that a prince had conquered a king.

Jean II was later transferred to the palace known as the Hôtel de Savoie on the river at London in conditions of some luxury, together eventually with a court of several hundred persons, some taken prisoner at Poitiers and others who came of their own free will to be at the French court-in-exile. In the autumn of 1359 Edward III invaded France again to claim the throne, but was defeated, not by French force of arms, but by logistics. Conditions are hard to imagine in the wasted territory of the north, where his army could neither find food for men nor pasturage for animals. Usually attributed to Napoleon, the saying, *'C'est la soupe qui fait le soldat,'* rendered in English as 'an army marches on its stomach', sums up a truth known for centuries. Either one takes sufficient provisions with the army or finds it by force on the campaign, but even threatened at sword-point the starving civilians had nothing to give up. On 13 April 1360, known as Black Monday, the misery culminated in a catastrophic storm causing floods, and Edward III decided that it was better to negotiate a treaty, which became the Treaty of Brétigny ratified by Jean II and Edward III that October in Calais. Edward claimed back many of the formerly Plantagenet Continental territories: Aquitaine – then known as Guyenne – plus Saintonge, the Agenais, the Limousin, Perigord, Quercy and Ponthieu, making altogether a third of France as it then was.

It is now generally acknowledged that destroying the entire economy of the defeated power is unintelligent, but in the Middle Ages the science of economics was unknown and punitive terms were the rule. The culminating damage to France was the ransom required for Jean II: 4 million *écus*, later reduced to 3 million, equivalent to 12 tons of gold. He managed to raise 400,000 *écus* and was allowed to return to France after leaving numerous important hostages as security and promising to pay the balance within a year, which was impossible. After a renewed campaign in 1359 was inconclusive, the Treaty of Bretigny in 1360 saw Jean le Bon freed and Edward III renouncing all claims to the French throne while being guaranteed full sovereignty over his current Continental possessions. Raising the ransom had caused so many economic problems for Jean II that he had to devalue the currency and introduce the *franc* – an unpopular move.

Prince Edward was 31 in 1361 when he married his 33-year-old second cousin Countess Joan of Kent, their consanguinity requiring papal sanction. Joan was widely reputed for her beauty and already had quite a history, having married 26-year-old Lord Thomas Holland when herself aged only 12 without obtaining the royal consent necessary for persons of their rank. After Holland left for the wars in Flanders and France, Joan's disapproving family arranged her marriage to the earl of Salisbury's son William Montagu, both spouses being 13 years old. Holland returned to England in about

1348, told Edward III about his marriage to Joan and appealed to the pope to arrange her return to him. Learning of this, her second husband, now earl of Salisbury himself, kept Joan under house arrest for several months until Pope Clement VI annulled his marriage, enabling Joan to return to her first husband. Over the next eleven years, she bore him five children. Two having died, she was a widow with three living children when marrying Prince Edward, in a ceremony of some magnificence. He had previously fathered at least four illegitimate sons. By his mistress Edith of Willesford he had a son christened Roger, whose silver spoon in the mouth at birth became tarnished: he ended as Sir Roger Clarendon, hanged and beheaded for treason by King Henry IV in 1402. Three other sons by unknown mothers were called Edward, John and Charles. Setting up his household with Joan in Berkhamsted Palace, it may have seemed that Prince Edward's warlike passions might be put on hold in this family setting. Such was not to be.

Also in 1361, Edward's brother Prince Lionel, duke of Clarence, was given the title Earl of Ulster and sailed to Ireland. An imposing fellow standing nearly 7 feet tall, he failed to impose his rule on the dissident Anglo-Norman lords of the country and abandoned the attempt in 1366. In contrast with Prince Edward's record of campaigns and martial enterprise, Lionel's main claim to lasting fame was as employer of Geoffrey Chaucer, retained as a clerk in his household.

Prince Edward departed from England with his family, sailing to La Rochelle with Joan in 1363 to set up court in Bordeaux. Ordered by his father to destroy the bands of unemployed mercenaries plundering the duchy and restore order, he found that many of the barons of Aquitaine, traditionally resentful of their overlords, refused to recognise this 'English prince', to pay their taxes and pledge allegiance to, or fight for, him. On only one principle they did agree: a refusal to sign up for a new crusade. The unfortunate King Jean of France returned to London in January 1364 to renegotiate the Treaty of Brétigny, but died there three months later. The leader of the bands of *routiers* came mostly from England or Gascony and so did not ravage Aquitaine, but used it as a safe haven in between their marauding in French territory. Accordingly on 14 November 1364 Edward III called upon Prince Edward to restrain their ravages, which were causing diplomatic problems.

PLANTAGENET PRINCES

It may have been Prince Edward's repression of the Gascon *routiers* that drove them to take service in the French warlord Bertrand du Guesclin's invasion of Castile. This forced King Pedro – who would have been Prince Edward's brother-in-law if Princess Joan had not died on the journey from England – to flee his realm, leaving his bastard half-brother Enrique de Trastámara to take the throne. Begging Prince Edward for military assistance, Pedro arrived at Bayonne with his family. Against the advice of his Gascon vassals, Edward declared grandly that a bastard should not inherit a kingdom in preference to the legitimate monarch. From London came Edward III's endorsement, leading the Gascon lords to agree to serve in Castile, providing their pay was guaranteed. Pedro had few funds, so Edward agreed to lend him the necessary finance, including 100,000 francs his father had received in Jean II's ransom. It was a complicated deal. Put simply, once restored, Pedro was to gift the province of Vizcaya to Edward, enabling him to reach the fortress of Castro Urdiales on the western border of Vizcaya, whose attraction was – as it had been for the Emperor Vespasian when he founded it and would be again for Napoleon in the Peninsula War – in the rich deposits of iron ore there. As surety, Pedro had to leave his three daughters hostage in Aquitaine. That Christmas in Bordeaux Prince Edward's wife gave birth to a son christened Richard, whose destiny it was to inherit the throne of England which his father failed to do.

Prince Edward left for the war in February 1367 reinforced with 400 men-at-arms and 400 archers from England under his brother John of Gaunt. Hearing he was coming to fight for Pedro, the Gascon *routiers* changed sides and joined him. With their help, he won the decisive battle of Nájera on 3 April 1367. Instead of being humbly grateful for the restoration of his kingdom, Pedro invented excuses for not handing over Vizcaya and not repaying the loan. While waiting through the hot summer on poor rations, many of Prince Edward's force fell ill and he contracted the disease that would kill him.

Back north of the Pyrenees, Edward was in debt and reduced to asking the Three Estates in the Parlamant de Guiyana – the bishops, the nobles and the towns – to approve a *fouage* or hearth tax of forty *sous* per taxable hearth to fill his empty coffers. This was reduced to twenty, and then ten *sous* per hearth, to be levied for five years but by no means all collected. Gaston Phébus the count of Foix who refused to swear fealty for Béarn was one of many vassals who protested, '*Et touz jours a il esperance que ses subgiz aideront a ses besoigns.*' He is always hoping his vassals will help him out. That idea conflicted with the principle in the realm of France that *Le roi doit vivre du sien* – the king must live from his own income,[9] i.e. the revenue from his personal possessions. Yet at the *parlamant* held in Périguex in September-October 1365 the bishop of Sarlat, Austens de Ste-Colombe, compared Prince Edward to Christ the son of God. Even Edward found that a bit of an overstatement.[10]

In April 1369 Edward found himself in open warfare with the new French monarch Charles V. The most notable event of this war was his capture of Limoges in 1370. At that time Limoges castle and its *citat* or citadel were two separate fortifications. Bishop Jehan de Cros was approached by emissaries of Charles V to surrender the city on terms. On 23 August 1370 he opened the gates to the French troops commanded by Duke Jean of Berry, which infuriated Prince Edward, increasingly short-tempered and ill with the amoebic dysentery – then known as 'the bloody flux' – that would kill him. Seventy-five miles to the west at Angoulême, Edward and John of Gaunt had an army of 1,200 men-at-arms, 1,000 archers and 3,000 infantry. Edward was in fact so ill that he could not mount or ride a horse and had to be transported in a litter slung between two horses. Nevertheless, regarding Bishop Jehan's treason as a personal insult, he wished to be present at an exemplary sack of the city. With the two princes were several war-hardened nobles from England and Aquitaine. They arrived outside Limoges city in the second week of September, when Edward ordered the undermining of its walls. On 19 September, his miners succeeded in demolishing a large section of wall which filled the dry moat with rubble. The town was then stormed through the breach, with the usual destruction and loss of life. A local chronicler summed up what happened then:

> *En l'an mil CCC LXX a XIX de septembre fut preise et ardude la Citat et meis a mort may de IIIc personas a cause de la rébellion qu'avian fach contre mossen Oudouart, duc d'Aquitaine.*

The *citat* was taken and burned and more than 300 persons put to death for their rebellion against the Lord Edward, duke of Aquitaine. Half of the unfortunate 300 were the inadequate garrison left by the duke of Berry, the others just citizens who got in the way. A later account put the number of dead at 1,800 and the famous chronicler Jean Froissart blew this up for the greater glory of Edward, averring that 3,000 were put to death. Bishop Jehan was not among them, having managed to get himself elected to the college of cardinals, presumably because he was a nephew of Pope Gregory XI.

The death of Prince Edward's 10-year-old son Edward of Angoulême, coming on top of his illness, left the bereaved father distraught. Returning to Southampton in early January 1371, he met his father at Windsor in time to prevent him ratifying a treaty with Charles of Navarre, afterwards retiring to his palace at Berkhampsted, a very sick and discredited prince. In remission during April 1376, he took part in the 'Good Parliament', which attempted to correct abuses of the administration, and refused to accept substantial bribes offered by the guilty Crown servants. Perhaps that stress was part of the cause of a rapid worsening of his condition.[11] Begging the king to protect his eldest surviving son Richard, who was about to become crown prince, he died in the Palace of Westminster[12] on 8 June 1376, aged 45. His body eventually reached Canterbury cathedral on 29 September and was there entombed. Above the bronze effigy still to be seen on the tomb are replicas of his surcoat, helmet, shield, and gauntlets, the originals being preserved in a glass case nearby.

Chapter 21

Richard II

Edward the Black Prince never became king because his father Edward III was still alive when he died in 1376. After the death of Edward III on 21 June of the following year, the custom of primogeniture required that the succession pass to his eldest surviving son or the issue thereof, and not to the next eldest surviving son of the dead king, who would have been John of Gaunt. The Black Prince's son, 10-year-old Prince Richard had been born in Bordeaux on 6 January 1367 and became the eighth Plantagenet king and effectively the last one, England being rent by the Wars of the Roses both before and after his death. The members of both houses of parliament feared that John of Gaunt, who had acquired much power during the king's last years, might usurp the throne, and hastily prepared the coronation of young Prince Richard, which took place on 16 July at Westminster.

To 'guide' – in fact to control – the actions of the boy-king, the parliament nominated a series of counsellors, from which John of Gaunt was excluded. So eventually were the first counsellors, being replaced by men nominated by parliament in January 1380. In adult life, Richard was tall and well built, but certainly not in the same mold as his father and grandfather. Some have accused him of being slightly mad, but today's verdict would most likely be that he had some characteristics perhaps unfortunate in a medieval monarch. He preferred to keep a small court of like-minded men, where art and culture were appreciated and warlike speech not encouraged.

The first crisis of the new reign came in 1381. The so-called Peasants' Revolt merits a volume to itself. In brief, life for the peasants held in serfdom[1] had always been hard but, after the Black Death reduced their numbers, roughly half the previous mass of agricultural labourers were expected to do the same amount of work. Although wages generally increased by 40 per cent, inflation consumed much of the difference. At the same time, the common people of the countryside were aware that ordinary working folk in the towns – many of whom were, or were descended from, runaway serfs – were acquiring more and more political power. The taxes levied by the king brought no advantages to either class as they had been largely spent on the enforcement of order and the long succession of pointless wars in France. Maintaining the English garrisons in Calais and Brest alone cost £36,000 per annum and sending an army to France cost up to another £100,000 a year. Such justice as there was in the countryside, was in the control of local gentry, who could impose on recalcitrant peasants penalties including branding with hot iron and imprisonment.

The timing of the revolt was important. The king was still a 14-year-old lad acting under the guidance of his uncles and other counsellors. His armed forces in England were mainly held in the north of the country, preparing for a Scottish invasion, and his most experienced military leaders were abroad. In November 1380 the parliament was informed that there was a hole in the Crown's budget which required immediately raising by taxation the enormous sum of £16,000. A *third* poll tax fell far short and royal commissioners were despatched nationwide to identify and punish those who refused to pay up. This caused resentment and violence against the commissioners, caught up in which, John of Gaunt narrowly escaped being lynched in London. Paranoia of the nobility led to a fear that a French invasion could cause the entire lower classes to rise up in support of the invaders. On 30 May 1381 the degree of violence against tax collectors grew to riot proportions. Four days later a mob several thousand strong was marching towards London and on 7 June a man named Wat Tyler was popularly hailed as the leader of the revolt. Under his command, they first occupied the city and castle of Canterbury, opening the prison and executing many they thought enemies of their cause. Next morning, Wat Tyler and several thousand supporters set off on the old pilgrim road to London, encountering on the way Philippa de Hainault, the widow of Edward III, and insulting her without doing any physical harm.

At Blackheath outside London a radical priest named John Ball preached a sermon. Being an educated man, he was careful to avoid accusations of treason by stressing that he and his listeners were the true friends of King Richard, while his courtiers were the king's real enemies. The bishop of Rochester, sent to clerically outrank Ball and urge them all to return home, was shouted down and hastily turned tail to save his skin. News of this reaching King Richard at Windsor castle on the night of 10 June caused him to take the royal barge down-river with his intimate courtiers to the safety of the Tower, where they decided that he should meet the rebels at Greenwich, on the river below Blackheath, for a parley. Guarded by four boatloads of men-at-arms, he was rowed down-river on the morning of 13 June, and had a brief long-distance exchange, terminated by his understandable refusal to step ashore. That afternoon, the rebels entered the city, the gates being opened for them by sympathetic Londoners. More or less at the same time another mob arrived at the Aldgate, also opened for them, and swept into the streets of the capital, where many sympathisers joined them. Targets of their violence included inevitably foreigners and anyone associated with the administration. Moving west, they destroyed the Savoy Palace owned by John of Gaunt, first emptying it of valuables, which they threw into the river to show they were not thieves and robbers, and then set fire to it. That evening, safely inside the Tower, the king and his inner circle watched the houses burning in the city and outside.

We know little about Richard's education, largely supervised by two of his father's courtiers. In 1388 a group of nobles, perhaps fearing that this close-knit pair might lead him astray as had Edward II's coterie, constituted themselves the Lords Appellant under a vague principle of law to prosecute their king's favourites.[2] Originally three in number, Duke Thomas of Gloucester, an uncle of Richard, Earl Richard fitzAlan of Arundel and Surrey and Earl Thomas of Warwick. To these were later added John of Gaunt's son Henry Bolinbroke and Earl Thomas of Nottingham. They established what was effectively a commission of regency valid for one year counted from 13 November 1386, but went further in lanching an armed rebellion against Richard in 1387. After they defeated the royal army at Radcot bridge outside Oxford, they reduced him to a titular king with no real power, and attacked his favourites in what was called 'the merciless parliament' of 1388. Archbishop Alexander of York had all his worldly wealth confiscated. Earl Robert de Vere of Oxford and Lord Chancellor Earl Michael de la Pole of Suffolk were condemned to death *in absentio*, having fled the realm in time. But the Lord Chief Justice, the Lord Mayor of London and several others were both condemned and executed.

PLANTAGENET PRINCES

When John of Gaunt returned to England in 1389 after his failed attempts to claim the throne of Castile in right of his second wife – which had cost him two daughters traded for treaties – things looked up for Richard, who bent his best efforts to revenge himself on the Lords Appellant. Arundel was beheaded. Gloucester was murdered in captivity in Calais, reputedly on Richard's orders. Warwick lost his title and lands, being imprisoned on the Isle of Man until Richard's reign ended. Both Mowbray and Henry Bolingbroke, duke of Lancaster – although a son of John of Gaunt – were exiled. In June 1399, while Richard II was on campaign in Ireland, Bolingbroke secretly returned to England with a few supporters, whose numbers rapidly grew, enabling him eventually to capture and imprison Richard II. He never reappeared, dying in prison, probably murdered on Bolingbroke's orders. John of Gaunt dying in February 1399, the parliament recognised Bolingbroke's right to the throne as a descendant of Edward III. On 13 October 1399 he was crowned Henry IV at Westminster abbey and made history by taking the coronation oath in English, marking the end of the Plantagenet dynasty of French-speaking kings, a transition emphasised when his son Henry V was also literate in English.[3]

Acknowledgements

The author thanks Jennifer Weller for the maps, Joe Gordon for the photograph of Conway castle and Rosemary Dyson for that of the Black Prince's effigy in Canterbury cathedral. All other photographs in this book are taken from the author's archives. If any copyright has been unwittingly infringed, please communicate with the author, care of the publisher. Additional research and photo reconnaissance was carried out in Bristol by Ted Turner and in St Albans by Jon Mein and Tony Berk, two very active members of St Albans and Hertfordshire Architectural and Archeological Society.

Thanks are also due to Series Editor Dr Danna Messer and at Pen & Sword Books, commissioning editor Claire Hopkins and production coordinator Laura Hirst.

Notes and Sources

Chapter 1: The life of princes

1. *Jordan Fantosme Chronicle*, ed. R.C. Johnston, Oxford Medieval Texts, 1981, lines 443-6, 449.
2. Although modern usage of the expression dates back only to Ludendorff's 1935 memoir of the First World War, *Der Totale Krieg*.
3. A comprehensive illustrative commentary on the tapestry may be found in R.H. Bloch, *A Needle in the Right Hand of God*, London: Random House, 2006.
4. D. Boyd, *Normandy's Nightmare War*, Barnsley: Pen & Sword Books 2019.
5. Although one recovered from the wreck of the *Mary Rose* measured 6ft 11in.
6. Similarly, modern saddles are padded at the sides, to spare the horse's spine.
7. See, in greater detail, D. Boyd, *Lionheart*, Stroud: The History Press 2014, pp. 214-17.
8. E. Oakeshott, *A Knight and his Weapons*, Chester Springs: Dufour 1997, pp. 29-32.
9. A comprehensive description of medieval arms and armour may be found in *War and Combat 1150–1270* by C. Hanley, Woodbridge: Boydell 1972.

Chapter 2: The death of kings

1. *Saga of Edward the Confessor*, London: Rolls Series 1894, Vol. III, pp. 424-8.
2. R. Bartlett, *England under the Norman and Angevin Kings 1075–1225*, Oxford: Oxford University Press 2000, p. 160-2.

3. R. Wickson, *Kings and Bishops in Medieval England 1066–1216*: London, Macmillan Palgrave 2015, pp. 3-5.
4. The epithet being Anglo-Norman for 'little boots', a reference to his short stature, unfortunately as in Caligula!
5. C. Warren Hollister, *The Strange Death of William Rufus* in *Speculum* (1973), pp. 637-53.
6. Succession to those 'born into the purple'.
7. Also known by her Anglo-Saxon name Edith, being descended from the West Saxon nobility.
8. Some sources say £10,000 or even £15,000.
9. It was thought by many that the crew was drunk, having been plied with alcohol by the noble passengers.
10. Called Foulkes in French sources.
11. Hollister, *Henry I*, New Haven: Yale University Press 2003, pp. 467-8.

Chapter 3: The civil war

1. *The Annals of Roger of Hoveden*, tr. H.T. Riley, London: H.G. Bohn 1853, Vol. I, pp. 243, 244.
2. *fitz* was a corruption of the Latin *filius* meaning 'son of'.
3. For a fuller account of the crusade, see D. Boyd, *April Queen: Eleanor of Aquitaine*, Stroud: The History Press 2011, pp. 62-102.

Chapter 4: The crusader queen

1. '*Elle était de celles-là qui aiment à être battues.*' A. Richard, *Histoire des Comtes de Poitou at Ducs d'Aquitaine*, Paris: Picard et Fils 1903, Vol. II, p. 110.
2. Ibid, p. 114.
3. Ibid, p. 115.
4. Although, when the author was growing up there, nobody in Faversham seemed to realise that Stephen's former port might have displaced London as the capital. Local memories went back only as far as the explosion of the powder mill in April 1916 when 200 tons of TNT ignited and killed 115 men and boys working there.
5. Richard, *Histoire*, p. 116.

6. Ibid, p. 115.
7. Dom J. Vaissete, *Abrégé de l'Histoire générale de Longuedoc*, Paris 1799, Vol. III, p. 87.

Chapter 5: Prince Henry

1. Gervase of Tilbury, *Otia imperialia*, eds. S.E. Banks and J.W. Binns, Oxford: Clarendon Press 2002, pp. 486-7.
2. Walter Map, *De nugis curialium*, eds. M.R. James, C.N.L. Brooke and R.A.B. Mynors, Oxford: Oxford University Press 1983, pp. 282-3.
3. *Opera Historica: The Historical Works of Master Ralph de Diceto, Dean of London*, ed. W. Stubbs, London: Rolls Series 1876, Vol. II, p. 19.
4. *Giraldus Cambrensis Opera*, ed. J.S. Brewer, Vol. I, London: Longman, Green and Longman and Roberts 1861, p. 355.
5. *Chronica magistri Rogeri de Hoveden*, ed. W. Stubbs, London: Rolls Series 1868–71, Vol. II, p. 46.
6. *Rotuli litterarum clausarum*, ed. T.D. Hardy, London: Eyre & Spottiswood 1833, Vol. I, p. 175b.
7. Richard, *Histoire*, p. 122.
8. Ibid, p. 124.
9. P. Bouquet, *Recueil des historiens des Gaules et de la France*, Poitiers: Oudin 1878, Vol. XVI, p. 1.
10. William fitz Stephen, *Life of Becket*, ed. J.C. Robertson, London: Rolls Series No 67, Vol. III, p. 29.
11. Sometimes called Neufmarché.
12. Continuator of William de Junièges, *Gesta normannorum ducum*.
13. Louis had been raised for a career in the Church until the accidental death of his older brother made him crown prince, a position for which he had little liking.
14. Richard, *Histoire*, p. 132.
15. Boyd, *April Queen*, pp. 156, 162-3, 176, 179-82, 181, 191, 195-6, 199-202, 216-17, 236.
16. *Materials for the History of Thomas Becket Archbishop of Canterbury*, eds. J.C. Robertson and J.B. Sheppard, London: Rolls Series 1875–85, Vol. VII.

NOTES AND SOURCES

17. Boyd, *Lionheart*, pp. 43-4.
18. Although the anonymous author of the *Life of William the Marshal* claimed that the prince was knighted later by the Marshal.
19. The title was not used during his lifetime, but refers to the lion rampant in his coat of arms, still incorporated in the upper right quarter of the British royal standard.
20. A more comprehensive description of the ceremony may be found in M. Strickland, *Henry the Young King 1155–1183*, New Haven: Yale University Press 2016, pp. 85-6.

Chapter 6: A king with no kingdom

1. Matthew Paris, *Historia Anglorum*, ed. F. Madden, London: Rolls Series 1865–69, Vol. I, p. 353.
2. Boyd, *Lionheart*, pp. 45-6.
3. Ralph de Diceto, *Opera Historica*, Vol. I, p. 350; *Expugnatio Hiberica : The Conquest of Ireland by Geraldus Cambrensis*, eds. A.B. Scott and F.X. Martin, Dublin: Royal Irish Academy, 1978, pp. 220-1.
4. Ralph de Diceto, *Opera Historica*, Vol. I, p. 352.
5. Now Clermont-Ferrand.
6. Bouquet, *Recueil*, Vol. XIV, p. 644.
7. Richard, *Histoire*, p. 166.
8. Ibid, p. 167.
9. Bouquet, *Recueil*, Vol. XVI, p. 644.
10. Richard, *Histoire*, p. 168.
11. According to Orderic Vitalis, the odd sobriquet is derived from the Norman French insult referring to Robert's less than imposing stature *courtheuse*, once translated into Latin by his father as *brevis ocrea*, or 'short greave'.
12. Strickland, *Henry the Young King*, p. 166, quoting *The Chronicle of John of Worcester*, eds. R.R. Farlington and P. McGurk, Oxford: Clarendon Press 1995, Vol. III, pp. 30-3.
13. Richard, *Histoire*, p. 179.
14. A more comprehensive account of the rebellion may be found in Boyd, *April Queen*, pp. 203-10.

Chapter 7: Death in misery

1. Strickland, *Henry the Young King*, p. 230.
2. A. Hyland, *The Horse in the Middle Ages*, Thrupp: Sutton 1999, p. 99.
3. Strickland, *Henry the Young King*, p. 241.
4. Benedict of Peterborough, *Gesta regis Henrici secundi benedicti abbatis: The Chronicle of the Reigns of Henry II and Richard*, ed. W. Stubbs, London: Rolls Series 1867, Vol. I, pp. 246-7.

Chapter 8: Prince Richard

1. Also sometimes spelled *Nequam* which, strangely, means 'worthless' in Latin. Yet the respect he gained as a theologian brought him the position of abbot of Cirencester abbey, which he held from 1213 to his death in 1217.
2. J. Attali, *Les Juifs, le monde et l'argent*, Paris: Fayard 2002, p. 197.
3. R. Bartlett, *England Under the Norman and Angevin Kings*, p. 140.
4. Richard, *Histoire*, pp. 153-4, 161.
5. Ibid, p. 161.
6. Ibid.
7. Ibid, p. 180.
8. Ibid, p. 198.
9. Now in the *departement* of Gers, southeast of Condom.
10. Richard, *Histoire*, p. 198.

Chapter 9: Richard the Lionheart

1. Created for the Great Exhibition in 1851.
2. Full name Sir James Cochran Stevenson Runciman.
3. S. Runciman, *A History of the Crusades*, Cambridge: Cambridge University Press 1954, Vol. III, p. 75.
4. *Itinerarium peregrinorum et gestae regis ricardi*, ed. W. Stubbs, London: Rolls Series 1864, Vol. I, pp. 17, 21, 27.
5. For a description of the battle, see Boyd, *Lionheart*, pp. 77-85.
6. The title of a papal bull was simply the first two words, in this case translated as 'having heard the terrible news'.

NOTES AND SOURCES

7. Pipe Roll, 1 Richard I, p. 5.
8. Roger of Hoveden, *Chronica*, Vol. III, p. 8.
9. Benedict of Peterborough, *Gesta regis henrici secundi,* Vol. II, pp. 87-8.
10. William of Newburgh, *Historia Rerum Anglicanum*, London: Sumptibis Societatis 1856, Vol. I, p. 346.
11. Benedict of Peterborough *Gesta Henrici secundi benedicti abbatis*, London: Longman 1867, Vol. II, pp. 73, 75, 78; Roger of Hoveden, *Chronica*, London: Longman 1868, Vol. III, p. xxxiii.
12. Hyland, p. 163.
13. Runciman, *A History of the Crusades*, Vol. III, p. 33.
14. B.Z. Kedar 'Reflections on Maps, Crusading and Logistics' in *Logistics of Warfare in the Age of the Crusades*, ed. J.H. Pryor, Aldershot: Ashgate Publishing 2006, p. 288 (abridged).
15. For more detail of the preparations and victualling, see Boyd, *Lionheart*, pp. 113-18.
16. A detailed account of the whole crusade may be found in Boyd, *Lionheart*, pp. 123-43.
17. Roger of Hoveden, *Chronica*, Vol. III, pp. 71-2; also Pryor, *Logistics of Warfare*, p. 266.
18. A. Maalouf, *The Crusades through Arab Eyes*, London: Saqi Books 1984, p. 190.
19. *Itinerarium Peregrinarum et Gesta Regis Ricardi*, ed. W. Stubbs, London: Rolls Series, 1864, Vol. II, p. 223.
20. More details in Boyd, *Lionheart*, pp. 142-8.

Chapter 10: Richard's perfect castle

1. D. Nicolle and C. Hook *The Third Crusade 1191: Richard the Lionheart, Saladin and the Struggle for Jerusalem*, Botley: Osprey 2006, p. 59.
2. Runciman, *History of the Crusades*, Vol. IV, p. 71.
3. Roger of Hoveden, *Chronica*, Vol. III, p. 195.
4. Originally in Norman French *aveir de peis*, meaning literally 'goods of weight'.
5. Ralph of Diceto, *Opera Historica*, Vol. II, p. 119.
6. Richard, *Histoire*, p. 293.

7. *Great Rolls of the Pipe*, published by the Pipe Roll Society (London), for the years 1191–1194.
8. M. Powicke, *The Loss of Normandy*. Manchester: Manchester University Press 1999, p. 239.
9. J. Bradbury, *The Medieval Archer*, Woodbridge: Boydell 2002, p. 77.

Chapter 11: Prince Geoffrey

1. J. Everard, *Brittany and the Angevins: Province and Empire, 1158–1203*, Cambridge: Cambridge University Press 2000, p. 43.
2. M.A. Craig, 'A Second Daughter of Geoffrey of Brittany', in *Historical Research*, Vol. 50, no. 121 (May 1977), pp. 112-15.
3. J. Everard and M. Jones, *The Charters of Duchess Constance of Brittany and Her Family*, Woodbridge: Boydell Press 1999, pp. 93-4. This book contains a treasure trove for Latinists on the charters and confirmation of charters by Constance and Geoffrey.
4. Often rendered as *de mortuis nil nisi bene dicendum est* in medieval Latin.
5. Boyd, *Lionheart*, p. 131.
6. Sometimes rendered as 30,000 marks, equivalent to the 20,000 pounds recorded in the annals of Margam Abbey, although Powicke held that both copies of the treaty specified 20,000 marks.
7. Also known as William de Briouze.
8. Richard, *Histoire*, p. 407.
9. S. McGlynn, *Blood Cries Afar*, Stroud: Spellmount 2011, pp. 139-40.
10. Ibid, pp. 139-40.
11. *Worcester Annals*, London, Bohn 1854, p. 314.
12. Guillaume le Breton, *Philippide*, Paris: Brière 1825, p. 170.
13. Powicke, *Loss of Normandy*, p. 243 quoting E.J. Tardif *Statuta et Consuetudines*, Vol. I, p. 62.
14. Ibid., p. 243.
15. Ibid., pp. 243-4, quoting *Philippide*, Vol II, pp. 300-08. Several English chroniclers averred that such an incident took place, not in Normandy but after the siege of Radnor in 1198. (*Brut y Tywysogion*, p. 252). Accepting poetic licence, similar tit-for-tat atrocities occurred in many places at many times under the *lex talionis*.

16. This account is to be found in M. Michelet, *History of France from the Earliest Period to the Present*, tr. G.H. Smith, New York: Appleton 1845, Vol. I, Part II, p. 273, quoting as the original source *Annals of Margam ap. Scr. R. Fr.* xix, p. 247.
17. *Chronicle of Walter of Guisborough*, ed. H. Rothwell, London: Camden Society, 3rd Series 1957, Vol. lxxxix, p. 144.
18. Bouquet, *Recueil*, Vol. XVII, pp. 682-3; Richard *Histoire*, pp. 424-5; Powicke, *Loss of Normandy*, p. 468.
19. Roger of Wendover, *Flores Historiarum*, ed. H.O. Coxe, London: English Historical Society 1841–5, Vol. III, pp. 224-5.
20. W.L. Warren, *King John*, London: Methuen 1991, p. 184.
21. *Worcester Annals*, p. 314.
22. The whole elaborate story may be found in S. Church, *King John*, London: Pan 2016, pp. 171-2.
23. Ibid, p. 185.
24. Boyd, *Plantagenet Princesses*, Barnsley: Pen & Sword 2020, pp. 102-05.

Chapter 12: Prince John

1. *Pipe Roll*, 5 John, p. 139.
2. E. Foss, *Judges of England*, London : Longman 1848, pp. 139-40 quoting *Rotuli Misae*, 11 John.
3. Ibid., p. 267, quoting *Rotuli Misae*, 14 John.
4. Boyd, *April Queen* 2011, pp. 183-4.
5. Benedict of Peterborough, *Gesta regis Henrici secundi*, Vol. I, p. 221.
6. Richard, *Histoire*, p. 233.
7. Ibid, pp. 228-9.
8. Ibid, pp. 224-5.
9. *Pipe Roll*, 1 Richard I, p. 5.
10. Powicke, *Loss of Normandy*, pp. 210-12.
11. Roger of Hoveden, *Chronica*, Vol. IV, pp. 96-7.
12. http://plume-dhistoire.fr/isabelle-dangouleme-epouse-de-jean-sans-terre.
13. Boyd, *Lionheart*, pp. 213-14.
14. Probably derived from Stochestede, meaning 'the stockaded place'.

15. Full text in Latin and English may be found in *Notes on the Charters of the Borough (now city) of Liverpool* by J.A. Picton – downloadable from: www.hslc.org.uk/wp-contents/uploads/2017/07/36-5-Picton.pdf.

Chapter 13: War on all sides

1. Boyd, *Plantagenet Princesses*, pp. 107-18. This extraordinary woman was given a new lease of life in 1956, when Seymour Lewis' play *Siwan a cherddi eraill,* or *Siwan and Other Tales,* became a staple of the Welsh Language 'A' level syllabus. Thus, a thirteenth-century princess has become a romantic heroine for two generations of Welsh-speaking teenagers.
2. The present castle is largely a later construction.
3. Abstract from a paper presented at International Medieval Congress in Leeds 2009 by R. Cassidy entitled 'Rose of Dover (d. 1261), Richard of Chilham and an Inheritance in Kent', Courtesy of *Archeologia Cantiana*, Vol. CXXI (2011).
4. Boyd, *Plantagenet Princesses*, pp. 84-90.
5. Rot. lit. claus I, p. 89.
6. Boyd, *Plantagenet Princesses*, p. 111.
7. T.F. Tout, *The History of England*, London 1889, p. 226.
8. G. Ronay *The Tartar Khan's Englishman* London, Cassel 1978, pp. 20-3.
9. Tout, *The History of England*, p. 227.
10. R.V. Turner, *King John*, Stroud: The History Press 2009, pp. 180, 182.
11. *Foedera, conventiones, litterae et acta publica*, ed. T. Rymer, London 1745, Vol. I, Part i-ii, p. 68.
12. Ibid, pp. 63-4.
13. Roger of Wendover, *Flores Historiarum,* Vol. III, pp. 363-4.
14. Roger of Wendover, *Flores Historiarum*, Vol. II, p. 180.
15. Ibid, p. 182.
16. McGlynn, *Blood Cries Afar*, note on p. 300.
17. J.C. Holt, *Magna Carta and Medieval Government*, London: Hambledon Press 1985, p. 122.
18. S. Church, *King John*, pp. 254-5.

NOTES AND SOURCES

Chapter 14: Henry III

1. M. Powicke, *The Thirteenth Century*, Oxford: Clarendon Press 1962, p. 1.
2. Ibid.
3. McGlynn, *Blood Cries Afar*, p. 35.
4. Ibid, pp. 47-8.
5. He appears as Philip the Bastard in Shakespeare's play *King John*.
6. L. Delisle, *Etienne de Gaillardon*, Paris : Biblothèque de l'Ecole de Chartes 1899, p. 21.
7. McGlynn, *Blood Cries Afar*, pp. 224-7.
8. Although Mathew Paris' sketch of the drama shows him being beheaded by a sword.
9. Boyd, *Plantagenet Princesses*, pp. 122-7.
10. Powicke, *Thirteenth Century*, p. 16.
11. Reputedly the originator of the custom of awarding a flitch of bacon to the happiest couple in the community.
12. The full saga may be found in Ronay, *The Tatar Khan's Englishman*.

Chapter 15: King v. barons, round 2

1. Boyd, *Plantagenet Princesses*, pp. 114-18.
2. McGlynn, *Blood Cries Afar*, p. 155.
3. K. Staniland, 'The Nuptials of Alexander III of Scotland and Margaret Plantagenet', *Nottingham Medieval Studies*, Vol. 30 (1986).
4. P. Ziegler, *The Black Death*, London: Penguin 1982, p. 32.
5. M.C. Howell, *Eleanor of Provence: Queenship in Thirteenth Century England* Oxford: Oxford University Press 1998, pp. 22-4, 112.

Chapter 16: Richard of Cornwall

1. The Brythonic Cornish language, mutually comprehensible with Breton, continued in general use until the eighteenth century before gradually giving way to English.
2. Now in Oxfordshire.

3. The name 'Bethlehem' is derived from two Hebrew words: *bet* meaning 'house' and *lechem* meaning 'bread'. Not surprisingly, there were many places known as *bet lechem* in the Holy Land, including one just five miles west of Nazareth where the prophet's family lived.
4. Quoted in *The Cambridge Companion to the Literature of the Crusades*, ed. A. Bale, Cambridge: Cambridge University Press 2019, Vol. 1, p. 93 (author's translation).
5. Ibid, p. 94 (author's translation).
6. S. Painter, *The Crusade of Theobald of Champagne and Richard of Cornwall, 1239–1241*, Madison: University of Wisconsin Press 1969, pp. 463–86.
7. M. Lower, *The Barons' Crusade: A Call to Arms and Its Consequences*, Philadelphia: University of Pennsylvania Press, p. 171.
8. Painter, *The Crusade of Theobald of Champagne and Richard of Cornwall*, p. 478.
9. Not the eponymous sultan of Egypt.
10. Lower, *The Barons' Crusade*, p. 148.
11. M. Prestwich, *Plantagenet England 1225–1360*, Oxford: Oxford University Press, 2007, p. 121.
12. A corruption of the Old French name for Germany: Allemaine.

Chapter 17: Edward I

1. Prestwich *Plantgenet England*, p. 177.
2. M. Prestwich *Edward I*, New Haven: Yale University Press 1997, pp. 11-14.
3. J.C. Parsons, 'Introduction' to *The Court and Household of Eleanor of Castile in 1290 [British Library additional MS 35294]*, Toronto: Pontifical Institute for Medieval Studies 2000.
4. For the relationship of Eleanor of Castile and Edward I, see Boyd, *Plantagenet Princesses*, pp 179-95.
5. M. Morris, *A Great and Terrible King: Edward I*, London: Windmill Books 2009, pp. 44-5.
6. J. Sadler, *The Second Barons' War*, Barnsley:, Pen & Sword Books 2008, pp. 105-9.

NOTES AND SOURCES

7. Prestwich, *Edward I*, p. 72.
8. J. Maddicott, 'The Crusade Taxation of 1268–70' in *Thirteenth Century England*, eds. P.R. Cross and S.D. Lloyd, Woodbridge: Boydel Press 1989, pp. 93-117.
9. J. Haldon, 'Roads and Communications in the Byzantine Empire' in *Logistics of Warfare*, p. 146.
10. *Logistics of Warfare*, p. 33.
11. Ibid, p. 275.
12. R. Gertwagen, 'Harbours and Facilities Along the Eastern Mediteranean Sea Lanes to Outremer', in *Logistics of Warfare*.
13. *Martino de Canale Les Estoires de Venise*, Florence: Editions Limentani 1972, p. 159.
14. Prestwich *Edward I*, p. 175.
15. Ibid, p. 151.
16. Morris, *A Great and Terrible King*, pp. 170-1.

Chapter 18: Edward II

1. S. Phillips, *Edward II*, New Haven: Yale University Press 2011, p. 47.
2. Ibid, pp. 55-7.
3. Ibid, pp. 43-6.
4. E.A.R. Brown, *The Marriage of Edward II and Isabelle of France*, in *Speculum 63* (1988), p. 574.
5. Unpublished research by the late uncle of the author.
6. Prestwich, *Edward I*, p. 557.
7. Boyd, *Plantagenet Princesses*, p. 199.
8. Phillips, *Edward II*, pp. 135-7.
9. Ibid, pp. 150-1.
10. Essay by James A. Schultz in *Constructing Medieval Sexuality, Minneapolis:* University of Minnesota Press 1997, p. 99.
11. *Annales londinenses*, ed. W. Stubbs, London : Rolls Series 1882–3, Vol I, p. 151.
12. H.S. Lucas, *The Great European Famine of 1315, 1316 and 1317* in *Speculum* Vol. 5 (1930), p. 355.
13. Phillips, *Edward II*, pp. 308, 330.

14. Quoted ibid, pp. 367-8.
15. A manuscript copy of the chronicle may be found in the British Library under the reference MS Cotton Vitellius c.vi, f.244. The Latin-English nineteenth-century edition edited by E.A. Bond was published in 1867 in the series *Chronicles and Memorials of Great Britain and Ireland during the Middle Ages* by London, Longmans, Green, Reader and Dyer as *Chronica Monasterii de Melsa, a Fundatione Usque ad Annum 1396, Auctore Thoma de Burton, Abbate. Accedit Continuatio ad Annum 1406, Rerum Britannicarum medii aevi scriptores.*

Chapter 19: Edward III

1. Boyd, *Plantagenet Princesses,* pp. 203-09.
2. Essay by *E. Jane Burns in Constructing Medieval Sexuality*, p. 114.
3. The mercenaries from Hainaut cost £41,000 according to C.J. Rogers, *War Cruel and Sharp* Woodbridge: Boydell 2000, p. 23.
4. Ibid, pp. 19-22.
5. A full account of a royal wedding banquet at York may be found in Boyd, *Plantagenet* Princesses, pp. 166-9.
6. The same instructions are in *speculum dominarum* (Bibliotheque Nationale de France, *manuscrits latins 6784*) quoted in essay by *Louise O. Fradenburg in Constructing Medieval Sexuality*, p. 141
7. P.C. Doherty, *Isabella and the Strange Death of Edward II*, London: Robinson 2003, p. 161.
8. Eventually increased to £4,000.
9. Froissart *Chronicles* downloadable from https://ehistory.osu.edu/books/froissart 0061, ∬113-115.
10. Ziegler, *The Black Death,* pp. 25-6.
11. Ibid, p. 150, citing *Originalia Roll 29*, Ed III, m.8.
12. Ibid, p. 81.
13. J.J. De Smet, *Chronicon Majus Aegidii li Muisis* in *Recueil des Chroniques de Flandres* Brussels: Hayez 1837, Vol. II, p. 280.
14. Ziegler, *The Black Death,* p. 152.
15. Ibid, p. 159 quotes several sources.

NOTES AND SOURCES

Chapter 20: Edward, the Black Prince

1. J. Speed, *The History of Great Britaine under the Conquests of ye Romans, Saxons, Danes and Normans*, London 1611, p. 567; T. Fuller, *The Holy State and the Prophane State*, Cambridge: Williams 1642.
2. *Foedera*, Vol. II, p. 919.
3. Today, this region has the appellation *Entre deux Mers*, taken by many to mean 'between two seas', but this is a mistranslation of the Occitan *entre dos mars*, which means between the tidal reaches of the two rivers.
4. Although Froissart believed this, he was perhaps reiterating the dinner after the taking of Poitiers in 1356.
5. N.H. Nicolas, *The Origins of the Royal Navy*, London: Bentley 1847, Vol. II, p. 112.
6. *The Life and Glorious Actions of Edward, Prince of Wales*, ed. A. Collins, London: Osborne 1740, pp. 42-3 (abridged).
7. Article by W. Hunt in *Dictionary of National Biography* 1889, citing several sources.
8. The rulers of Aquitaine had traditionally been dukes.
9. L. Cordia, *La Théorie de l'Impôt en France*, Paris: Institut d'Etudes Augustiniennes 2005, pp. 249-53.
10. G. Pepin, *Towards a New Assessment of the Black Prince's Principality of Aquitaine 1369–1372* in *Nottingham Medieval Studies lii* (2008), courtesy of www.academia.eu.
11. Other possible diagnoses include nephritis, cirrhosis or a combination of these.
12. It is asserted by Caxton, in his continuation of the *Polychronicon*, that the prince died previously at his manor of Kennington and that the body was brought to Westminster on 8 July, Trinity Sunday, a holy day he had always kept with special reverence.

Chapter 21: Richard II

1. A serf was virtually a slave, tied to the land where he or she was born, and the property of its owner.
2. A. Tuck, 'Lords Appellant (act. 1387–1388)', in *Oxford Dictionary of National Biography*, Oxford University Press, 2004.

3. French survived for centuries as the second language of the privileged classes, who used it when they did not want commoners such as their servants to understand what they were saying, hence the oft-quoted phrase *Pas devant les domestiques*, which survived well into Victorian times. French remained the language of the law, all judges and lawyers being able to speak it until 1731, when legal French ceased to be used in common law cases although some expressions continued in legal use well into the nineteenth century. For example, the custom of *coverture* described an unmarried woman as *feme sole* and used *feme covert* for a married woman, who had no separate legal *persona* and was 'covered' by her husband's responsibility – in fact, controlled by him in all respects.

Index

Acre 80, 83, 86-9, 135, 147-9, 158-60
Adam fitzRoy 171, 174
Adam of Churchdown 58-9, 64
Adelaide de Maurienne 23
Adelard of Bath 26
Adelin 14, 16
Adeliza of Louvain 14, 18
Aelith of Aquitaine 32
Agnès de Maurienne 31
Agnès de Méranie 101, 113
Aimery of Limoges 65
Aixe-sur-Vienne castle 66
Al-Adil, brother of Saladin 86-9
Alais, daughter of Louis VII 60, 70, 77, 84
Albéric Clément 86
Alexander II of Scotland 124, 126, 134, 135; 140
Alexander Seton 181
Alfonso II of Aragon 67, 74
Alfonso VIII of Castile 119
Alfonso VIII of Castile 142
Alfonso X of Castile 151, 154, 160
Alice de Leygrave 164
Alix de Blois 99
Alix de Thouars 101
Alix of Maurienne 49, 109
Al-Kamil, Egyptian sultan 147
Alphonse, son of Edward I 160, 164

Amaury de Montfort 149
Amboise 47
Amélie de Jarnac 131
Andrew Harclay 174
Anglesey 161
Anjou, Angevins 19, 93, 122, 137
Anglo-Saxons 2, 36
Anglo-Scandinavians 9
Angers 31, 54, 60
Angevin empire *see* Plantagenet empire
Angoulême 114, 120, 131, 189-90, 197
Anjou 27, 41, 50
An-Nasir Dawud, sultan 149
Antioch 79
antipope Viktor 41
Aquitaine 31, 33, 43, 47, 72, 76, 93, 96, 100, 102, 107, 110, 114, 136, 139, 154, 160, 174
archbishops: Alexander of York 201; Anselm 12, 15; Boniface of Savoy 139, 151, 156; Edmund Rich 137, 152; Geoffrey of York; Hugh (de Puiset) of Durham 45, 82; Hubert Walter 112, 119; Hugues de Rouen 41; Joscius of Tyre 79; Konrad of Hochstaden 151; Robert de Torigni 40-1; Roger (de Pont-Levé) of York 44, 46; Rotrou de Rouen 49, 53, 59;

Stephen Langton 121-3, 125, 129, 135-6; Theobald of Bec 21, 33, 34, 40, 41; Walter de Gray 139, 142; Walter Reynolds 168, 169, 176; William de Corbeil; William Edendon 186: see also Becket, Thomas
Argentan 50, 74, 75
armour 1, 4, 5, 8, 84, 198
Arnaud de Châtillon 79
Arnoud de Bouville 76
Arsuf, battle 7, 88
Arthur, mythical king 146
Arthur of Brittany 85, 98, 99, 100-1, 103-6, 112, 114
Arundel 18
Ashkelon 89, 149
'auld alliance' 120
avoirdupois 92
Avranches 48
Aylesbury 131
Aymar of Limoges 94
Aymer de Valence 169
Aymer Taillefer of Angooulême 114

Baha al-Din 88
Baibars, Mameluke 150, 159
bankers 162, 170
Barfleur 14, 16, 31, 34, 55, 58, 93, 110
barons 15, 17, 18, 42, 74, 76, 82-5, 96-7, 99-101, 103, 121-4, 125, 129, 134, 137-139, 142-4, 147, 151, 156-8, 167-8, 170, 173
barons' wars 117, `118, 134, 145, 152, 156
bastards 14, 18, 101, 117, 118, 171, 174
Batu Khan 135
Baudouin II 16
Bayeux 3, 44

Bayeux tapestry 2, 3, 9-11
Baynard's castle 121
Bay of Biscay 74
Bayonne 74
Béatrice, daughter of Henry III 138-9
Béatrice of Provence 138
Béatrice of Savoy 137, 160
Béatrice of Valkenburg 153
Beaugency 27-8
Beaulieu abbey 127, 150
Bedford castle 136
Beit Nuba 89
Belin 28
Berengaria of Barcelona 70
Berengaria of Navarre 70, 85-6, 92
Bergerac 189
Berkhamstead castle 129, 146, 153, 195, 198
Bernard of Clairvaux 25, 27, 73
Berry 59-60, 110
Bertrand du Guesclin 196
Bertran de Born 61, 65-68, 74, 77, 80
Berwick-on-Tweed 82, 125, 180-1
Bishops 15, 27, 33, 34, 41, 44, 47, 59, 67, 73, 85, 176: Adam Orleton 173, 175; Austens de St Colombe; Bertrand of Bordeaux 73; Bertrand of Agen; Geoffroi de Lauroux 23, 32, 33 ;Gilbert Foliot 47; Henry of Winchester 16, 18, 20; Henry Woodlock 167; Jehan de Cros 197; John dee Gray 119; Maurice of Le Mans 12; Peter des Roches 128, 131, 135-6; Richard de Belmeis 38; Roger of Salisbury 17, 83; Walter Langton 165-6; William Longchamp of Ely 82, 84

INDEX

Black Death 185-6, 190, 199
Blanca of Castille / Queen Blanche 113, 119, 124, 130-133
Blanche Nef 14, 34
Blois 41
Blood Libel 141
Bohemund V of Antioch 149
Bonneville-sur-Touques
Bordeaux 23, 28, 33, 77, 138, 189, 195-6
Boulogne 54 , 113-14, 132, 182
Bouvines, battle 122, 124
Brabant, Brabanters 52, 54, 55, 75, 111
Breakspear, Nicolas 42
Brest 200
Bristol 19, 106, 129, 175
Brittany 43, 54, 56, 96-7, 99-101, 106, 110, 114, 137, 192
Brough castle 106
Builth Wells castle 162
Bures 74
Burgh-by-Sands 166
Burgos 154
Bur-le-Roi 48
Bury St Edmunds 32, 54

Caen 64, 65, 183, 189
Caernarvon castle 172
Calais 132, 183-4, 190, 200
cannibalism 83
Canterbury cathedral and city, 1, 43, 46, 48, 49, 55, 63, 74, 119, 133, 138-9, 158, 198, 200
Capetian dynasty 43, 131
Cardiff 13
cardinals : Henry of Pisa 41; William of Pavia 41; Peter 60; Stephen Langton 119-20; Talleyrand of Périgord 193
Carlisle 52

Carlos de la Cerda 190
castellans 75, 104, 129
Castelnaux 119
Castile 196, 202
Castle Rising 180
Castro Urdiales 196
Cathars 136
Caversham 135
Central Asia 135
Châlus 94-5, 100
Champagne 41, 43
Channel Islands 101, 134
Charlemagne 151
Charles II of Navarre 191-3, 198
Charles IV of France 174, 181-2
Charles V of France 197
Charles d'Anjou 138, 150, 158, 159
Charles de Valois 167
charters 73-4, 113, 115, 143
Château Gaillard 93-4, 113-14
Châteauneuf-sur-Epte castle 40, 5
Châteauroux castle 59, 60
Chaumont castle 41, 97
Chester 115
Chinon castle 28, 41, 49, 50, 56, 60, 74, 80, 84, 95, 122, 129
Christmas courts 15, 27, 41-2, 44, 47, 48, 49, 60, 64, 65, 70, 74, 75, 90, 110, 121, 168
chroniclers: Ambroise 87; Gervase of Tilbury 37; Giraldus Cambrensis 37, 48; Henry of Huntingdon 16; Jean Froissart 184; Ralph of Diceto 37, 48; Walter Map 71; Richard of Devizes 7; Roger of Hoveden 19, 37; Walter Map 37
Church, the 1, 2, 10, 15, 35, 47, 54, 55, 94, 100, 108, 143, 159, 162
Cinque Ports 32, 117, 132
Cistercian order 108

221

Clan Comyn 140
Clipstone 162
Conan III of Brittany 96
Conan IV 96, 97
Constance of Brittany 43, 43, 89, 96-7, 99-101, 113
Constance of Castile, consort of Louis VII 40
Constantinople 9
Constitutions of Clarendon 42, 44, 48
Conwy castle 161
Corfe castle 106, 123
Council of Oxford 110
Crécy, battle 183, 190
crusades 2, 11, 25, 26, 49, 57, 58, 71, 77-9, 83-5, 91, 99, 111, 115, 118, 134, 136, 139, 141-2, 147, 157-9, 162, 170, 195
Cyprus 85, 158

Danes, Danelaw 10
Daniel of Beccles 22
Dartsmouth, 83
David I of Scotland 27
David, son of Robert the Bruce 179, 181, 183-4
Denise de Déols 59
Despensers, father and son 172-5
Devizes 13, 128
Dictum of Kenilworth 145
Dieppe 182
diffidatio 103, 122, 144, 176
Domesday Book 10
Domfront 46
Dover 16, 63, 120, 123, 126, 130, 132, 134, 157, 160
dowries 13, 40, 77, 119, 135, 138
Duchy of Cornwall 146
Dumfries 166
Duncan Boyd 166
Dunkirk 55

Durham 184
Dürnstein castle 90

Easter courts 41, 44, 58, 70, 90
Easter parliament 151
Edict of Expulsion 162
Edinburgh 124
Edith of Willesford 195
Edmund of Woodstock 174
Edmund, son of Henry III 138, 141-2
Edmund, son of Richard of Cornwall 151, 153, 157
Edward Balliol 180-1
Edward of Angoulême 198
Edward of Caernarvon 162-4; as King Edward II 166-77, 180, 184-5
Edward of Woodstock / the Black Prince 186, 188, 190-9
Edward, son of Edward II 174-6; as Edward III 177-82, 185-6, 188-90, 192-6, 199-200, 202
Edward, son of Henry III 138, 142-5, 153-59; as King Edward I 160-4, 164, 167
Edward the Confessor 12, 135, 139, 140, 167
Egidio Boccanegra 182-3
Egypt 148-9
Eleanor, daughter of Edward I 160
Eleanor, daughter of Henry II 119
Eleanor, daughter of King John 152
Eleanor de Clare 175
Eleanor of Aquitaine 23, 25-9, 31-9, 42, 45, 48-51, 53, 56, 69, 71-4, 80-2, 84-6, 90-3, 95, 99-101-3, 105-7, 109, 112, 119, 158
Eleanor of Brittany 90, 98, 105-6, 114
Eleanor of Castile 142, 156, 158-60, 164-5

222

INDEX

Eleanor of Provence 138-9, 142-4, 155-6, 161-2, 165
Enrique de Trastámara 196
Ermengarde de Beaumont 135
Esnecca ship 38
Etienne de Blois, see Stephen of Blois
Etienne de Tournay 111
Eudon II de Porhoët 96
Eustace de Vescy 103, 122
Eustace of Blois 21, 32, 33
Eustace the Monk 132-4
Evesham, battle 145, 156
Evreux 112
Exchequer 57, 118, 129, 134, 172
excommunication 47, 67, 101, 103, 121, 123, 124, 126, 136, 160, 169-71

Falaise, and treaty of, 41, 54, 57, 103-4
famine 137, 141-2, 151, 171-3
Farnham 126
Faversham 32, 123
Flagellants 186
Flanders 113-14, 132, 165, 182-3
Fontevraud abbey 80, 95, 100, 102-3, 108, 109
Forest Charter 134
forest laws 29, 81
Foulkes de Bréauté 130
Frederik II of Germany 147, 149
Friedrich VI of Swabia 80
Friedrich Barbarossa, emperor 80
Fulk of Anjou and Maine 15, 16
Fulk of Jerusalem 26

Gascony 119, 136, 142-3, 154, 157, 163, 165, 170, 181
Gaston Phébus 196-7
Genoa 135

Geoffrey Chaucer 195
Geoffrey of Anjou 15, 16, 17, 26, 27, 67, 97
Geoffrey of Val Richer 94
Geoffrey, as prince 43, 44, 45, 49, 51-2, 56, 58, 62-3, 65-6, 74-6, 85, 97; as duke of Brittany 97-9, 101, 106, 110, 112
Geoffrey the Bastard 57, 81, 84, 110
Geoffroi de Preuilly 60
Geoffroy de Rancon 76
Geoffroi of Anjou 16, 117
Gerberoi 53
Germany 13, 91
Gilbert de Clare 146
Giles of Oudenaerde 164
Gilles le Musis 186
Gisors castle 40, 53-4, 63, 79, 97
Gloucester 18, 112, 128, 136, 175-6
Godefroi de Bouillon 71
Godred of Man 45
Grand Council 44, 112, 122, 136, 189
Grandmont abbey 46, 67
Guildford 126
Guillaume de Braose 102, 104, 105
Guillaume Longuespée 118, 121-2, 124
Guillaume des Roches 101-2
Guy de Beauchamp, earl of Warwick 169
Guy de Lusignan as king of Jerusalem 79, 83; as knight later 102
Guy de Montfort 153, 160
Guy de Thouars 99
Guy Ferre 164

Hailes abbey 153
Harby 163

Hastings 2, 6, 10, 182
Hawise, wife of Oliver the
　Bastard 118
hawking 43, 108
Heinrich V 13, 14, 15
Heinrich VI Hohenstaufen 90-1
Henri de Reynes 140
Henry I Beauclerc 12-16, 18, 37,
　38, 96, 111, 175
Henry II 16, 21, 22, 26-51, 53-5,
　59-60, 63, 65, 68-73, 75-7, 79-
　82, 84, 96-7, 99, 101, 103, 106-7,
　109, 110-11, 118-119, 128, 129
Henry III 106, 116, 118, 128, 131,
　134-46, 150-2, 155-6, 158, 160
Henry Bolingbroke 201-2
Henry de Grosmont 186, 189, 191
Henry de Lacy 168
Henry fitzWarin 115
Henry of Almain 153, 156-7, 160
Henry of Cornwall 153
Henry of Lancaster 177, 180,
　189, 192
Henry Percy 184
Henry, son of Edward I 160-1
Henry Spigurnel 170
Henry the Young King 19, 37, 38,
　40-9, 51-7, 59-60, 61, 63-7, 70,
　73-6, 80, 97, 98, 110, 111
Hertford castle 129
Hodierna 69-70
Hoël III of Brittany 96
Holy Land 16, 25, 54, 78-9, 83,
　109, 147, 159
Holt, J.C. 127
homosexuality 30, 173
Horns of Hattin, battle 79
horses 3, 7, 15, 84-5, 88-9, 108,
　123, 125, 132, 157, 169, 182-3
Hubert de Burgh 104, 129, 132,
　135-6, 137

Hugh Bigod 19, 54, 55, 143
Hugh de Lacy 110
Hugues III of Cyprus 159
Hugues IX of Lusignan 114, 131
Hugues X of Lusignan 131,
　138-9, 151
Hugues le Brun 109
Hull 83
Humbert of Maurienne 49, 75, 109
Humphrey of Toron 89
Hundred Years War 182
hunting 42, 108

Ile d'Olèron 113
Isle of Ely 153
illness 34, 35, 83, 90, 126, 137,
　158, 162-3, 185-6, 196
Ingeborg of Denmark 113
interdict 60, 111, 113, 119, 121
investiture contest 119
Ipswich 19, 46
Ira et malevolentia 103
Ireland 47, 59, 74, 105, 110, 120,
　154-5, 168, 195
Isabel, illegitimate daughter of
　King John 117
Isabella of Angoulême 114, 120,
　123, 128-9, 131, 139
Isabelle, consort of Edward II
　165-9, 171-8, 180-1
Isabel of Gloucester 81,
　110-11, 114
Isabel of Pembroke 146-7, 150
Isabel of Striguil 80
Italy 13

Jaffa 87
James Douglas 178
Jacques de St George 162
Jean II de Valois 191-3, 195-6
Jean de Savigny 127

224

INDEX

Jean de Valerant 105
Jeanne de Navarre 179
John of Berry 197
Jean, son of Philippe IV 189
Jean Tristan, son of Louis IX 158
Jehan de Brienne 148
Jerusalem 2, 71, 78, 79, 88-90, 149, 159
Jews 2, 30, 71, 82, 84, 141, 144, 151, 157, 160, 162
Joan aka Siwan, illegitimate daughter of King John 117, 121
Joan, daughter of Edward III 186
Joan, daughter of King John and Isabella 131, 135, 140
Joan of Kent, wife of Black Prince 194-5
Joanna, princess 89, 108
Joan of Acre 160
Joan of the Tower 179, 181
Johannes of Bohemia 190
John, as prince 45, 47, 49, 56, 59, 81-5, 89-93, 99-100, 107, 108-9; as king 100-7, 109-17, 119-22, 125-6, 128, 133, 146
John Ball 200
John of Alençon 112
John of Eltham 171, 177
John of Gaunt 186, 190, 196, 197, 199-202
John of Salisbury 25, 28
justiciars 112, 118, 136-7, 139

Kenilworth 145, 153, 170, 175-6
King Harold 2, 6, 9, 10
King's Lynn 126
knights, knighthood 1, 3, 4, 6, 8, 18, 39, 45, 48, 50, 54, 59, 60, 63-4, 66-7, 71, 74-6, 83-4, 86, 89, 93, 102-4, 110, 112, 120, 122, 125, 131-2, 139, 144, 193

La Châtre 60
La Réole 136, 189
La Rochelle 113
languages 1, 2, 3, 9, 10, 13, 35, 71, 90, 108, 135, 165
Lagny 61, 64
Lake Galilee 79
La Rochelle 51, 163, 195
Lateran Council 95
Latrun 89
legates, papal 44, 47, 48, 54, 60, 74, 77, 118, 121, 125, 128, 129, 133-4, 136, 145, 192
Leicester 52, 54
Le Mans 3, 41, 50, 54, 67, 92, 102
Lent 41, 54, 80, 85, 94, 110
Leonor, daughter of Alfonso X 154-5
Leopold V of Austria 80, 86, 90
Le Perche 50
Les Andelys 93, 104
Lewes, battle 144, 156
Lewis, M 134
lex talionis 104
Limassol 86
Limoges 27, 50, 65-6, 73-4, 197
Limousin 46, 58, 68, 75, 110
Lincoln 19, 57, 130
Lionel, brother of Black Prince 195
Liverpool 115-16
Llandeilo Fawr 161
LLywellyn ap Gruffudd 156, 161
Llywellyn ap Iorwerth 121
Llewellyn Fawr 117
London 17, 18, 20, 35, 122, 124, 128, 134-5, 144, 193
Lords Appellant 201-2
Louis VI 13, 23, 26
Louis VII 23, 25-30, 32, 33, 34, 39-41, 43-7, 49-56, 58, 60-3, 70, 72-5, 77, 96-8, 107, 158

225

Louis d'Evreux 167
Louis, son of Philippe Auguste 113, 124-6, 128, 129-34, 144; as King Louis VIII 136-7
Louis IX 138, 141-4, 148, 150, 157-9
Loudun 50, 56
Lusignan family 102, 109, 142, 152
Lyon 84

'mad parliament' 143
Magna Carta 103, 122-3, 125, 129, 134, 157
Mainard 37, 43
Maine 27
Maino de Maineri 179
Mainz 91
Margam abbey 105
Margaret, daughter of Henry III 138, 140
Margaret de Clare 166
Margaret of Huntingdon 96
Margaret of Norway 165
Marguerite de Bourbon 147-8
Marguerite of Provence 138, 142, 144
Marguerite, wife of Young King 39-42, 45-6, 48, 49, 58-60, 64 -6
Marguerite, second wife of Edward I 163, 165
Marie, daughter of Philippe-Auguste 101
Marie de Champagne 91, 99
Marie de Coucy 140
Marlborough 70, 135
Marseille 85
Martel 66
Mary Maunsel 164
Matilda, consort of Henry I 13
Matilda, Empress 13-22, 26, 28, 31-2, 125

Matilda of Boulogne 20, 31
Matilda, Princess 40, 100
Maude, illegitimate daughter of King John 117
Maud of Brittany 98
mêlées 61-2
Melisande, consort of Fulk 16
Mercadier 111
mercenaries 19, 32, 52, 55, 58, 65-6, 75-7, 92-3, 102, 110-12, 114, 120, 122, 125, 127, 144, 150, 170, 178, 195-6
Messina 85, 99, 100, 103
Michael de la Pole 201
Mise of Amiens 144
milites herlewini 70
Milo, chaplain 79, 95, 100
Mirebeau 50, 56, 65, 102, 106
Mongols 159
Montlouis 55, 56, 75, 110
Montmirail 43, 72, 97
Mont St Michel 40, 41, 48
Mortain 111-12
Muslims 2, 54, 71, 78, 83, 86, 88-9, 109, 149, 158

Nantes 44, 96, 98, 101
Napoleon 194
Narbonne 192
Navarre 85
Neckam, Alexander 69
Neaufles castle, 40
Neubourg 40, 41
Newark 126-7
Nice 85
Nicolaa de la Haye 130
Nicholas Breakspear 108
Nonancourt 60
Normandy 9, 11, 12, 13, 15, 16, 17, 27, 38, 45, 46, 49, 52, 54-56, 60,

INDEX

68, 93, 96, 101-2, 112, 117, 120, 122, 143, 156, 183, 192
Northumberland 58
Norwich 19
Nottingham 83, 92, 124-5, 179-80

Odo of Bayeux 10
Old Sarum 56, 75
Oliver, bastard of King John 118, 130
Oliver Cromwell 162
Order of the Garter 186, 190
Ordainers 169
ordinances 169-70, 173
Ordinance of Labourers 185
Orvieto 160
Ottakar II of Bohemia 151
Otto of Brunswick 100
Ouistreham 55
Outremer, see Holy Land
Oxford 19, 20-1, 38, 69, 82, 170

Pacifiques 110
Paris 26, 27, 28, 31, 39, 51, 54, 58, 62, 65, 74, 92, 93, 100, 131, 143, 160, 166
Parlamant of Aquitaine 195-6
Patrick of Salisbury 109
Peace of God 102, 103, 109
Peasants' Revolt 199-200
Pedro of Castile 196
Pembroke, earl of 170, 173-4
Perigueux 189
Perigord 111
Peter de Maulay 105, 106
Peter de Montfort 143, 145
Peter de Savoy 143
Peter des Roches 118
Peter fitzHerbert 118
Peter of Blois 70-1
Peter of Brittany 149

Philip de Faulconbridge 131
Philip of Flanders 1, 52, 54, 55, 58, 63-5, 79, 113, 121
Philippa of Hainault 174, 177, 179-81, 184, 188, 200
Philippe III 159-60
Philippe IV 162-3, 165-6, 168, 170, 181, 189
Philippe VI 181-4, 190
Philippe Auguste 61, 63, 66, 78, 79-80, 84-6, 89-94, 98, 100-1, 103-4, 106, 111-14, 119-20, 122, 124, 126, 131, 133
Philippe d'Orléans 171
Philippe, son of Jean II 193
Piers Gaveston 166-71
pilgrimage 58, 145
Pipe Rolls 93
plague 185
Plantagenet empire 38, 82, 85, 100-101
Plantagenet, eytmology 17
Plymouth 193
Poitiers 28, 29, 46, 54, 58, 65, 72-4, 102, 109, 192, 193
Poitou 31, 51, 72, 75-7, 93, 102, 107, 110, 119, 122, 136, 150
Ponthieu 160, 165-6, 181
Pontigny monastery 44
popes 2: Adrian IV 42, 108; Alexander II 10; Alexander III 41, 43-4, 47, 51, 54, 60, 70, 74, 77; Alexander IV 142, 144; Anastasius IV 32; Clement III 82; Clement V 169; Clement VI 195; Eugenius III 25-7 ; Gregory VIII 79; Gregory IX 147, 148, 150; Gregory X 158, 160; Gregory XI 198; Honorius III 126, 129, 134, 136; Innocent III 101, 103, 119, 120-3, 126;

227

Innocent IV 142; Leo III 151;
Nicholas II 158; Urban II 11, 49;
Urban IV 144
Port-Mort 113
Portsmouth 63, 82, 83, 92,
117, 182
Provisions of Oxford 143, 144,
155-6
Provisions of Westminster 143

Qalandiya 89

Ralph de Déols 59
Ralph Neville 184
Ramón Berengar IV of Provence
137, 150
Ranulf de Blondeville 99, 100,
115, 129
Ranulf de Gernon 19
Ranulf de Glanville 82
Ranulf of Chester 27
Raoul de Fougères 97
Raymond of Antioch 25
Raymond of Toulouse 50, 74, 90
Reading abbey 38
Reigate 126
Reims 63
Reconquista 48
Reginald, sub-prior of
Canterbury 119
Reims 113
Rhodes 158
Rhuddlan castle 161
Rhys ap Gryffydd 81-2
Richard de Clare 143-4, 156
Richard de Luci 118
Richard de Warenne 117
Richard fitzAlan 201
Richard fitzRoy, bastard of King
John 132-3
Richard fitzYves 119

Richard Lionheart 3, 7, 38, 43,
45, 47, 49, 51-2, 54-5, 57-8, 60,
62-3, 65-72, 75-91, 93-5, 98-101,
103, 107, 110-15, 128, 131, 168
Richard of Cornwall 136, 138-9,
142, 144, 146-51, 156 ; as King
of the Romans 151-3
Richard, son of Richard of
Cornwall 151
Richard, son of Black Prince 186,
196, 198-200; as Richard II
198-202
Richard, son of William the
Marshal 137
Richmond 55, 96, 101
Rigord 98
Robert Baldock 175
Robert Burnell 158, 160-1
Robert Courtheuse 11-13, 53
Robert d'Arbrissel 108
Robert d'Aubigny 123
Robert de Boyt 166
Robert de Counrtenay 132
Robert de Vere 201
Robert de Vieux Pont / Vipont
104-6
Robert fitzWalter 103, 121-4, 135
Robert of Dreux 30
Robert of Gloucester 18-21, 26,
59, 105
Robert of Leicester 52-4
Robert the Bruce 165-6, 169,
173-4, 179-80
Robert the Chaplain 135
Rocamadour 47, 66
Rochester castle 123-5
Rochester cathedral 123
Roger Mortimer 174-80
Roger of Neubourg 40
Rohese of Dover 118
Romans 33, 35

INDEX

Rome 25, 70, 74, 121, 129, 152
Rotrou of Le Perche 66
Rouen 31, 33, 39, 55, 67, 77, 93, 104
Roxburgh 82
Runnymede 103, 122

Saffuriya 79
Saint Emilion 113
Saintes 32, 54, 75, 76, 150
Saint-Germain-en-Laye 44, 72
Saint Jean d'Angély 27, 113
Saint Paul's cathedral 37, 91
Saint-Puy 76
Saladdin 78, 79, 83, 86, 88-90
Sancha of Provence 138, 150-1, 153
Sancho VI of Navarre 74, 93
Sandwich 130, 132-3
sanitation 71, 84, 186-7
Santiago de Compostela 23, 58
sapping 86, 94, 123
Saracens, *see* Muslims
Savaric de Mauléon 121, 124, 129
Savoy 160, 162, 201
Savoyards 139, 151, 155
Scarborough 169
Sées 54
shipping 84-5, 90, 117, 120, 121, 124-5, 130, 132, 157, 163, 174, 182-3
Sicily 85, 142, 158
Sigurd of Gloucester 9
Simon V de Montfort 138, 140, 142-5, 148, 152, 156
Simon the Younger of Montfort 153
Simon de Pateshill 116
Siwan, *see* Joan
Sluys, battle 183
Southampton 110, 182, 198
Stamford 103, 122
Stanhope Park, battle 178

stannary towns 131
Statute of Jewry 141
Statute of Labourers 185
Stephen Harding 108
Stephen of Blois 16, 17, 18, 19, 20, 27, 31-3, 123, 125
Stirling castle 165

Taillebourg 55, 76-7, 138, 150
Tatar-Mongol yoke 135
taxes 74, 79, 91, 93, 103, 115, 117, 120, 122, 136, 137, 151, 159, 161, 172, 185, 191, 196, 199-200
Templars 30, 39, 40, 41, 78, 90, 120, 135
Teobaldo o trovador 147-9
Thanet 125
Theobald of Blois 41
Thomas Becket: as layman 39-42, 108; as archbishop 42-4, 46-9, 55, 57, 63, 70, 72-5, 81, 146
Thomas Holland 194-5
Thomas of Gloucester 201
Thomas of Lancaster 167-73, 176
Thomas of Nottingham 201
Thomas of Warwick 201
Thomas Rokesbury 178
Thomas Seton 181
Tiberias 79
tin 140, 146 – *see* also 'stannary towns'
Tinchbray, battle of 13
Tintagel 146
Toulouse 33, 79, 192
Touraine 27
Tournai 186
tournaments 58, 60-2, 122, 134, 160, 166, 190-1
Tours 80
Tower of London 123, 126, 137, 144, 156, 174-5, 184, 201

229

treason 75, 133
treaties: Berwick 184; Bretigny 194; Lambeth 133; Kingston 133; Le Goulet 101, 113; Louviers 93
Tripoli 79
Tunis 158
Turcopoles 88
Turnberry castle 165
Tyrell, Gautier or Walter 11-12

Viterbo 153, 91, 117
Vendôme 93
Verneuil 52-3
Vexin 27, 40, 41, 97
Vézelay 84
Vikings 28, 33

Wallingford castle 21, 38, 147, 166
Walter IV de Brienne 150
Waltham abbey 163
Wareham 18
Warwick 169-70
Wat Tyler 200
Westminster 11, 15, 35, 45, 78, 82, 111-12, 126, 128, 135, 138, 140, 151, 152, 155-6, 160, 163, 166, 177, 189, 198-9, 202
William II Longuespée 148
William IX, duke of Aquitaine 71
William X, duke of Aquitaine 23
William de Bohun 186

William de Clinton 186
William des Roches 113
William Longchamp 91
William Montagu 180, 186, 194-5
William of Anjou 16
William of Blois 32
William of Blyborough 164
William of Gloucester 59
William of Hainault 174
William, Prince 33, 38
William Rufus 11, 12, 14, 175
William the Breton 104
William the Conqueror 2, 9, 10, 11, 53
William the Lion of Scotland 45, 55, 57-8, 60, 82, 120
William the Marshal 3, 61-7, 80, 109, 112, 128-30, 132, 134-5, 141, 146, 152
William of Cassingham 125, 130
Winchelsea 130, 132
Winchester 17, 20, 34, 41, 56, 58, 81, 116, 121, 125-6, 128, 139, 146
Windsor 44, 122, 156. 164, 168, 180, 198
Wissant 16, 54
Wool 113, 161, 172, 182
Worcester 38, 106, 109, 127

York city and Minster 57, 59, 84, 121, 140, 169, 173, 179